W9-BMW-585

WORKING A SCENE

WORKING A SCENE
An Actor's Approach

Charles McGaw
The Goodman School of Drama
A School of The Art Institute of Chicago

Holt, Rinehart and Winston
New York Chicago San Francisco Atlanta Dallas
Montreal Toronto London Sydney

Library of Congress Cataloging in Publication Data

McGaw, Charles J.
　　Working a scene.

　　Includes index.
　　1. Acting.　2. Drama—Collections.　I. Title.
PN2080.M3　　　792'.028　　　76–54967
ISBN: 0–03–080086–2

Design by Arthur Ritter

Copyright © 1977 by Holt, Rinehart and Winston
All Rights Reserved
Printed in the United States of America
7　8　9　0　　　081　　　9　8　7　6　5　4　3　2　1

PREFACE

The primary purpose of this book is to help the actor to find a specific way of working on a scene. There is, of course, no single right way. Different actors work differently, and different kinds of scenes may require different approaches. But each actor needs to seek and develop an individual way of working that is right for both actor and material. For every student actor who has developed some basic method, there are a dozen who have no way of working at all. Most students depend on trial and error, putting their faith in that most elusive of helpers —the inspiration of the moment. The results are unpredictable, and the actor's ability to repeat them is problematical. Described here is one specific way of working that student actors may explore and test. This way may then be modified as necessary to meet the particular demands of any special problem.

A second purpose is to provide students and teachers with readily available materials for scene study from contemporary and classic plays. Finding practice materials is usually a time-consuming process. Not only are instructors expected to make suggestions for each new assignment, but students often spend many hours searching for the "right" scene—hours that might better be spent in exploring and rehearsing suitable material at hand. The scenes selected here therefore present a variety of challenges. Each scene is placed in context by briefly relating it to the play from which it is taken. The first scenes are explored in some detail. New problems arising in later scenes are recognized and discussed as they occur.

The approach is concisely described in two short sections—*Exploring a Scene* and *Rehearsing a Scene*. The brevity of the description assumes that the student is beginning scene work either after having studied principles of acting from a basic text in a course devoted principally to acting exercises, or that the scene work will be supplemented by the study of acting fundamentals and their application in basic exercises.

C.McG.
Chicago, Illinois
December 1976

v

CONTENTS

WORKING A SCENE

PART 1
Introduction

Exploring a Scene

Questions and Answers

Exploring a scene means discovering within it a series of physical and verbal actions that the actor will perform in specific circumstances, in a specific place, at a specific time. The work entails other problems, but it logically begins with the actor's finding some answers—specific, not general—to some fundamental questions about the character he[1] is going to create and develop. He phrases both the questions and the answers in first person because the actor must involve *himself* with his character's problems.

> *What* am I doing?
> *Why* am I doing it?
> *Who* am I?
> *Where* am I?
> *When* am I there?

In modern plays partial answers are often directly stated by the dramatist, sometimes in considerable detail, in the stage directions. Answers are always stated or implied in the dialogue—in what the character says about himself or what other characters say about him. Usually, the answers *given* by the dramatist must be supplemented with additional details supplied by the actor's imagination. These *supplied* answers must, of course, be a logical extension of the circumstances given by the playwright.

Finding the Intentions and the Obstacles

Fundamentally, acting consists in performing a series—in a complex role, sometimes a very long series—of specific actions. The answer to "What am I doing?" provides the physical actions that must be carried out during the scene.

Behind the actions, however, there must be a purpose. So the answer to "Why am I doing it?" is perhaps the most important of all. Why am I in the scene? The key word in answering this question is *want*. What do I want to achieve? What do I want to happen as a result of my actions? A specific answer gives the actor an *intention,* a reason for being onstage. Dramatic conflict requires that opposed to each want there be an *obstacle,* some opposing force that makes it difficult to reach the desired goal. The obstacle is usually a conflict between the characters. It may, however, be a psychological block within a character. Or two characters may be united against some other force. Suspense and interest, both for the actor and for the audience, are generated by the actor's wanting to overcome an obstacle, and committing himself fully to the task. So involved here are three more questions demanding definite answers.

> What do I want?
> Why do I want it?
> What obstacles must I overcome to get it?

---

[1]The use of *he, him,* and *his* to refer to indefinite sex or to groups composed of both sexes is done for convenience in the writing of this book and is not to be thought of as a sign of sexism.

3

The answers to *What* and *Why* and the answers to *Who, Where,* and *When* are interdependent. We tend to think that a person's character, what a person is, determines his behavior. Onstage, however, as in life, a person's character is *revealed* through his actions and through his reasons for doing them. So the actor begins to discover who his character is by finding out what he does and why he does it.

Why, Where, and *When* all affect the actions that a character chooses to realize his intentions and how he will carry them out. Some people choose to resolve differences of opinion by the action of courteous conversation; some choose physical violence that may lead to injury or even death. At one period in history quarrels were often settled with rapiers, at another with dueling pistols. Too many people in today's society resort to knives or revolvers. Here are other examples of ways in which *Where* and *When* determine behavior.

A flirtation is not carried on at a formal party the way it is at a beach picnic.

The permissiveness of modern society allows language that was quite unacceptable in any earlier period.

Women in large hoopskirts cannot move the way women can move in slacks.

A plot to commit a crime is likely to be discussed in whispers if there is any danger of being overheard.

Character Relationships

Answers to all of these questions influence character relationships; and the nature of the relationship between the characters demands careful consideration. It may be simple and straightforward. It may be, particularly in modern psychological drama, subtle and complex. The actor should always explore the relationship through a study of the text and through his own imagination, and define it as unequivocally

as possible. Its nature will determine to a large extent how he carries out his intention, how he behaves in order to achieve what he wants. Consider how different relationships between two partners who are working on an important business transaction would influence their behavior and determine the way they attempt to realize their intentions. Consider how it would be

if they were in complete agreement and shared a mutual confidence and respect,

if they were in serious disagreement and shared a mutual confidence and respect,

if one doubted the other's honesty and goodwill,

if one was contemptuous of the other's intelligence and ability,

if one was extremely cautious and the other was very daring.

There are many possibilities for different relationships within the same situation. The actor needs to examine these possibilities and make choices that are in accordance with the playwright's concept.

Relation to Objects

Relating to objects with which he is involved in performing his actions is also one of the actor's challenges. The relationship consists in responding to the sensory stimuli of the object, and often in giving it the particular dramatic significance required by the situation. Drinking a liquid—beer, for example—involves a number of sensory stimuli such as taste, temperature, the quality of the container. In addition, the character may have a definite relationship to the beer. In *A Streetcar Named Desire,* Stanley Kowalski returning from the hospital where his wife is giving birth to their first child, drinks beer in celebration, exults in it, and finally pours it over his naked chest. The relationship and the action become a dramatization of Stanley's sensuality. In a play about lives of Elizabeth Barrett and Robert Browning, Elizabeth is required by her domineering father to drink a tankard of ale each night before retiring as an aid to restoring her health. The ale is highly distasteful to her, but she drinks every drop rather than provoke her father to a display of temper. The relationship and the physical action dramatize her father's tyranny from which she ultimately escapes through her elopement with Robert Browning.

Objects become very good partners when the actor imbues them with a meaningful relationship. We will call establishing and maintaining a relationship to an object a *sensory task*. We must remember that other characters provide a sensory, as well as a psychological stimulus, and should often be regarded as sensory objects.

Using the Lines

The actor gives a good deal of thought, both at home and at rehearsal, to the lines that the playwright has given him to speak. He should think of the lines as actions—verbal actions, if you will—that serve him in accomplishing his intention. He needs to discover how he can use each line to help him get what he wants, and he needs to consider both its surface (textual) and its implied (subtextual) meaning. On the surface (textually) the line "It's raining" is a simple statement about the condition of the weather. It may have, however, a number of implied or subtextual meanings, such as

We'll have to move the party indoors.
Now those flowers we planted ought to grow very well.
No, you can't go outdoors to play.
I told you you ought to get the roof fixed.
I love to walk in the rain.

The actor speaks the text, but *thinks* the subtext. And it is his responsibility to think the subtext as

clearly as he speaks the text. It is usually in the subtext that we find the dramatic significance of a line. An actor's failure to discover and communicate this significance may lead a director to remark, "I know what you're saying, but I don't know what you mean by saying it."

Conceiving the lines as verbal actions, and using them as an active means of accomplishing an intention and influencing the behavior of other characters, is too often neglected by students. An actor has no right to speak a line until he has discovered a reason for saying it.

Finding the Beats

In each scene in order to accomplish his overall *want*, that is to achieve his major intention, the actor will have to realize a number of minor intentions, the exact number and nature depending upon the circumstances and the obstacles that have to be overcome. What the actor does to accomplish each minor intention is called a unit of action or a *beat*. The term *beat* is supposedly a mispronunciation of the word *bit* by Russian teachers of the Stanislavski system in the United States. They used the word to emphasize that an actor cannot effectively play an entire scene without breaking it into smaller bits or units.

Each beat or unit is a necessary step in accomplishing the larger objective, so the actor must discover each beat, play it clearly, and relate it to the intention of the whole scene. Effectual development of the scene demands the playing of beat *one* before progressing to beat *two*, of beat *two* before progressing to beat *three*, and so on throughout. A definite "terminal point" at the end of each unit makes clear that one step toward the major objective has been accomplished. After a moment of transition, a vigorous "attack" at the beginning of the next unit indicates that something new is starting, giving both actor and audience a sense that the scene is moving forward.

We can illustrate with a scene that we will call *The Burglary*. As the burglar, your major intention is to rob the house. To accomplish this objective, you must realize a number of smaller intentions that entail playing a number of specific beats:

> You must break into the house.
> You must locate the wall safe where the money and jewelry are secured.
> You must open the safe.
> You must remove the valuables.
> You must escape from the house.

The sequence of physical actions required to accomplish each of these minor intentions is called a unit or a beat.

For each intention there must be an *obstacle,* something that is working against your getting what you want. Too often, actors minimize or ignore the obstacle and, consequently, eliminate the conflict that is the essence of drama. In this scene, besides the obvious physical obstacles occasioned by having to break through a door or window, to locate the safe in the dark, to work the combination, and so forth, there are such obstacles as *time* (you must accomplish your intention before you get caught), as *background* (are you an expert thief who as a matter of pride must not fumble or are you a novice whose ineptitude is a constant obstacle?), and as *character* (do you have to combat any sense of guilt or fear?). Seek for all obstacles that are inherent in the situation!

Characters in a play do not, of course, always succeed in accomplishing their intentions. In this situation you might be caught, the police might be called. A new set of circumstances would require new intentions, and the beats would consist of a different sequence of physical and verbal actions.

In working a scene the actor should always find the beats, state the intention and obstacle for each one, and mark the beginning and the end of each beat in his script.

In Summary

The analysis of the scene to find answers to the basic questions, to discover intentions, obstacles, relationships, subtext, and beats should be made before actual staging is begun—that is before the actors start working "on their feet." It can and should begin with the individual actors working by themselves at home. Early rehearsals should then be devoted to discussion of the answers the actors have discovered during their initial study. They will derive a direction from such analysis and discussion that makes it possible for them to perform specific physical and verbal actions for the purpose of satisfying clearly stated intentions. Without this work the actor resorts to intuitive responses that are not dependable and that lead him to a display of "general emotion" rather than to the meaning of the scene.

As choices are made, the actor should write them in his script, thus providing him with a "score" to which he can refer whenever it is necessary to review the specific things he has to do. He may have to interleaf his script to provide enough writing space, and he should write always in pencil since further study during rehearsal may bring him to other choices. Once answers have been found, the actor must not regard them as Holy Scripture. Throughout his association with any role, he should be alert to new and better answers as experience with the text and with his partners increases his depth of understanding.

Rehearsing a Scene

When an actor is working with a director, he will naturally adhere to the rehearsal procedure that the director establishes. In class related scene study actors are usually working in small groups without a director's guidance. In either situation there are principles and procedures an actor needs to recognize.

1. An actor's basic work on a scene or a play is done at home. By himself—with pencil in hand—he studies the script. He finds answers to the questions raised above. He states his intentions. He discovers his relationships and sensory tasks. He breaks his role into beats. He works by himself preparing what he is going to bring to the rehearsal.

2. Rehearsals are for testing what the actor has discovered, for further exploration, and for establishing relationships with his partners. The actor who attempts to do all his work at rehearsal can hope to realize only part of his potential. Rehearsals are fruitful to the extent that the actors bring something to them.

3. After each rehearsal the actor reviews carefully what has happened and incorporates whatever has been constructive into the creation and development of his character. In this way each succeeding rehearsal gives evidence of growth and progress. It is discouraging and defeating to work with actors who do not retain what has been accomplished at the preceeding rehearsal and who, consequently, begin each time at approximately the same stage of development.

4. At each rehearsal the actor commits all of his energy and attention to the work at hand. He is not content with anything less than his best effort. He accepts it as a challenge rather than as a defeat when his best effort does not produce the results he is seeking. When one approach to a problem does not work, he tries another. He is never willing immediately to accept the first solution that comes to mind, although he may ultimately return to it as the best one.

5. He maintains contact with other actors. He realizes that almost always his intention, his *want,* is to influence the behavior of the other characters. He uses his actions and his lines to accomplish this purpose. He develops an "eye technique" so that at early rehearsals when he is working with a script in his hand, he can get his eyes off the page and make direct eye contact with his partners. Acting is a cooperative group effort. Very little creativity results when actors in rehearsal or performance work by themselves rather than with their partners.

6. As a rehearsal technique, improvisational exercises can serve a valuable function. The actors set up circumstances outside of the play, but in which the characters have

been, or might have been involved. Intentions are determined before the beginning of the improvisation, and the actors attempt to realize them through verbal and physical actions which arise as necessary or appropriate during the playing of the exercise. Two major benefits to be gained from improvisation are 1) a fuller understanding of the character and his relationship to other characters in the scene, and 2) the experience of having to maintain real contact with a partner throughout. Because an actor cannot know in advance what obstacles his partner may make for him, he must be ready to make moment by moment adjustments. Both of these benefits should carry over into rehearsing and playing the scene as written by the dramatist. It is often said there is an improvisational quality about all good acting. This statement means that, even though the actor is speaking the dramatist's lines and carrying out prescribed actions, he is, at the same time, moment by moment, making real adjustments to the demands of the situation.

7. During rehearsals the actor, aided by the director if there is one, should attempt to discover all physical activity that is either stated or inherent in the text, and should use his imagination to invent further activity that is appropriate to the character and the circumstances. Such activity imparts reality to the scene for both the actor and the audience. It also gives the actor an increased sense of belonging onstage. While too much activity (popularly called "business") can make a scene too "busy," most student actors tend to use too little imagination in this regard rather than too much. This is particularly true in plays written before the modern period, before dramatists such as Ibsen, Strindberg, and Shaw began to supply the actor with detailed stage directions. In rehearsing a Shakespearean play it often takes some imagination even to

discover where the actors may logically *sit down*. The quality of an actor's imagination is very evident in the amount and kind of physical activity he invents.

8. At some point in rehearsal the actor must complete memorization of his lines. Circumstances will alter cases, but in general memorization should be completed about half-way through the rehearsal period. Too early memorization may mean that patterns are established that will have to be altered as the actor gains fuller understanding of his character. Too late memorization deprives the actor and his partners of gaining the feeling of security that comes only after memorization has been completed. It is an actor's responsibility to memorize the lines as the dramatist has written them and to speak them accurately at each repetition.

9. After the exploration of the text and before the actors begin to move around, it is necessary to devise a ground plan, an arrangement of exits and entrances, windows, furniture, and so forth. In modern plays it is often described in some detail in the text, and an acting version may include a diagram from an earlier production. These sources should not be ignored because they may serve very well. On the other hand, the actors and the director, if there is one, may be able to plan an arrangement that better suits their immediate purpose.

One consideration is that the ground plan be appropriate to the Where and When of the play. The formal arrangement of an eighteenth-century drawing room is not appropriate for a log cabin. The major requirement, especially in class related scene study where the matter of decor is usually ignored, is that it serve the needs of the actors in carrying out their intentions and in maintaining helpful physical relationships among the characters. Once a ground plan has been established a good deal of the movement has been prescribed. So the most important consideration is what the ground plan will make the actor do, or what it will permit him to do.

In regard to the ground plan, as to all other choices, the actor should remain experimental and flexible—ready to make changes if they seem desirable.

10. Rehearsals should always begin with a warm-up. Working either separately or together, the actors should do eight to ten minutes of vocal and physical exercises that will reduce tensions, induce relaxation, and prepare their voices and bodies for concentrated work. The nature of the exercises is best prescribed by voice and movement teachers. Each actor needs, however, to develop a warm-up routine that meets his individual needs. It should be vigorous and stimulating, but not exhausting. Do not begin rehearsals (or performances) without a warm-up! It is as necessary for an actor as for a dancer or singer. During working rehearsals, it is in order for an actor to ask for time-out for a short "re-warming," if he feels that tensions are interfering with his work. Elimination of excess tension is necessary to creativity, and it is an ever-present problem.

The following analyses of scenes from *The Crucible* by Arthur Miller and *When You Comin Back, Red Ryder?* by Mark Medoff illustrate the principles set forth for exploring a scene. It is suggested that these exploratory analyses be carefully studied and applied in rehearsal before beginning work on other scenes.

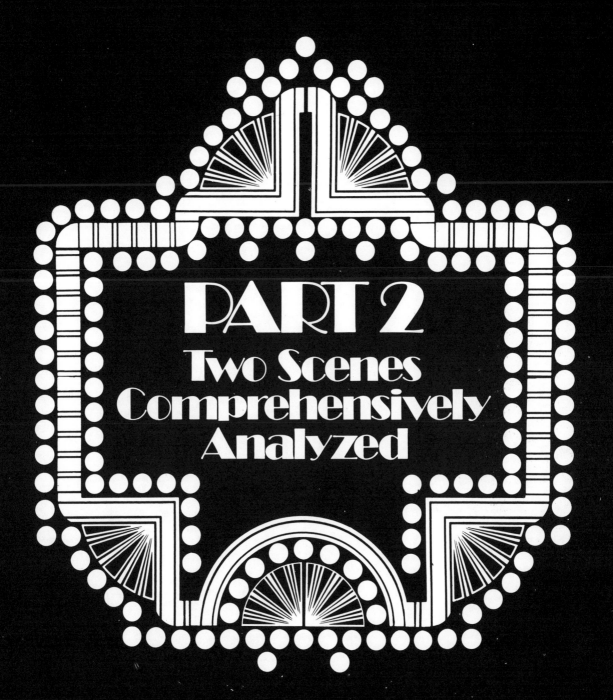

PART 2
Two Scenes Comprehensively Analyzed

The Crucible

ARTHUR MILLER

Exploratory Analysis of a Scene from Act II: 1 man, 1 woman

Background *The Crucible* deals with the famous witchcraft trials in Salem, Massachusetts, in 1692. The theme is the frightening effect of injustice and misapplication of authority. Although the dramatist made some use of dramatic license, the story is told essentially as it happened in fact. A group of irresponsible girls, ranging in age from ten to eighteen, partly for sport and partly for spite, claimed certain people in Salem were afflicting them by means of witchcraft. Encouraged by some of their elders, these "children" brought charges against scores of innocent and defenseless people. Before sanity was restored, twenty people had been hanged and many more had suffered great loss in reputation, health, and property. The most disturbing thing about the whole affair was that those elders who were responsible for the tragedy were not villains. They were "good people" who, although they may have been fighting for some personal gain, believed they were doing right for God and country.

The prime mover among the girls was one Abigail Williams. In Miller's play she has been dismissed from Elizabeth Proctor's service because she was discovered in an adulterous relation with Elizabeth's husband John. Abigail resents the stern treatment she has received and fosters ambitions of maintaining her relationship with John, possibly as his wife. Although later in the play she "cries out" against Elizabeth, accusing her of being a witch, in an earlier scene she has told John that the girls' apparent afflictions have "naught to do with witchcraft."

Who JOHN PROCTOR. About thirty. An earnest, hardworking, clear-thinking farmer. He is an independent spirit who makes up his own mind and does not readily follow the suggestions of others. He is a man who strives mightily to do good as he sees it. Outraged at the hysteria that has taken hold of his neighbors, he fights it in the best way of which his simple honest nature is capable.

ELIZABETH PROCTOR. About thirty. John Proctor's wife. An honest farmwife of plain appearance. Hardworking, but "not altogether well" since the birth of her last child. Although reserved and detached, she is firm in her judgments and outspoken in expressing them. She is guided in her behavior by a strict moral code based upon an uncompromising Puritan ethic. Consequently, Elizabeth has centered too much of her life and thought upon her husband's single infidelity.

(MARY WARREN. She does not appear in this scene, but the references to her make identification necessary. She has replaced Abigail in Elizabeth's service. Usually meek and timid, as one of the girls involved in the court proceedings, she has for the first time a feeling of self-importance and is beginning to assert herself against John's and Elizabeth's authority.)

Character Relationships Not given to romantic love, John nevertheless has a genuine respect and affection for his wife. He has made every effort to atone for what he unquestionably accepts as a sinful act with Abigail. He treats Elizabeth with genuine consideration (goes on "tiptoe") and displays as much affection as his undemonstrative nature permits. He is deeply concerned with providing for his wife and family and with maintaining their good name.

Elizabeth treats John with considerable sternness, refusing to forgive or forget his transgression. Her severity is caused by her Puritanism, which maintains that man should pay for his sins, and also by the fact that she is not confident of her ability to retain his love. She discharges her wifely and motherly duties with exacting care. That she is devoted to John and capable of great sacrifice is abundantly clear in later scenes. This aspect of their relationship should not be ignored here.

What and Why The physical and verbal actions that constitute the scene are performed to realize these overall *intentions*.

ELIZABETH: "I must make John go to Salem to expose and denounce Abigail." The realization of this intention is vital to her because she believes it will put an end to the hysteria that is ravaging the community, as well as to any hold Abigail may still have over John. She employs a number of different tactics each initiating a new beat, as we shall see when we get into the text. Elizabeth's initial tactic, one she has been using for some months, is constantly to make John feel guilty for his single transgression.

JOHN: "I must please Elizabeth and restore normalcy to my household." His wife's behavior during the past seven months since Abigail's dismissal has created an unbearable situation. He is not yet aware of the gravity of the proceedings in Salem. His intention, like Elizabeth's, is one to which an actor can totally commit herself.

Obstacles: These intentions bring the two characters into the direct conflict that is vital to dramatic interest. Even though a denunciation of Abigail would be right and justified, John recognizes he would meet with disbelief in the village, a firm denial from Abigail, and a loss of his good name at the exposure of their relationship. He cannot risk such consequences. Elizabeth, whose fears now far exceed those of a wronged and jealous wife, cannot accept John's refusal to go to Salem. Because of the obstacles they create for each other, both actors are unable to realize their intentions, and they are stalemated at the end of the scene.

When and Where 1692 in Massachusetts. John Proctor's farm about five miles from the village of Salem. The scene is the common room of the farmhouse, a room which served many functions, a combined living, dining, and cooking room (since most of the food was prepared at the large stone fireplace). Besides the fireplace, the room contains a doorway to the outside, a doorway to the back part of the house, and a stairway leading up to the bedroom. It is sparsely furnished with a washstand, a table with a bench behind it, and several stools. The ground plan opposite will serve the scene well, although the actors should feel free to create any arrangement that helps them to carry out their physical actions and puts the characters into meaningful physical relationships. During scene work it is well to experiment with several different arrangements for the purpose of arriving finally at the most effective ground plan.

A Note on the Language Arthur Miller has used in some instances a kind of archaic syntax to create a feeling of Puritan Massachusetts in the seventeenth century. It never obscures the meaning, and it should not present the actor with any real problem. As with any dialect or colloquial speech, the actor needs to master it so that it becomes a natural way of speaking. It should not call attention to itself.

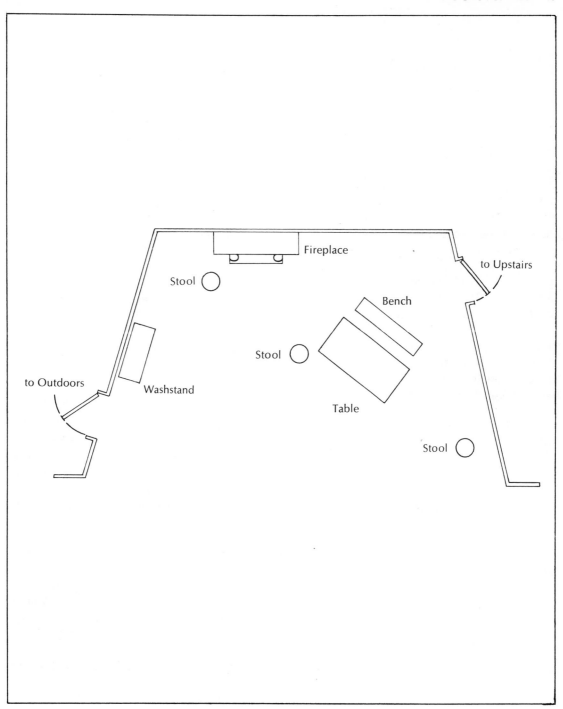

Fireplace

to Upstairs

Stool

Bench

Stool

to Outdoors

Washstand

Table

Stool

Ground Plan for *The Crucible*

The Crucible

ARTHUR MILLER

ACT II

As the curtain rises the room is empty. From above Elizabeth is heard softly singing to the children. Presently the door opens and John Proctor enters carrying his gun. He glances about the room as he comes toward the fireplace, then halts for an instant as he hears her singing. He continues on to the fireplace, leans the gun against the wall as he swings a pot out of the fire and smells it. Then he lifts out the ladle and tastes. He is not quite pleased. He reaches to a cupboard, takes a pinch of salt, and drops it into the pot. As he is testing again, her footsteps are heard on the stair. He swings the pot into the fireplace and goes to a basin and washes his hands and face. Elizabeth enters.

These physical actions involve the actor playing John in a number of relations and sensory tasks. Opening the door he hears Elizabeth singing and smells a good supper cooking. Perhaps Elizabeth will be less difficult tonight. The action at the fireplace involves smelling, tasting, feeling the warmth of the fire and the heat of the stew. The action of washing requires other sensory responses.

ELIZABETH: What keeps you so late? It's almost dark.

Elizabeth: BEGIN *Beat 1*
Her first two lines make up her first beat. Her intention may be stated as "I must find out if John is late because he went to Salem." Her subtext for the first line could be: "I hope you're late because you went to Salem." Her meaning in her second line, which ends the beat and constitutes a terminal point, is: "So you finished your planting instead of going to Salem as you knew I wanted you to."
John: BEGIN *Beat 1*

PROCTOR: I was planting far out to the forest edge.

He knows what Elizabeth means. His subtext might be: "No, I didn't go to Salem, I got the whole farm planted instead, which should bring us a good crop in the fall." This line is his initial effort to restore normalcy by trying to get Elizabeth to concentrate on the farm and the daily routine. He wants her to think about their future prosperity rather than about her past disappointments.

Reprinted by permission of International Creative Management. Copyright 1952, 1953, 1954, by Arthur Miller.

ELIZABETH: Oh, you're done then.

PROCTOR: Aye, the farm is seeded. The boys asleep?

ELIZABETH: They will be soon. *And she goes to the fireplace, proceeds to ladle up stew in a dish.*

PROCTOR: Pray now for a fair summer.

ELIZABETH: Aye.

PROCTOR: Are you well today?

ELIZABETH: I am. *She brings the plate to the table, and, indicating the food:* It is a rabbit.

PROCTOR, *going to the table:* Oh, is it! In Jonathan's trap?

ELIZABETH: No, she walked into the house this afternoon; I found her sittin' in the corner like she come to visit.

PROCTOR: Oh, that's a good sign walkin' in.

ELIZABETH: Pray God. It hurt my heart to strip her, poor rabbit. *She sits and watches him taste it.*

PROCTOR: It's well seasoned.

ELIZABETH, *blushing with pleasure:* I took great care. She's tender?

PROCTOR: Aye. *He eats. She watches him.* I think we'll see green fields soon. It's warm as blood beneath the clods.

Elizabeth: END *Beat 1*
She makes a strong terminal point letting him know she is not happy about what he has done.
John does not accept her rebuff. He continues to pursue his intention.
Elizabeth: BEGIN *Beat 2*
She retreats into a passive resistance. Her answers are terse, her manner unresponsive. Her intention: "I must make John aware that things are not going to be normal until he goes to Salem and denounces Abigail."
During the next several speeches the actors are provided with physical activity and sensory tasks related to the serving and eating of the stew. This is the kind of activity that creates reality for both actor and audience. The actor always has an advantage when he is given or invents such physical actions. Sensory work should be done carefully and truthfully. It should involve as many senses as possible, with the actor relying upon his sense memory of taste, touch, smell, sight, and sound.
Although there are several references to Elizabeth's not being "altogether well," the nature of her illness is never specified. It does not significantly affect the action except that it provides an additional reason that Mary Warren should not be disobedient and adds poignancy when Elizabeth is jailed for witchcraft. Here is an example of the need for the actress to supply details from her imagination, and use them in her characterization. It might be she has not fully recovered from the birth of her last child, and we learn in Act III that she is again pregnant. Because it is not of major importance it should not be overemphasized.
It is possible she stripped the rabbit only because, in anticipation of John's having gone to Salem, she wanted to prepare a good supper for him. Note that she does not eat supper with her husband. She remains ready to serve him.
There is sly humor here which should not be lost. She is not used to compliments, and she wants to conceal the fact that she is pleased.
John has sensory task of eating good food. Verbal action for the purpose of realizing his intention.

ELIZABETH: That's well.

PROCTOR, *eats then looks up:* If the crop is good I'll buy George Jacob's heifer. How would that please you?

ELIZABETH: Aye, it would.

PROCTOR, *with a grin:* I mean to please you, Elizabeth.

ELIZABETH—*it is hard to say:* I know it, John.

He gets up, goes to her, kisses her. She receives it. With a certain disappointment, he returns to the table.

PROCTOR, *as gently as he can:* Cider?

ELIZABETH, *with a sense of reprimanding herself for having forgot:* Aye! *She gets up and goes and pours a glass for him. He now arches his back.*

PROCTOR: This farm's a continent when you go foot by foot droppin' seeds in it.

ELIZABETH, *coming with the cider:* It must be.

PROCTOR: On Sunday let you come with me, and we'll walk the farm together; I never see such a load of flowers on the earth. Massachusetts is a beauty in the spring!

ELIZABETH: Aye, it is.

There is a pause. It is as though she would speak but cannot. Instead, now, she takes up his glass and plate and fork and goes with them to the basin. Her back is turned to him. He turns to her and watches her. A sense of their separation rises.

PROCTOR: I think you're sad again. Are you?

ELIZABETH—*she doesn't want friction, and yet she must:* You come so late I thought you'd gone to Salem this afternoon.

PROCTOR: Why? I have no business in Salem.

Terse answer. She will not yield to his want even though she knows what it is.

This is an example of telling physical activity supplied by the dramatist. The action serves the intentions of both actors.

This "cider business" is also telling. It gives John an opportunity to remind Elizabeth that she too is not quite perfect. The direction, He now arches his back, *should communicate John's awareness of the small advantage he has gained. Elizabeth realizes it. Here is an example of how actors can establish contact and "play off of each other."*

John has sensory task of drinking cider.

This line is a kind of climax of John's first beat. He is suggesting that they do something together. Something he would love to do and share with her. He should have a picture in his mind of the beauty of the farm and their walking together.

John: END Beat 1

Elizabeth: END Beat 2

This stage direction is the terminal point. They both recognize they have failed. She will not resume their normal pattern. He will not face the matter of going to Salem.

John: BEGIN Beat 2

His subtext might be: "I see you can't forget about it, so let's talk things over." His intention is: "I want to give Elizabeth a chance to speak what's on her mind."

Elizabeth: BEGIN Beat 3

Her subtext is suggested in the stage direction. Her intention is: "I must make John face the situation as it is." Definitely make the line the beginning of a new beat. Get to the point.

He wants to sound casual. He wants it to mean "I have no farm business to conduct in Salem."

Don Murray and Maria Tucci appear as John and Elizabeth Proctor in Arthur Miller's *The Crucible*. The 1976 production at the American Shakespeare Theatre in Stratford, Connecticut, was directed by Michael Kahn. (Photograph: Martha Swope)

ELIZABETH: You did speak of going, earlier this week.

PROCTOR—*he knows what she means:* I thought better of it since.

ELIZABETH: Mary Warren's there today.

Subtext: We both should recognize it would be better not to go to Salem.

This line has a double subtext: (a) I have to confess I couldn't stop Mary from going to Salem against your orders, and (b) the situation in Salem is much graver than you think it is.

PROCTOR: Why'd you let her? You heard me forbid her go to Salem anymore.

ELIZABETH: I couldn't stop her.

PROCTOR, *holding back a full condemnation of her:* It is a fault, it is a fault, Elizabeth—you're the mistress here, not Mary Warren.

John's reprimand would be more severe if it were not for the fact that he does not want to create more friction than already exists.

ELIZABETH: She frightened all my strength away.

PROCTOR: How may that mouse frighten you, Elizabeth? You—

ELIZABETH: It is a mouse no more. I forbid her go, and she raises up her chin like the daughter of a prince and says to me, "I must go to Salem, Goody Proctor; I am an official of the court."

PROCTOR: Court! What court?

Goody is a shortened form of Goodwife, the customary title for married women in Puritan times. He is not asking a question. His intent here and in his next several speeches is to belittle what Elizabeth is saying. His subtext: What silly little court can Mary be an official of?

The tactic she is using now is to impress him with the seriousness of the situation.

ELIZABETH: Aye, it is a proper court they have now. They've sent four judges out of Boston, she says, weighty magistrates of the general court, and at the head sits the Deputy Governor of the Province.

PROCTOR, *astonished:* Why, she's mad.

Subtext: You can't be taking her seriously. She must be making this up.

ELIZABETH: I would to God she were. There be fourteen people in the jail now, she says. *Proctor simply looks at her unable to grasp it.* And they'll be tried, and the court have power to hang them too, she says.

PROCTOR, *scoffing, but without conviction:* Ah, they'd never hang—

Elizabeth is beginning to succeed in her intention.

ELIZABETH: The Deputy Governor promise hangin' if they'll not confess, John. The town's gone wild, I think. She speak of Abigail, and I thought she were a saint, to hear her. Abigail brings the other girls into the court, and where she walks the crowds will part like the sea for Israel. And folks are brought before them, and if they scream and howl and fall to the floor—the person's clapped in jail for bewitchin' them.

PROCTOR, *wide-eyed:* Oh, it is a black mischief.

ELIZABETH: I think you must go to Salem, John. *He turns to her.* I think so. You must tell them it is a fraud.

PROCTOR, *thinking beyond this:* Aye, it is surely.

ELIZABETH: Let you go to Ezekiel Cheever—he knows you well. And tell him what she told you last week in her uncle's house. She told you it had naught to do with witchcraft, did she not?

PROCTOR, *in thought:* Aye, she did, she did. *Now a pause.*

ELIZABETH, *quietly, fearing to anger him by prodding:* God forbid you keep it from the court, John. I think they must be told.

PROCTOR, *quietly, struggling with his thought:* Aye, they must, they must. It is a wonder they do believe her.

ELIZABETH: I would go to Salem now, John—let you go tonight.

PROCTOR: I'll think on it.

ELIZABETH, *with her courage now:* You cannot keep it, John.

PROCTOR, *angering:* I know I cannot keep it. I say I will think on it.

Elizabeth considers Abigail a whore, and wants to communicate her contempt of the respect with which she is now being treated.

Elizabeth should SEE *the image of the Red Sea parting superimposed upon a picture of the crowds making way for Abigail as she enters the court. Working with specific images is a useful technique. Elizabeth has succeeded in making him recognize the gravity of the situation. Subtext: I see now that Abigail really is a dangerous little bitch.*

Another example of how actors can "play off of each other." John's turn expresses his continuing reluctance to go to Salem. It motivates her "I think so," which is more emphatic than her previous sentence. In "thinking beyond this," he is considering the consequences he might have to face if he denounced Abigail.
Her tactic is to assume he is going and is ready to consider a specific course of action.

What the actor is thinking while he is onstage is an important consideration. His thought process must be related to his effort to accomplish his intention, and it must be actively repeated at each rehearsal and performance.
Elizabeth watches him carefully, measuring just how much pressure she can apply at this point.

John can use his imagination specifically to picture in his mind what the scene might be if he went to Salem.
She is playing her intention more aggressively. Not only must he go to Salem, he must go immediately. The emphatic word, toward which the speech builds, is "tonight."
He is still presenting her with an obstacle.
The conflict between them is quiet, but intense. This beat is approaching a climax.
John: END *Beat 2*

ELIZABETH, *hurt and very coldly:* Good, then, let you think on it. *She stands and starts to walk out of the room.*

PROCTOR: I am only wondering how I may prove what she told me, Elizabeth. If the girl's a saint now, I think it's not easy to prove she's a fraud, and the town gone so silly. She told it to me in a room alone—I have no proof for it.

ELIZABETH: You were alone with her?

PROCTOR: For a moment alone, aye.

ELIZABETH: Why, then, it is not as you told me.

PROCTOR, *his anger rising:* For a moment, I say. The others come in soon after.

ELIZABETH, *quietly, she has suddenly lost all faith in him:* Do as you wish, then. *She starts to turn.*

PROCTOR: Woman. *She turns to him.* I'll not have your suspicion anymore.

ELIZABETH, *a little loftily:* I have no—

PROCTOR: I'll not have it!

ELIZABETH: Then let you not earn it.

PROCTOR, *with a violent undertone:* You doubt me yet?

ELIZABETH, *with a smile to keep her dignity:* John, if it were not Abigail that you must go to hurt, would you falter now? I think not.

PROCTOR: Now look you—

ELIZABETH: I see what I see, John.

PROCTOR, *with solemn warning:* You will not judge me more, Elizabeth. I have good reason to think before I charge fraud on Abigail, and I will think on it. Let you look to your own improvement before you go to judge your husband anymore. I have forgot Abigail, and—

Elizabeth: END *Beat 3*

These two lines are both terminal points, bringing an end to this part of the conflict. Elizabeth further emphasizes the end of the beat by starting to walk away.

John: BEGIN *Beat 3*

His intention: "I must make Elizabeth understand why I can't go to Salem." He must explain the reason for his resistance. He wants to reason with her. He changes his tempo.

Elizabeth: BEGIN *Beat 4*

John's line introduces a new circumstance to which Elizabeth must adjust. She feels John has deceived her. Her intention: "I must make John know I cannot trust him any more."

Elizabeth: END *Beat 4*

Again a terminal point emphasized with a movement away from John.

John: BEGIN *Beat 4*

Elizabeth's suspicion, which John feels is quite unjustified, triggers a new beat. His intention: "I must attack her lack of faith." His "Woman," followed by a pause as she turns, provides him with a strong opening.

He has put her momentarily on the defensive.

In this direct attack John's speeches are building this beat and this scene to a climax, and to an effective terminal point.

ELIZABETH: And I.

PROCTOR: Spare me! You forget nothin' and forgive nothin'. Learn charity, woman. I have gone tiptoe in this house all seven month since she is gone. I have not moved from there to there without I think to please you, and still an everlasting funeral marches round your heart. I cannot speak but I am doubted, every moment judged for lies, as though I come into a court when I come into this house!

ELIZABETH: John, you are not open with me. You saw her in a crowd, you said. Now you—

PROCTOR: I'll plead my honesty no more, Elizabeth.

ELIZABETH—*now she would justify herself:* John, I only—

PROCTOR: No more! I should have roared you down when first you told me your suspicion. But I wilted, and, like a Christian, I confessed. Some dream I had must have mistaken you for God that day. But you're not, you're not, and let you remember it! Let you look sometimes for the goodness in me, and judge me not.

ELIZABETH: I do not judge you. The magistrate sits in your heart that judges you. I never thought you but a good man, John—*with a smile*—only somewhat bewildered.

PROCTOR, *laughing bitterly:* Oh, Elizabeth, your justice would freeze beer!

Inherent in this line is a physical action, probably a hand gesture, that he has not moved even a few feet without thinking whether she would approve.

Again, Elizabeth is on the defensive. This is an example of making an adjustment.

As a good Christian woman, she is certain of her moral rightness. His attack on her and his defense of himself have finally no effect. This is her final word. END *Beat 5.*
John: END *Beat 4*
This line is John's summation of Elizabeth's uncompromising Puritan "goodness." Neither has accomplished his intention, a fact that both recognize; he with some feeling of bitterness, she with some feeling of righteousness.

A Note on Playing Elizabeth   This is the first scene in which Elizabeth appears. She registers here as a "good woman in the worst sense of the word." The temptation to make her softer and more attractive should be resisted. To do so partially deprives John of the motivation for his intention, and it deprives Elizabeth of making the change she undergoes throughout the rest of the play as effective as it should be. She is armed with a sincere belief that she is right. This honesty justifies her behavior and gives her character the required dimension.

Improvisations for The Crucible   Working improvisationally in some or all of the following circumstances will help the actors to a fuller realization of the scene:

1. Working individually, Elizabeth and John perform chores that were a necessary part of their lives. Puritan farmers labored very hard from daylight to dark working with their hands, arms, backs—and, of course, without the aid of any machinery.

   Elizabeth may chop wood, carry armloads

into the house, build a fire in the fireplace.

Draw water from the well in heavy buckets, carry them into the house; or heat the water outdoors in large iron kettles, wash clothes, spread them out to dry.

Work in garden planting, weeding, picking crop, preparing it for cooking.

As immediate preparation for the scene, get children (she has three boys) ready for bed, conduct prayers, sing to them.

John may split rails for building a fence.

Spade or otherwise prepare soil for planting.

Plant seeds walking "far out to the forest edge."

As immediate preparation for the scene, walk home from the forest edge carrying gun and a heavy bag of seed. Remember the farm is "like a continent." *Think* about the situation you are coming home to and plan how you are going to get Elizabeth back to normal.

2. Working together, improvise in circumstances before the incident with Abigail, when John and Elizabeth had a good relationship:

Walk the farm together, enjoying its beauty and planning for the future. Exploring this experience should give special meaning to John's line in the scene when he asks Elizabeth to repeat the experience.

Have breakfast before beginning the hard day's work.

Put the boys to bed, enjoying each other and the children.

3. Improvise the scene in which Elizabeth confronts John with her suspicion about his relationship with Abigail and he confesses that she is right. This exercise should give special meaning to John's speech beginning, "No more. I should have roared you down when first you told me your suspicion." Follow this by improvising a scene the next morning when Elizabeth is giving John his breakfast.

Sources for the Play and the Period Often actors need to consult source materials, read, and study pictures that will increase their knowledge and understanding. The need is likely to be most apparent in plays set in other times and places, but it may also exist for plays dealing with contemporary problems. The following books contain helpful information about life in seventeenth-century New England —customs, manners, morals, dress; or information about the Salem witch trials on which *The Crucible* is based:

Paul Boyer. *Salem Possessed.* Cambridge, Massachusetts: Harvard University Press, 1974.

Charles Wentworth Upham. *Salem Witchcraft.* New York: Ungar Publishing Company, 1959.

When You Comin Back, Red Ryder?

MARK MEDOFF

Exploratory Analysis of Scene from Act I: 1 man, 1 woman

Background   Mark Medoff writes in a preface "In 1948 I am eight, my brother six, and . . . we meet the Durango Kid for the first time at the Airway Theatre in Louisville. I remember the Kid as the Superman of cowboys. . . . A mild-mannered rancher until trouble hits, the Kid then transmogrifies into a scourge in black mask and tight black togs who rides a white horse to ninety minutes of rectified wrongs. . . .

"I believe in the Durango Kid, as I come to believe in Cisco and Red and all the others. I'm not concerned that my heroes surround themselves with lepers and idiots, that they seem to have an abiding lack of interest in women —except as objects to save from other guys—or that their lives are as simply and cleanly plotted as my own. The Saturday matinee is an institution of my childhood, a schoolroom as surely as the one I attend at I. M. Bloom School Monday through Friday. My brother and I learn about justice and reenact what we learn in back of our apartment. We charge down the hill on our bikes, I the Durango Kid, the principal player (and to this day I cannot stand it otherwise), my brother and our cronies my assistants——peddling hell-bent-for-leather to the rescue

of a girl whose name I cannot remember, from whom I accept a brief thank you for all of us, if I am feeling beneficent, before leading my forces off to gun down her defilers with loaded fingers or cap pistols.

"Why would I suspect then, when I am eight, that when I return to Louisville for the first time in twenty-five years the Airway Theatre will house a furnace company?"

When You Comin Back, Red Ryder? asks what has happened to our heroes!

Who   STEPHEN/RED.   A boy of nineteen. He is plain looking in an unobtrusive way—small, his hair slicked straight back off his forehead. He wears a short sleeve sportshirt open one too many buttons at the top, the sleeves rolled several times toward his shoulders—an unconscious parody in his dress of the mid-fifties. He smokes Raleigh cigarettes and has a tattoo, "Born Dead," on his forearm. He has created an image of himself after the model of a Western movie hero. He sees himself escaping into a fantasy world "drivin a Chevrolet Corvette Stingray convertible the color of money and livin in his own apartment."

ANGEL.   A few years older than Stephen/Red. She is overweight, her white waitress uniform stretched across the rolls of her body. Her hair is framed by a bow made of limp, thick pastel yarn. She wears a wedding band on the ring finger of her right hand. She carries a very small purse. Angel rather complacently accepts things as they are because she wants to keep things as pleasant as possible. She tolerates her nagging mother. In her time away from her job she makes do with Lyle Striker with whom she watches television and carries on a little sex play. Lyle runs a filling station and motel next to the restaurant. He is a good-natured man, sixty years old, partially crippled.

Character Relationships   Angel epitomizes for Stephen/Red the life he wants to escape from. Her ready acceptance of things as they are, including her figure and the regulation about the coffee cups, makes him feel scornful and superior. She has a "crush" on Stephen, and true to her characteristic of making the best of things she accepts his treatment of her. She also accepts as likely that he will go away. "Stephen don't mean nothin by all the noise he makes. He just needs to make a lot of noise. . . . I wish that if he was gonna go, he'd just get it over with and go."

What and Why   The physical and verbal ac-tions that constitute the scene are performed to realize these *intentions:*

STEPHEN/RED: "I want to keep Angel from sticking her nose in my business."

ANGEL: "I want Stephen to pay some atten-tion to me."

Obstacles: The two intentions are op-posed, presenting each of the characters with a major obstacle. Both characters present them-selves with further obstacles because of *who* they are. Stephen has difficulty maintaining his image because of his own inconsequentiality. The contrast between who he is and who he would like to be provides comic incongruity. Angel's desire to keep everything as pleasant as possible compels her frequently to remind Stephen that he is disregarding the bosses' regu-lations. It's within her character to want to do her job well.

When and Where   The time is the late sixties or early seventies. The place is a diner on the desert in southern New Mexico—a counter with stools, some tables with chairs, a juke box. On one of the windows: FOSTER'S DINERS—ARIZ., N. MEX., TEX. The lettering has begun to chip away and although the diner is clean, its day has gone. The ground plan on the opposite page will serve the scene.

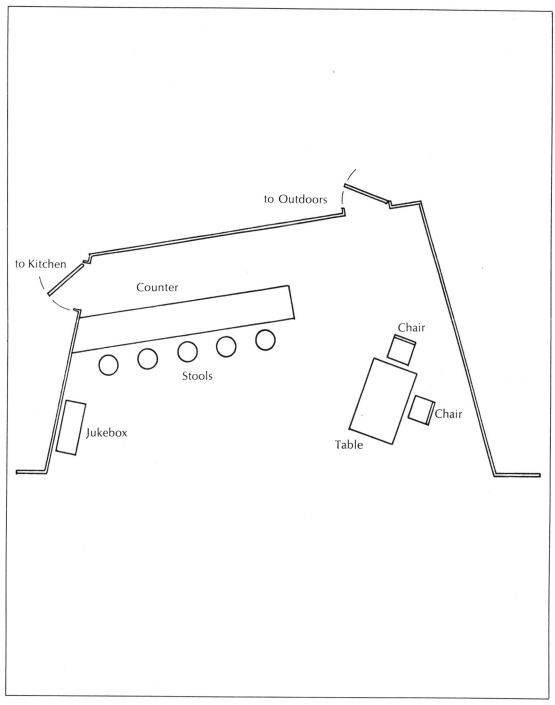

to Outdoors

to Kitchen

Counter

Chair

Stools

Chair

Jukebox

Table

Ground Plan for *When You Comin Back, Red Ryder?*

When You Comin Back, Red Ryder?

MARK MEDOFF

ACT I

The jukebox plays. Morning lights come through the windows. STEPHEN/RED *sits at the far end of the counter reading a newspaper, his feet propped on the second stool, the newspaper tabled by his knees and thighs.* STEPHEN *hears someone coming. He knows who it is. He moves to the jukebox, reaches behind it, and rejects the record that's playing.* ANGEL *enters.*

ANGEL: Good mornin, Stephen.

(STEPHEN does not look at her, but glances at the clock which reads 6:05 and makes a strained sucking sound through his teeth—a habit he has throughout—and flips the newspaper back up to his face. Unperturbed, ANGEL *proceeds behind the counter.)*

I'm sorry I'm late. My mom and me, our daily fight was a little off schedule today.

(STEPHEN loudly shuffles the paper, sucks his teeth.)

I said I'm sorry, Stephen. God. I'm only six minutes late.

STEPHEN: Only six minutes, huh? I got six minutes to just hang around this joint when my shift's up, right? This is really the kind of dump I'm going to hang around in my spare time, ain't it?

ANGEL: Stephen, that's a paper cup you got your coffee in.

(STEPHEN is entrenched behind his newspaper.)

Reprinted by permission of James T. White & Company and Curtis Brown, Ltd. Copyright © 1974 by Mark Medoff.

Stephen is playing the character he would like to be. Carefully chosen movements, postures, and physical attitudes help him to believe it.

Why does he turn off the jukebox when he hears Angel coming?

Angel: BEGIN *Beat 1*
She wants to set a cheerful tone. Her intention: "I want to get a pleasant greeting from Stephen."
Stephen: BEGIN *Beat 1*
His intention: "I want to bug Angel for being late."

This sucking sound always has a subtext, and Angel always understands what it is.

Angel establishes here the good nature with which she accepts her mother's nagging. It is often necessary to establish relationships with characters who never appear.
Stephen's actions of sucking his teeth and staying behind the newspaper are to accomplish his intention of keeping Angel out of his private world. Throughout the scene he ignores, resists or refutes everything she says. The scene is structured on Angel's various efforts to get to him, to get his attention. With each new tactic, she begins a new beat. Stephen retaliates. He initiates few beats himself.
Angel: BEGIN *Beat 2*
Beat 1 does not come to a terminal point; it is interrupted by Angel's noticing the paper cup, and

STEPHEN: Clark can afford it, believe me.

ANGEL: That's not the point, Stephen.

STEPHEN: Oh no? You're gonna tell me the point though, right? Hold it—lemme get a pencil.

ANGEL: The point is that if you're drinkin your coffee here, you're supposed to use a glass cup, and if it's to go, you're supposed to get charged fifteen instead of ten and ya get one of those five cent paper cups to take it with you with. That's the point, Stephen.

STEPHEN: Yeah, well I'm takin it with me, so where's the problem?

(STEPHEN has taken the last cigarette from a pack, slipped the coupon into his shirt pocket and crumpled the pack. He basketball shoots it across the service area.)

ANGEL: Stephen!

(She retrieves the pack and begins her morning routine of filling salt and pepper shakers and sugar dispensers, setting out place mats, and cleaning up the mess Stephen evidently leaves for her each morning. STEPHEN reaches over and underneath the counter and pulls up a half empty carton of Raleighs and slides out a fresh pack. He returns the carton and slaps the new pack down on the counter.)

ANGEL: What're ya gonna get with your cigarette coupons, Stephen?

(STEPHEN reads his paper, smokes, sips his coffee.)

ANGEL: Stephen?

(STEPHEN lowers his newspaper.)

STEPHEN: How many times I gotta tell you to don't call me Stephen.

the new beat begins before the old one is finished. Her intention: "I want to make contact with Stephen."
Clark is the proprietor of the restaurant.

Angel cheerfully accepts the regulations; Stephen flaunts his disregard for them.

Stephen: END *Beat 1*
A physical action to enhance his image and to irritate Angel. It makes a terminal point to Beat 1.

Angel: END *Beat 2*
She has failed to accomplish her intention. Her line makes a terminal point.
Physical action that creates reality. Here it also serves as a transition between beats.

His action of slapping down the cigarettes in true Western fashion is to reassert his image.
Angel: BEGIN *Beat 3*
Her beat is motivated by Stephen's action. She has wanted to know about the coupons for some time. Her intention: "I want Stephen to share something with me."
He is trying to ignore her.

She won't be ignored.
Stephen: BEGIN *Beat 2*
His assumed name is important to his image. His intention: "I want Angel to treat me like a cowboy hero."

ANGEL: I don't like callin ya Red. It's stupid callin somebody with brown hair Red.

STEPHEN: It's my name ain't it? I don't like Stephen. When I was a kid I had red hair.

ANGEL: But ya don't now. Now ya got brown hair.

STEPHEN: *(Exasperated.)* But *then* I did and then's when counts.

ANGEL: Who says *then's* when counts?

STEPHEN: The person that's doin the *countin!* Namely yours truly! I don't call you . . . *Caroline* or . . . *Madge,* do I?

ANGEL: Because those aren't my name . . . My name's Angel, so—

STEPHEN: Yeah, well ya don't look like no angel to me.

ANGEL: I can't help that, Stephen. At least I was named my name at birth. Nobody asked me if I'd mind bein named Angel, but at least—

STEPHEN: You could change it, couldn't you?

ANGEL: What for? To what?

STEPHEN: *(Thinking a moment, setting her up.)* To Mabel.

ANGEL: How come Mabel?

STEPHEN: Yeah . . . Mabel.

ANGEL: How come? You like Mabel?

STEPHEN: I *hate* Mabel. *(He stares at her, sucks his teeth.)*

ANGEL: Look, Stephen, if you're in such a big hurry to get out of here, how come you're just sittin around cleaning your teeth?

STEPHEN: Hey, look, I'll be gone in a minute. I mean if it's too much to ask if I have a cigarette and a cup of coffee in peace, for chrissake, just say so. A person's supposed to unwind for two minutes a day, in case you ain't read the latest medical report. If it's too much to ask to just lemme sit here in *peace* for two minutes, then say so. I wouldn't want to take up a stool somebody was waiting for or

---

Angel is a realist.

Her lack of imagination turns Stephen off.

He is setting her up for a let down.

He knows she is going to fall for this.
Subtext: I'll be glad to be Mabel if you like it.
Stephen: END *Beat 2*
His line is a strong terminal point. A cruel, and rather crude put-down. It forces Angel to try a new tactic. She tries mild sarcasm motivated by his teeth-sucking.
Angel: BEGIN *Beat 4*
Her intention: "I want to get back at Stephen."

Stephen: BEGIN *Beat 3*
His intention: "I want to put her down." A tactic of realizing his overall intention of keeping Angel out of his business.

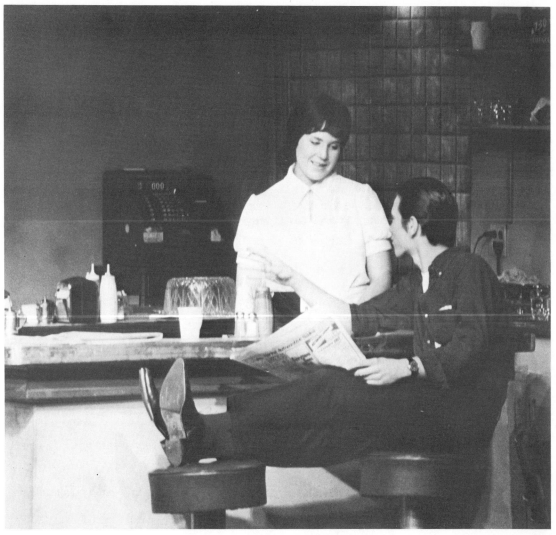

Angel and Stephen/Red in a Goodman Studio production of *When You Comin Back, Red Ryder?* by Mark Medoff. Note Angel's relationship to Stephen/Red. (Photograph: Goodman School of Drama)

anything. Christ, will ya look at the waitin line to get on this stool.

ANGEL: *(Pause.)* Did you notice what's playing at the films?

Makes strong terminal point, resorting to sarcasm.
ENDS *Beat for both Stephen and Angel.*
Angel: BEGIN *Beat 5*
The pause is a transition during which she is planning another tactic. Her intention: "I want him to ask me to go to the movies."

STEPHEN: Buncha crap, whudduya think?

ANGEL: *(Pause.)* I saw ya circle somethin in the gift book the other mornin.

STEPHEN: What *gift* book?

ANGEL: The Raleigh *coupon* gift book.

STEPHEN: Hey—com'ere.

(ANGEL *advances close to him. He snatches the pencil from behind her ear and draws a circle on the newspaper.*)

There. Now I just drew a circle on the newspaper. That mean I'm gonna get me that car?

ANGEL: Come on, Stephen, tell me. What're ya gonna get?

STEPHEN: Christ, whudduyou care what I'm gonna get?

ANGEL: God, Stephen, I'm not the FBI or somebody. What are you so upset about? Just tell me what you're gonna get.

STEPHEN: *(Mumbling irascibly.)* Back pack.

ANGEL: What?

STEPHEN: Whudduya, got home fries in your ears?

ANGEL: Just that I didn't hear what you said is all.

STEPHEN: *Back. Pack.*

ANGEL: Who's gettin a back pack?

STEPHEN: The guy down the enda the counter. Chingado the Chicano. He's hitchin to Guatemala.

ANGEL: You're getting a back pack? How come?

STEPHEN: Whuddo people usually get a back pack for?

ANGEL: Ya gonna go *campin*?

STEPHEN: No I ain't gonna go *campin*. I'm gonna go gettin the hell outta this town, that's where I'm gonna go *campin*.

ANGEL: When? I mean . . . when?

STEPHEN: When? Just as soon as I get somethin taken care of.

ANGEL: When will that be?

Another put-down.

Angel. BEGIN *Beat 6*

She has another transitional pause and then a new attack. She is back to the Raleigh coupons.

Her intention: "I want to know if Stephen's saving coupons has anything to do with his going away."

He is setting another trap.

Angel moves gingerly into the trap.

In performing the entire play, that car *needs special emphasis. Later Stephen's wanting to buy a car enters into the plot.*

Angel always wants things to be as pleasant as possible. She speaks reasonably, not irritably.

He wants the words to be unintelligible.

He gives exaggerated emphasis to the B, K, and P sounds.

He's leading her on, and he knows that she will take him seriously.

He is mimicking Angel on the word campin.

Her strongest effort to realize her intention.

He has to get enough to get a used car for his mother.

STEPHEN: When will that be? When I get it taken care of—when d'ya think. Lemme have a donut.

ANGEL: *(Getting him a donut.)* Where ya gonna go?

STEPHEN: Where am I gonna go? I'm gonna go hitchin that way *(Pointing left.)* or I'm gonna go hitchin that way *(Pointing right.)* and when I get to some place that don't still smella Turdville here I'm gonna get me a decent job and I'm gonna make me some bread. *(He picks up the donut and bites into it.)*

ANGEL: Rye or whole wheat, Stephen?

STEPHEN: This is some donut. I think they glued the crumbs together with Elmer's.

ANGEL: Rye or whole wheat, Stephen?

STEPHEN: *(With his mouth full.)* Believe me, that ain't funny.

ANGEL: Don't talk with your mouth full.

STEPHEN: Christ, my coffee's cold. How d'ya like that? *(He looks at her.)*

(She pours him a fresh cup of coffee in a mug. She sets it down by him. He looks at it a minute, then pours the coffee from the mug into his paper cup.)

STEPHEN: I told ya I'm leavin in less'n two minutes.

ANGEL: That's right, I forgot.

STEPHEN: Yeah, yeah.

ANGEL: You better let your hair grow and get some different clothes if you're gonna hitch somewhere, Stephen. You're outta style. Nobody's gonna pick up a boy dressed like you with his hair like yours. And with a tattoo on his arm that says "Born Dead." People wear tattoos now that say "Love" and "Peace," Stephen, not "Born Dead."

STEPHEN: Love and peace my Aunt Fanny's butt! And who says I want *them* to pick me up, for chrissake? You think I'm dyin for a case a the clap, or what? I got a coupla hundred truck drivers come through here in the middle of the night that said they'd all gimme a

Her relationship to Stephen—the "crush" she has on him—needs to be fully played.

Stephen has sensory task of eating donut.
Angel's verbal action is to get back at Stephen.
He ignores her joke. He wants to deny her the satisfaction of knowing that it has registered.
She persists in getting back at him.
He can give it, but he can't take it.

She was taught in childhood to observe this regulation.
Sensory task of drinking cold coffee. His look says, "Pour me another cup of coffee."
These physical actions dramatize their conflict.
Stephen should pointedly relate his action to his intention.

He wants to reproach her for the mug.

Subtext: Like hell you did! Makes terminal point.
ENDS Beat for both Stephen and Angel.
Angel: BEGIN Beat 7
She has to make a choice between at least two possible intentions here. She, either a) wants to get back at Stephen by telling him he is not such a hot shot, but way behind the times, or b) in spite of the rebuffs she has received, she wants realistically to help him with his problems in getting away. She should explore both possibilities in rehearsal.
The speech is a verbal action to build up his image.

ride anytime anywhere they was goin. You think I'm gonna lower myself to ride with those other morons—you're outta your mind.

ANGEL: Two hundred truck drivers? Uh-uh, I'm sorry I have to call you on that one, Stephen. If it wasn't for Lyle's station and his motel, Lyle'd be our *only* customer.

Being a realist, she can't let this one pass. Her verbal action is to make him face the facts.

STEPHEN: You know, right? Cause you're here all night while I'm home sacked out on my rear, so you know how many truck drivers still stop in here, now ain't that right?

ANGEL: In the three weeks since the by-pass opened, Stephen, you know exactly how many customers you had in the nights? You wanna know exactly how many, Stephen?

She is playing more strongly the intention of her previous line.

STEPHEN: No, Christ, I don't wanna know how many. I wanna have two minutes of peace to read my damn newspaper—if that's not askin too much! Is that askin too much? If it is, just say the word and I'll get the hell outta here and go to the goddamn cemetery or some-where.

Stephen wants to make Angel drop the issue. When confronted with facts he can't face up to them.

(LYLE STRIKER *enters.*)

He makes strong terminal point in an effort to get Angel off the subject.

Lyle's entrance would require an adjustment by both Stephen and Angel.

Some Notes on *When You Comin Back, Red Ryder?*

1. The environment, characters, and situation will certainly be familiar to young American actors without carrying on any research. If their knowledge does not come from direct observation, it will have been supplied by watching movies and television. The substandard speech should not present a problem; it is all too familiar in our mouths and in our ears. Like the language in *The Crucible,* it should be spoken naturally without calling attention to itself.

2. The scene has good opportunities for sensory work. In addition to small tasks, like drinking coffee and eating the donut, both characters have specific and different relationships to the diner and its environment. Stephen is disdainful of everything about it. Angel accepts it and works to keep it clean and pleasant. These contrasting relationships can be established in the handling of objects. The time of day also affects behavior. It is early morning. Stephen has been up all night. Angel has just got up. The actors themselves are sensory objects. Angel finds Stephen attractive. Stephen finds Angel unattractive. The actors would do well to relate to features in each other that they like or do not like.

3. Preparatory improvisations should be helpful.

Stephen: Improvise the last of his night shift, alone, without customers, waiting for Angel to take over.

Angel (with the help of another actress): Improvise the daily fight with her mother which occurs each morning before she comes to work. She will have to supply from her imagination the exact details of this relationship and the cause of the quarreling.

PART 3
Scenes for
Analysis
and Rehearsal

A Far Country

HENRY DENKER

The soul of man is a far country which cannot be approached or explored.

HERACLITUS

Exploratory Analysis of a Scene from Act II: 1 man, 1 woman

Background   The central character is Sigmund Freud, now for half a century recognized throughout the world as one of the most influential scientists of modern times. He opened the door to the hidden recesses of the human mind by developing a comprehensive theory about its structure and function. He demonstrated that many illnesses with no apparent organic explanation can be treated by psychiatry and psychological analysis. His name is a household word, and the adjective *Freudian* has a permanent place in our language.

It was not always so. In the play, which is based on actual events and authentically researched, he is a young doctor struggling to find ways to treat patients whose illness cannot be diagnosed in medical terms, and who therefore cannot be cured by conventional medical means. His experiments with shock treatment, hypnosis, and finally with "remembering and talking" lead to vilification in the press, censure from his professional colleagues, distrust and anger from his patients, and disruption in his family. The play dramatizes what it purports to be the first successful attempt at a form of psychoanalysis performed upon Elizabeth von Ritter, a young woman, who, with no apparent cause following the deaths of her father and sister, developed excruciating leg pains that

made it impossible for her to walk without crutches.

Who   DOCTOR SIGMUND FREUD. In his thirties. Already accepted by the Medical Academy, he has all the potential of a successful professional career as a practicing physician, which would provide, at the least, a comfortable life for himself, his young wife, and his family. (His first child is expected within a few months.) His increasing interest in mental illness, however, is rapidly curtailing the possibility of such a future. He has become a man beset with a dream that he must realize. He is not, in the usual sense, a fanatic. He enjoys good living. He is realistic about his successes and his failures. He recognizes the risks he is taking. He is a devoted son and husband, and he combats family opposition with tolerance and humor. He is Jewish, which, at least in his mother's opinion, means that to assure success he must behave conventionally and take care not to irritate people in authority.

ELIZABETH VON RITTER. In her twenties. From a wealthy family—attractive, accomplished, socially graceful—Elizabeth has accepted as a permanent, and possibly worsening condition the unexplainable pain in her legs. For several years she has walked only with crutches; she has

39

resigned herself to a wheelchair as her ultimate fate, with writing, painting, and sewing for charity as her life activities. Having been examined and treated by many doctors during the past six years, she sees her illness as incurable and further treatment as useless. More or less good-naturedly, she seeks help only to please her brother-in-law, her attitude in the doctor's office being "let's get it over with so I can go home and endure the pain." During her first visit with Freud, he taunts her with wanting to accept her illness rather than wanting to cure it. She is piqued enough to return.

Character Relationships The norm of Elizabeth's attitude toward her doctors has been described above. Early on with Freud there is a difference. His forthrightness, his lack of pretension, his need to succeed, all combine to make her want to continue her visits and to cooperate in her treatment. She becomes dependent, and this dependency induces an ambiguous response. She seeks to fulfill her need of him by maneuvering their relationship onto a personal basis with romantic subcurrents. At times she bitterly resents her dependency and the fact that he is not helping her. Her feelings fluctuate within a love/hate spectrum.

Entirely professional, Freud is aware of Elizabeth's feelings and treats them with respect. He wants to heal, as all good doctors do, and to that extent his relationship is personal. He *needs* to effect a recognized cure, both to substantiate his theories and to restore his confidence. Immediately before Elizabeth's first visit, he has returned from France, a tense and defeated man after having experienced a complete professional failure.

When and Where Vienna, 1893. Freud's office and consulting room in his apartment. The time and place affect the behavior of the characters. Dress and manners were more formal than they are today. Professional men wore cut-away coats, vests, high starched collars with cravats as they went about their business. On the street high hats, gloves and walking sticks were the order of the day. Women's dresses were ankle length, featuring bustles and tightly corsetted waists. Gloves were necessary away from home. Women's dresses determined their posture and their movement. The Viennese have always taken pride, sometimes to the point of feeling superior, in their sophistication, good manners, and good living. This general quality of life should become a part of the characterizations.

The Actors' Work Analyze the scene for intentions, obstacles, beats, physical and verbal actions, relationships, subtext, sensory tasks. Write the results of your analysis on your script, to provide you with a score for playing your role.

The Ground Plan Study the lines and stage directions to determine what items are needed to carry out the physical actions, and then arrange them in a way that will help you. The play is written to be done in a realistic setting representing a comfortable, book-filled office-consulting room of the period. For scene work only the furniture and properties actually used are essential.

A Far Country

HENRY DENKER

Time: afternoon, two weeks after Elizabeth's first visit.

At rise: we discover ELIZABETH *seated in an armchair, with her feet on the hassock.* FREUD *sits opposite her, using a shiny object on a chain like a metronome to focus her attention while he tries to hypnotize her. Her crutches are resting against the upstage wall.*

FREUD: Concentrate . . . follow closely . . . let your eyes follow and be relaxed . . . Now think of sleep . . . tired and you want only to sleep . . . sleep . . . sleep . . . Now your arms are getting heavy . . . let them go. Your hands. Let them fall away. Good. Elbows—let them drop—your shoulders—let them go . . . Let them fall. Good. Now, Elizabeth—the sky is very dark—and you are floating . . . floating. *(Cautiously, since it would be the first time she is under)* Elizabeth . . . do you hear me? *(She nods like one in a hypnotic trance)* Raise your right hand . . . raise it. *(She obeys)* Now lower it. Good *(She does)* Hold it out . . . rigidly. Good. Lower it. *(She holds out her arm, straight and stiff.* FREUD, *to test, presses down on her arm but she resists)* Elizabeth . . . when I instruct you, you will move your legs. And when you do this, you will *not feel pain.* Understand? No pain! Now move your legs!

ELIZABETH *(Eyes still closed, she taunts him)*: Well, I finally found out what you wanted me to do! *(She opens her eyes, but he does not join her joke)* You're angry with me.

FREUD: Yes.

ELIZABETH: I'm sorry. I try. Believe me, I do. Is there something terribly wrong with me?

In playing various roles an actor has need for a wide knowledge and understanding of human experience. Both Freud and Elizabeth need to learn about hypnosis—how it is induced and how the subject responds. It is necessary that Freud's efforts at hypnosis be made in a professional manner.

Reprinted by permission of the William Morris Agency, Inc., on behalf of the author. Copyright © 1961 by Henry Denker.

FREUD (*To cover his own concern and reassure her*):   Not everyone is susceptible.

ELIZABETH: And if one isn't? Then there's nothing you can do for her, is there?

FREUD: I've seen patients not responsive one day who were the next.

ELIZABETH (*Suddenly, and tense*): It's been the "next day" for twelve days now! And nothing has happened.

FREUD (*He presses her hand*): We must be patient. That will be all for today.

(*He turns away to get her crutches but the moment of contact has an effect on ELIZABETH. To keep from being sent away she asks*)

ELIZABETH: When I leave here, what do you do?

FREUD (*Turning back without her crutches*): Do?

ELIZABETH: The rest of your time . . . your days . . . your nights? . . .

FREUD (*Lightly*):   Oh. People always think that doctors lead such interesting lives. The truth is, we do the same as everyone else. Work, read, go to the theatre, argue about politics . . .

ELIZABETH: Even with your wives?

FREUD (*More soberly*):   Sometimes.

(*He starts to turn back but she arrests him with—*)

ELIZABETH: Do you ever think about what *I* do when I leave here?

FREUD: Write poetry . . . paint . . . sew for the poor, if I remember.

(*He begins to be aware of her desperate effort to stay on*)

ELIZABETH: I have a confession to make . . . My poetry . . . it's not very good.

FREUD: But you mentioned some professors at the University . . .

ELIZABETH: They were being gentlemen more than scholars, I'm afraid. (*Changing the sub-*

Elizabeth's response to physical contact with Freud is an example of actors' playing "off each other." It is an important action in establishing her relationship with Freud.

The stage direction More soberly *indicates that Freud is thinking a subtext. His wife's independence of mind frequently provokes arguments, and her concern about his future is reaching a crucial stage.*

ject quite suddenly) Sometimes, sitting out there waiting for you, I see her . . . She's a very devoted person. And she carries herself with a kind of independence that one has to admire.

FREUD: Independence is hardly an adequate word for her.

ELIZABETH: Oh?

FREUD (He gets her crutches during this):   She's a tyrant. Sometimes I scarcely dare treat a patient without consulting her. But I have to make some concession. After all, we can't afford to pay her what she's worth.

ELIZABETH: I didn't mean Kathy.

FREUD: Oh? Madame Freud?

ELIZABETH: Yes.

FREUD: Yes. Interesting, that you call her "independent."

ELIZABETH: If a woman has the man she needs and loves, nothing can touch her or harm her.

(He holds out the crutches but she doesn't take them)

FREUD: Have you . . . ever been in love?

ELIZABETH (Ignoring his question):   Where did you meet?

FREUD: In my own home.

ELIZABETH: Oh?

FREUD: Very brazen of her, wasn't it?

ELIZABETH: Well . . .

FREUD: No, the truth is, she came to visit my sister. I had only one glimpse of her . . . and . . . I was lost!

ELIZABETH: That's the way love should be. At first sight.

(Elizabeth starts to lower her legs, but she is obviously in pain)

FREUD: Are they worse today?

ELIZABETH: Oh, no.

FREUD: The way you move them—

Freud and Elizabeth need to create definite images of the two women they are discussing and keep them vividly in mind.

In an effort to realize her intention of personalizing their relationship, she is making a point that she wants to talk about his wife.

What is Elizabeth's subtext?

She may be thinking about Freud, or she may be thinking about her brother-in-law with whom it develops she has been in love since before her sister's marriage. Actors must make choices.

A major sensory task for Elizabeth is realizing the pain in her legs.

(He is bending to examine them. She fends him off)

ELIZABETH: No! Please!

It will soon be clear that she has a strong reason for not wanting him to examine her legs.

Goodman Theatre Center production of *A Far Country* by Henry Denker, showing guest artist William Smithers as Sigmund Freud treating Elizabeth Von Ritter with a Faraday machine. Production directed by John Reich. (Photograph: Voris Fisher)

(He does not insist, draws back. She rises)

FREUD: You haven't answered *my* question.

ELIZABETH: I've only been close to one person in my lifetime. Charlotte.

FREUD: Your sister.

ELIZABETH: And my friend. If you'd known her, charming, sensitive, bright . . . and for all her suffering, kind, and pleasant.

FREUD: Since her death you've been alone.

ELIZABETH: Even now, in the morning sometimes, before I'm fully awake . . . I'm "aware" of her. I sit up suddenly, look around the room expecting . . . but of course she's not there. Oh, the impression I must be giving you. You must think I'm shut off from the world, a recluse! Do you?

FREUD *(He can't deny it)*:   No—

ELIZABETH: Well, I'm not. I go to concerts, the theatre. And we have parties . . . sometimes. Teas, very often. In fact, our house in Doebling is one of the most popular in the entire suburb. It's always so alive, so interesting. Conversation, laughter, musicales, people . . .

FREUD *(Pointedly)*:   Young people?

ELIZABETH: Young people. And when the weather is good, we . . . I . . . I serve out in the garden. In the spring with the flowers, people say, "Let's go to von Ritters for tea and roses."

FREUD: You said "we" . . .

ELIZABETH: It used to be that Charlotte and I would serve . . . She would sit there in this . . . you see, her heart made her an invalid . . . this bower of roses . . . she would sit there and pour, cut the cake and I would carry the . . . *(She breaks off suddenly)* Of course, now I sit there, pour, and others move about and carry and serve. If there's one thing I can't bear, it's women who chatter. You must come visit one day. I know, I'll send the carriage for you. And for Madame Freud, of course. (FREUD *does as is usual now, goes to the door and opens it for her, but she stops him with—)* I mean to tell you . . . every day . . . I do admire these. I have from the first time.

Elizabeth needs to make the memory of Charlotte very real. Work with specific images drawn from experience and/or imagination. See and experience the images at each rehearsal. (See suggestions for improvisation at the end of the scene.)

(She indicates the collection of statuettes)

FREUD: My one vice . . . my only extrava-
gance. Aside from cigars.

ELIZABETH: I thought they were gifts . . . from
your wife.

FREUD: No. That one is . . . *(He goes to the
collection on the desk)* Ernutet . . . Egyptian
goddess of fertility.

ELIZABETH *(She interrupts him)*:   This one! It
was on your desk the first day, was it not?

FREUD *(Turning back to her)*:   Yes. A new piece
I brought with me from Nancy.

*(FREUD takes the Janus from the shelf and holds it.
Since she has both hands occupied with
crutches, he displays it to her carefully)*

ELIZABETH: A head of Janus! Or must one say
the heads of Janus? *(Admiring it)* Magnificent!
Is it Etruscan?

FREUD: My collection, like your poetry, may
not be quite what it seems. A copy. In fact,
most of these are.

ELIZABETH: But a very fine copy! *(As she ad-
mires it, and they are physically close, she says
suddenly)* As long as we are exchanging
confidences . . . I've written several poems
. . . to you.

FREUD: I would like to read them.

ELIZABETH: Would you?

FREUD: Yes.

ELIZABETH: I . . . There are no endings . . .
eleven poems . . . and not one ending.

FREUD: Some day, when they have endings
will you let me read them?

ELIZABETH: Someday, perhaps. Though . . .
there are some poems no one will ever see. I
destroy them . . .

---

*It is established in Act I that Freud collects statu-
ettes.*

*Freud has a reason for showing her this particular
figure. Elizabeth will never be fertile until she is
cured of her illness. It is her awareness of his meaning that prompts her interruption.*

*Janus was a mythological god with two faces. Freud
bought this statuette during his unsuccessful trip
to France. Showing it to his wife in Act I, he relates
his own career to the two faces: "This fierce one . . .
looking back on the lean years. This one, looking
ahead to the fat years . . ."*

*Subtext is very important. It develops that
Elizabeth suffers from extraordinary guilt feelings,
which she does not altogether understand, about
her sister and her attraction to her brother-in-law.
The poems no one will ever see doubtless attempt to
express these feelings, and possibly her growing
attraction to Freud. Here is another example of how
early scenes must be a preparation for later scenes.*

FREUD: Why? Are you afraid of something? Are you?

ELIZABETH: I can't describe it.

FREUD: Try. Please?

ELIZABETH: You wouldn't understand. No one could.

FREUD: If you tried . . . I might.

ELIZABETH *(feeling the overt symptoms of an anxiety attack)*:   I . . . please . . . I . . . it's getting dark in here. I . . . I can't breathe . . . it's a feeling . . . sometimes I feel that I'm falling . . . yes, falling . . .

FREUD: No earth beneath you . . . only a void . . . dark . . . empty void . . . *(She looks at him suddenly, pleading yet wondering)* Yes! There are others who feel as you do!

ELIZABETH: Then, maybe you can . . . oh, God . . . I can't . . . I can't . . . they hurt so!

(She trembles so, her crutches fall away. She is about to collapse but he catches her and assists her to the couch. He kneels quickly, examines her legs. What he sees makes him stand back, shocked)

FREUD: Elizabeth, how did you get those bruises?

ELIZABETH: Last night . . . I . . . stood in a long dark corridor . . . suddenly at the end of it, a door opened. A bright light. And a man. He beckoned to me. I wouldn't move. Till I saw it was you. I started toward you. As I reached the door, you slammed it in my face. I beat on it. Cried out, "Open! Help me! You promised. I believed you. Now help me!" You didn't . . . open. I woke. In terror. Alone . . . in the dark. "I will do it without him, without crutches," I said. Dragged myself from the bed. Rose to my feet. Even took a step . . . then they crumpled . . . I fell . . . lay there on the floor . . . hating them and I . . . I beat them and beat them and beat them! God, she buried the wrong daughter! *(During the above, Freud has been unable to comfort or reassure her. With her final outburst and tears, he turns, looks to the Faraday machine and decides to at least divert her. The movement makes her ask)* What is that?

Learn specifically what the symptoms of an anxiety attack are.

Relive the experience of this dream as you tell about it.

The Faraday machine is a device for administering shock treatment, named for Michael Faraday, who made important discoveries in electromagnetism.

In Act I Freud has said, "This is the latest 'scientific discovery.' Yes, that's what we nerve specialists call it. And we use it at the slightest provocation. We use it for cases of paralysis with no physical basis. We use it for pain with no discernible cause. We use it and use it and use it! But not one of us has ever seen it cure anything! Perhaps I exaggerate. Actually it does divert the patient from his pain, gives him a momentary sense of well being. But it cures nothing." It is necessary that the actor learn to use the machine properly.

FREUD: It may soothe your pain. *(He turns on the machine, holds aside her skirt and runs the glass over her lower legs, creating sparks)* There, now. Well?

ELIZABETH *(Assessing it)*:   I feel no change.

FREUD *(He turns, adjusts the batteries)*:   Now?

ELIZABETH: No difference.

FREUD *(Applying the rod)*:   You feel no difference at all?

ELIZABETH: Can't you make them stronger?

FREUD *(Giving it no special significance, he turns up the current, applies the rod)*:   Now?

Elizabeth must learn what the experience of having a shock treatment is. She must concern herself with both a physical and an emotional response.

ELIZABETH: Wait! Yes! That *is* better!

FREUD *(Puzzled that she can think so)*:   Better?

ELIZABETH: The pain is going away! More, please! Make the sparks stronger! Stronger! *(Puzzled, yet intrigued by the phenomenon. He deliberately adjusts the current and observes that though it obviously hurts, she says)* Much better! Much much better! Oh, yes . . . yes . . .

(Her exhilaration becomes very great till he suddenly turns off the machine. She looks up at him, puzzled)

FREUD: Elizabeth . . . you're sure it feels better . . . that the pain's not so bad?

ELIZABETH: Oh, yes! For the first time in a long time, the pain almost went away.

FREUD: And now, when you move them?

ELIZABETH *(She tries to move them and there is obviously some pain there)*:   Well, naturally, when I move them.

FREUD *(Still unconvinced)*:   But it did feel better?

ELIZABETH: Oh, yes. I like this treatment. I like it very much. Why haven't you tried it on me before?

(The doorbell rings)

FREUD: . . . I wanted to observe you thoroughly first.

(He goes to pick up her crutches from the floor)

ELIZABETH: We shall have to use it tomorrow. And every day from now on. Won't we?

FREUD: Elizabeth! I *know* that current of such intensity is very painful. I've tried it myself. Yet you insist you feel better?

ELIZABETH: Infinitely better. It was worth enduring the current. I think you've found exactly the treatment for me, Doctor.

FREUD: As long as you feel better.

(He opens the office door and starts leading ELIZABETH *out)*

Notes on *A Far Country*

1. While dramatists and actors may exercise dramatic license to make a play theatrically effective, in dealing with historical characters, especially ones who are close to our times (Freud lived until 1939), attention must be paid to a degree of accuracy. We have noted the necessity of Freud's treating Elizabeth in an acceptably professional manner. Fortunately the playwright has provided many details of his behavior. It would be well for the actor to augment this information by reading and, if possible, by interviews with doctors and patients.

2. Elizabeth is a challenge to any actress. She will need to draw upon both research and imagination. The leg pains must become real to her and they must be specifically located. She will need to depend upon memory of her own experience with physical pain; then she must recognize that the physical action involved is not to *feel* pain, but to *relieve* it. She needs to learn to walk with crutches. She needs to create and keep vividly in mind the past experiences that she describes and that are responsible for her condition. For her this is, in a sense, a "memory piece," and a study of the entire play is necessary for a complete characterization.

3. A reading of the play will suggest several possibilities for improvisations enlisting, if possible, the help of other actors:

— Situations involving Charlotte, such as Elizabeth and Charlotte entertaining at tea in the rose garden.
— Elizabeth pouring tea and cutting cake after Charlotte's death.
— Elizabeth nursing her father or her sister during their illnesses.
— Elizabeth entering the room to find Charlotte dead.
— Freud delivering a lecture to the Medical Academy. The texts of many of Freud's lectures are readily available.
— Freud taking his patient to Nancy when he has hope of her recovery through hypnotic treatment by another doctor.
— Freud returning with his patient to Vienna when he has no hope of her recovery.

FOR READING AND STUDY

Ernest Jones. *The Life and Work of Sigmund Freud, Vol. 1 The Formative Years and the Great Discoveries,* Chapter X-XVII. New York: Basic Books, 1953.

Sigmund Freud. "The Question of Lay Analysis: Conversations with an Impartial Person." The Standard Edition of the Complete Psychological Works of Sigmund Freud, Vol. XX. London: Hogarth Press, 1959.

The Journey of the Fifth Horse

RONALD RIBMAN

Based, in part, on the story "Diary of a Superfluous Man"

Exploratory Analysis of Two Related Scenes from Acts I and II: 1 man, 1 woman

Background The significance of the title becomes clear in a speech in which one of the characters describes a coach ride. "The driver, a lunatic of a fellow, was absolutely insensitive to anything other than meeting his schedule. Although the four horses we had were good and we were flying along, this madman insisted on adding a fifth horse. This poor horse was completely out of place, completely superfluous. . . . And how was this unnecessary horse fastened to the carriage? Absolutely all wrong. By means of a short thick rope that constantly cut into his flank so that his flesh was at all times positively lacerated. How he expected the beast to run naturally when its entire body was arched in pain I don't know. And what was this lunatic's reaction when I informed him that we would do better without this superfluous horse? . . . He began lashing the horse, a dozen additional strokes across its back and swollen belly, and screaming out to the wind. 'What the hell. It's been tied on, and if not to run then what the hell for?' "

In the play, the diary of the Superfluous Man has, after his death, been brought to a publisher.

As the publisher reads the diary, scenes from it come to life on the stage.

Who NIKOLAI ALEXEEVICH CHULKATURIN, the Superfluous Man. About twenty-five years old in the scenes with which we are concerned. Two passages from his diary tell us who he is:

"Think, dear Christ, have you made me anything more than Lawyer Levinov's fifth horse? If I had never lived it would have made no difference to anyone. My entire existence has been superfluous. That is the central fact of my being: the central word that sums up my total meaning. Think, dear Christ, is that not so? Have you not made me a fifth horse fastened uselessly to the coach of life? For whose benefit do I run? For whose benefit am I beaten?"

"Upon meeting my friends on the street of the university: 'Why it's Chulkaturin,' they say, and when I approach, the circle of friends parts as if a slightly leprous thing had been thrust in their midst. And the eyes which had

51

been set upon my eyes begin dropping from my face to my chest to my knees to the bottom of my feet, and everybody stands absolutely struck-still desperately trying to remember what it was they were saying before I arrived. Once I am ten feet past, the circle once again shrinks, the eyes once more rise, and the conversation moves like fish hustling down the Don. Oh Christ, that the circles of this world might shrink and find me standing locked inside!''

Chulkaturin is a landowner, educated, intelligent, sensitive.

ELIZAVETA KIRILLOVNA. Aged seventeen. Daughter of a wealthy landowner living in a small Russian town. She is called LIZA. She is so devoted to a pet bullfinch that she gives little attention to anything else. Her annoyed father complains about a ''daughter who arranges flowers all day and tickles bullfinches.'' Aside from birds and flowers, her mind is occupied with romantic images of her older brother's university friends, one of whom is to visit them later in the summer. He is a dashing cavalry officer, Captain Ivan Petrovich Narvinsky.

Character Relationships Chulkaturin, who was briefly a roommate of Liza's brother Illya, visits Illya's parents, near whom he is living temporarily, in order to make their acquaintance. Liza—charming, pretty, coquettish, full of romantic nonsense about anyone associated with her brother—makes him feel that he is not superfluous. Chulkaturin immediately falls in love with her. He writes in his diary: ''Is it possible that one day you could open the door to some stranger's house and fall in love? Yes, it is possible. That was the exact moment I fell in

love. I say that without reservation. The moment the door swung open into that household was the exact moment I came to love and to shut out all the impossible loneliness and misfortune of all the years before. . . . I now for the first time placed myself in contact with one whose steps would not flee from me, one whose eyes would behold my face and not turn away. It didn't matter that now I stood in front of a birdcage and forced myself to whistle. Not even forced myself. I whistled joyfully.''

When and Where Russia, in and near St. Petersburg, in the late nineteenth century. A full realization of these scenes requires a knowledge of manners, customs and dress of the period in order to understand how they affect behavior.

The Actors' Work Analyze the scenes carefully. Discover the overall intentions of the characters with the obstacles that must be overcome. Find the beginning and end of the beats, the sensory tasks, subtexts; consider how the verbal and physical actions help the actors to realize their intentions. Invent additional physical actions as necessary.

Make a score of your role by noting the results of your analysis in the appropriate places in your script. Continue to enlarge and refine your score during rehearsals. Make your notes in pencil so you can erase and change them as your understanding of your character grows. Review your score often throughout the working period.

Ground Plans After completing your initial analysis, give attention to the ground plans. Decide what exits and entrances, what furniture and properties you need. Then arrange them so they will serve you. The requirements here are simple.

The Journey of the Fifth Horse

Two Related Scenes

RONALD RIBMAN

FROM ACT I

*The drawing room of Kirilla Matevich Ozhogin,
Liza's father.* LIZA *is dancing about the cage and
whistling to the bird. She pokes her fingers into
the cage and makes bird sounds:* Eech, eech.
Ooooch, oooch. Eech, eech. *There is a knock at
the door which brings her out of her trance. She
goes to the door.* CHULKATURIN *comes in. He is
rather overdressed, almost foppish, somewhat ill
at ease. He tends to make little mistakes in
manners due to his anxiety.*

CHULKATURIN: Excuse me, I am Nikolai Alexeevich Chulkaturin.

Pronounce: nee'kō li̅ a̍ lĕk sā'vĭtch chool kä toor′ ĭn [1]

LIZA: I am Elizaveta Kirillovna, Illya's sister.
(They just stand looking at each other.)

Pronounce: ĕ lĭz a vĕ'ta kĭ rĭl'ōv na

CHULKATURIN: Is there anything wrong? I sent a
  messenger to say that I was to follow.

LIZA: Oh, no, there is nothing wrong. Illya used
  to talk so much about his University friends
  . . . We are expecting another of Illya's friends
  to call later this summer, you must know him

Pronounce: eel'ya

Copyright ©, 1967, by Ronald Ribman. ALL RIGHTS RESERVED
CAUTION: Professionals and amateurs are hereby warned that
The Journey of the Fifth Horse is subject to a royalty. It is fully
protected under the copyright laws of the United States of
America, the British Empire, including the Dominion of
Canada, and all other countries of the Copyright Union. All
rights, including professional, amateur, motion pictures, recitation, lecturing, public reading, radio broadcasting, television and the rights of translation into foreign languages are
strictly reserved. In its present form the play is dedicated to
the reading public only.

  The Journey of the Fifth Horse may be given stage presen-
tation by amateurs upon payment of a royalty of Thirty-five
Dollars for the first performance, and Twenty-five Dollars for
each additional performance, payable one week before the
date when the play is given, to Samuel French, Inc., at 25
West 45th Street, New York, N. Y. 10036, or at 7623 Sunset
Boulevard, Hollywood, Calif. 90046, or to Samuel French
(Canada), Ltd., 27 Grenville Street, Toronto 5, Ontario,
Canada.

  Royalty of the required amount must be paid whether the
play is presented for charity or gain and whether or not
admission is charged.

  Stock royalty quoted on application to Samuel French, Inc.

  For all other rights than those stipulated above, apply to
Flora Roberts, Inc., 65 East 55th Street, New York, New York
10022.

[1]Pronunciation of Russian names is difficult for English-
speaking actors. An effort has been made to suggest accept-
able pronunciation. Actors working a production of a Russian play should seek authoritative guidance.

53

. . . Captain Ivan Petrovich Narvinsky.

CHULKATURIN: No, I don't think so.

LIZA: Illya used to talk about him all the time. He's the terribly handsome one that I was absolutely forbidden to meet. The one who went into the Army.

CHULKATURIN: No, I'm afraid I don't recall . . .

LIZA: Shall I try to place you? I know all of Illya's friends.

CHULKATURIN: Well, I don't think that outside of being roommates we were very . . .

LIZA (Clapping her hands):   You were the roommate who never came in from parties earlier than four in the morning. The boy who never attended a single lecture for two years.

CHULKATURIN: No. I think that was the roommate your brother had during his senior year. We were roommates during the second year, the first half of the second year. Then Illya moved out.

LIZA: Oh. (Pause.) Then you must be the one Illya had that terrible fight with over some dreadful woman. He wrote papa all about it in a letter.

CHULKATURIN: No. Illya and I never had a quarrel. That was Peter Richter from Prussia.

LIZA: If you give me time I will remember just exactly your place in my brother's life, because Illya wrote me every week from Petersburg and I'm sure I know everything he did. (Pause.) You were the one who gambled at the races. (A line of pain momentarily crosses CHULKATURIN's face but the girl does not see it.)

CHULKATURIN: That was Ivan Vorontzoff. I never went to the races.

LIZA: You did not own a white stallion? (CHULKATURIN shakes his head.) You know what I think? It will come to me suddenly. Oh!

CHULKATURIN: What's the matter?

LIZA: I hope you have not come all this way just to see Illya, because he's not here. He left to go abroad for the Czar; he is in the diplomatic

Pronounce: ee vän' pĕ trō' vitch   när vĭn' skee

This line tells us Liza's intention. She needs to supply from her imagination descriptions of friends that Illya has written about and to study Chulkaturin to see whether he "fits" any of them.

Pauses, to be effective, must be "filled." Here Liza is studying Chulkaturin closely, trying to think which one of Illya's friends he might be.

Liza should write details from Illya's letters in her score.

Pronounce: ee vän   vō rōnt' zawf

"Oh" means that Liza has just thought of something and begins a new beat. Her mind darts about very rapidly.

service now you know since last April, but I'm sure he wrote you about that. (CHULKATURIN *shakes his head.*) No? He must have forgotten. Poor Illya, it was a very busy time for him so you must excuse him. He left for Austria a month after his wedding to Frieda Semeonova who is a blood relative of Prince Adrian. I'm sorry you were unable to come to the wedding. So many of Illya's friends and yours from the University came, but you must have been busy. *(It is obvious from the look on CHULKATURIN's face that he realizes what a small part he must have played in ILLYA's life, and that ILLYA did not even consider him enough of a friend to extend a wedding invitation to him. He is saved from any further embarrassment by LIZA's running over to her bullfinch.)* Isn't it darling? Illya gave it to me when he left. I have been teaching it to sing. *(To the bird.)* Sing for the gentleman, Popka. *(She whistles to the bird, then turns to CHULKATURIN.)* He really sings his heart out when he wants to. Come. *(Motions for CHULKATURIN to come over to the cage. He stands close to LIZA as she talks.)* See, he is not afraid of you at all. That's a good sign. It is a well-known fact that birds and animals can instinctively look into the hearts of people and know if they are good or bad. Did you know that?

CHULKATURIN: No.

LIZA: Oh, they can. If you trust the judgment of your pets they will always tell you who your real friends are. See how he is not afraid of you.

CHULKATURIN: Then we shall become friends.

LIZA *(To bird)*:   Brave little bird. That's a brave little bird. *(To CHULKATURIN.)* I would find it impossible to love someone that an animal feared, wouldn't you?

CHULKATURIN: I don't know.

LIZA: Will you whistle for Popka? See if he will sing to you.

Pronounce: sĕm yōn' a va

Chulkaturin's thoughts, his response to Liza's lines, are fully as important as the lines themselves.

It is an irony of the play that while Chulkaturin is falling in love with Liza, she is chattering on without any real feeling toward him.

CHULKATURIN: Oh, I don't think I could.

LIZA: Please. (CHULKATURIN, *after a moment's hesitation, begins to whistle.*)

Notice the physical and verbal action with the bird, leading to a climax when Chulkaturin whistles, is the terminal point of the scene and a climactic moment in Chulkaturin's life. It is, perhaps, the first time he has ever felt that he "belonged," that he was not superfluous. It is a fine example of how the dramatist (and the actors) can use action to communicate dramatic meaning.

FROM ACT II

A public garden near LIZA's *home. A few weeks later. Sound of* LIZA's *laughter is heard.* LIZA *bursts into the open and whirls herself around.* CHULKATURIN *appears and watches her as she is lost in her reveries. She spirals to the ground.* LIZA, *resting on her extended arm, slowly opens her eyes and stares at* CHULKATURIN. *The moment is poignant and* CHULKATURIN *breaks the mood abruptly by striding forward in cheerful embarrassment.*)

CHULKATURIN (*A bit too loud*):   Well, you see you have fallen. That's what you get for running so fast. Come. Let me help you up.
(*Extends his hand to her. She looks at him for a moment and then turns away. He drops his hand.*)

LIZA: I'm all right. Please, just a moment.

CHULKATURIN (*Stands by her, uneasily feeling that something should be said but not knowing, or rather not daring, to say what is in his heart. Instead, he makes conversation*):   I suppose they will be wondering what happened to us. I cannot imagine how we came to be separated from your parents. (*Pause in which there is no answer.*) Well, we've certainly taken our exercise for the day. If the summer continues at such a pace we shall all be in fine health. I haven't run this far since my father raced me in the meadows of Lambswater. (*Pause. Change of tone. Serious.*) You grow older you run less.

Chulkaturin wrote in his diary of this moment: "I could not move. I could not breathe. There were wild flowers in her hand. Her cheek pressed to the floor of the forest as if feeling the unheard music of grass and earth. I clung to the edge of the clearing afraid to approach, afraid to be seen, afraid of the moment into which I had transgressed. Though love had brought me, I came only as a stranger."

His inability to respond to Liza's games has its effect on her.

LIZA *(Suddenly turning to him)*:   You think it was childish of me to run?

CHULKATURIN: No. No, I didn't mean to imply that.

LIZA: Well, it was. Perhaps it will be a long time before I run again. *(Her mood changes from seriousness to fresh exuberance.)* Come. Sit down beside me. *(Extending her hand to him as he had before to her.)*

CHULKATURIN: We ought to sit on the bench. Your dress is going to be covered with grass stains.

LIZA *(She drops her hand as he, before, had dropped his. She becomes thoughtful for a second and then that passes and she smiles again, playfully)*:   If you make me sit on the bench, I shall fold my hands in my lap and not allow you to become what you should become.

CHULKATURIN: And what is that?

LIZA: What do you think that is?

CHULKATURIN: I don't know.

He desperately wishes he knew what she wants him to become.

LIZA: Guess.

CHULKATURIN: I can't.

LIZA: Then you shan't become it. *(She plays with the wildflowers.)*

Liza ends the beat.

CHULKATURIN: Tell me.

LIZA: What would you like to become?

CHULKATURIN: I don't know.

LIZA: Poor Nikolai Alexeevich Chulkaturin doesn't know what he would like to become. Shall I be kind and tell you then? *(Pause, and she breaks into a smile.)* King of the May! The king of all the hearts of young ladies. Here and now I shall give you your new identity. But you must kneel properly and lower your head. Come. On your knees, or else I shall be forced to find another to be King of the May and you shall have lost your identity for good. Don't dally. Shall you be crowned or not? *(There is a moment in which they look at each other directly in the eyes, and then* CHULKATURIN *goes on his knees and lowers his head. She begins putting the wildflowers in his hair.)* What fine

Consider carefully what each is thinking during this look. It is significant in realizing their relationship.

silky hair you have, Nikolai Alexeevich. Have there been many young ladies who have loved you for your fine brown hair?

CHULKATURIN: There has been no one.

LIZA: Perhaps you have forgotten them. The woods are full of the sighs of young girls. I think there must be many girls you have loved and forgotten.

CHULKATURIN: Do not think that there have been others.

LIZA: You must hold still. If you raise your head the flowers will fall.

CHULKATURIN: There has been no one who has loved me. Do not think that of me.

LIZA: I think men must be very cruel creatures to play with the heart of a girl and then not even remember her name. Men are like that according to my brother. *(She laughs.)*

CHULKATURIN: Why do you laugh?

LIZA: Illya says that the hearts of young girls are strewn about the world like grains of sand upon the shore and that there are not as many stars in the night sky as unremembered girls. Do you think that is true?

CHULKATURIN: I think that is poetic.

LIZA: And is that the same as true? What is your answer to that, Nikolai Alexeevich who has fine silky hair?

CHULKATURIN: You are making fun of me.

LIZA *(Stops as if suddenly wearied)*:   Yes. *(She stands up and turns to face the sun.)*

CHULKATURIN: Have I offended you?

LIZA *(Wearily)*:   No.

CHULKATURIN: Then what is the matter? Why are you staring into the sun.

LIZA: Must I have reasons for everything? Is it not enough reason to stare at the sun because it is up there, because it is flaming across the sky, because we may never see the light again, because, because, because, because. *(The mood becomes a trifle lighter as if she attempted to recover.)* Have I found enough "be-causes" to satisfy you? *(He is hurt. She reaches out to him, sincerely.)* Poor Nikolai, it is I who

This idea titillates her romantic nature. It is an ironic speech in light of what happens to her.

His inability to enter Liza's romantic world reaches its climax here.

have offended you. Am I completely intolerable to be with?

CHULKATURIN *(As he stands up, the flowers fall off his head)*: No. You cannot offend me. How could you ever think that you . . .

LIZA: See how soon every flower must fall. *(Brushing her hand through his hair to dislodge the other flowers.)* Every flower. *(To* CHULKATURIN.*)* Don't be angry with me, ever, Nikolai. *(She takes his hands in hers and kisses them.* CHULKATURIN *bends down to kiss her, but she almost flippantly turns away.)* Papa thinks young girls should be placed in hibernation along with Siberian Mastodons until we become eighteen years old, then we are to be melted from the ice and returned to our homes in time for marriage. Isn't that terribly clever of papa? *(She begins to cry.)*

CHULKATURIN *(In surprise and confusion)*: Liza, why are you crying?

LIZA *(Tears running)*: Isn't that terribly clever. I suppose I should take my dear bullfinch to sing to me in the ice and . . .

CHULKATURIN: What is wrong? Please don't cry. Please, Liza, Liza. Please! *(She turns her back to* CHULKATURIN *and, bowing her head, runs off.* CHULKATURIN *picks up the fallen flowers.)*

The falling flowers become a symbol of their relationship.

She cries sentimental tears picturing herself and "Popka" frozen in the ice.

Establish a relationship to the flowers.

Notes on *The Journey of the Fifth Horse*

1. Note that the dramatist uses words like *reverie* and *trance* in regard to Liza's behavior. She lives in a dream, unconnected with reality—quite literally "out of this world."

2. In preparing an entire play, it is vital that each scene be realized in relation to the major climax; in other words each scene must be a preparation for the final scene. The outcome of the relationship between Liza and Chulkaturin needs to be considered here. It gives these scenes a special "rue," and it gives an ironic foreshadowing to many of the lines. These undertones should be noted in the scores.

When Captain Ivan Petrovich Narvinsky arrives, Liza ignores Chulkaturin and gives all of her attention to the dashing cavalry officer. When he leaves a few weeks later, he is deserting a saddened pregnant girl. His love being real, Chulkaturin still asks permission of Liza's father to marry her: "I do forgive. . . . She is not of less value to me because of fools. . . . She will be loved as no woman has ever been loved. She will be respected. I swear that to you." Liza refuses in favor of an old family friend. Chulkaturin remains alone in the garden asking: Who cares that I came here? What was it for—the bird in the cage, the wildflowers, the dreams?

3. Suggestions for improvisation:

Liza: Receive a letter from Illya telling of his friends in St. Petersburg, read and answer it.

Do an extended improvisation establishing her relationship with the bullfinch; feed him, care for him, teach him to sing.

Chulkaturin: Improvise a monologue expressing his thoughts during a situation in which he feels utterly superfluous; for example, after meeting his University friends, being left alone at a party, realizing no one is listening to what he is saying during a conversation.

Improvise his behavior as he describes it after his first meeting with Liza. "I danced that night. I opened every window to the summer air, struck every candle, from every corner of the room dispelled every shadow. I took the wine from my landlord's table and brought it to my room. I took the books from the shelves and threw them in the closet. I locked the closet. . . . The world was to become involved with me . . ."

Ludlow Fair

LANFORD WILSON

Exploratory Analysis of a Scene from a One-Act Play: 2 women

Background   The title is suggested by a collection of poems by A. E. Housman called *A Shropshire Lad,* many of which speak in a melancholy way of youthful love and the quest for love. Sometimes the questing took place at Ludlow Fair.

The play is a study of two working girls, probably college graduates, sharing an apartment in New York City (it could be any city) and their relationship with men. Rachel has no trouble getting men, but for one reason or another she never keeps them long. Her most recent affair with a fellow named Joe ended abruptly when she had him arrested for stealing four hundred dollars from the apartment. She is deeply troubled about whether she has done the right thing. Agnes is troubled because she doesn't attract boyfriends, at least not the kind she would like to attract. She is more sensible than Rachel and more objective.

Who   RACHEL. Mid-twenties. Attractive. Taking stock of herself in the mirror to discover what is the matter that she is always in so much trouble, she is critical but pleased, "Five foot two. Five foot six, actually: Girls are bigger than ever. Lovely dark hair, fine hair. Opalescent skin. Lovely hips. Fine breasts. Nice legs. Nice, hell, great legs. Not bad ears; good hands. Slightly blah eyes, frankly; but then you can't have every-thing. *(Echo, breaking away. To herself.)* Can't have everything. What you are is probably a louse. A fool, of course, and a probable louse. Moral to a fault. And where you are a probable louse, Joe is a first-class, A-one definite louse without a doubt, and it is good to have a first-class louse out of your hair." Rachel comes from North Carolina (Agnes says from Dogpatch), and sometimes a Southern accent shows through.

AGNES. Mid-twenties. Busty, no raving beauty, but not unattractive. Quick-witted, she is the kind of girl that is considered "a great deal of fun." Her description of her upcoming lunch date, "The boss's son. Tonsils. *(Nasally.)* He talks like that. And with a Harvard accent yet. . . . He looks like one of those little model men you make out of pipe cleaners when you're in grade school. If I ever saw Charles without his clothes, he's so pale and white, I swear to God I'd laugh myself silly. He's Jewish, too." Agnes works in the office of Standard Universal (Plumbing) Fixtures.

Character Relationships   These are two girls who share an apartment for economic and social convenience. They will stay together until one of them finds it more convenient to live somewhere else; or until one of them establishes a permanent arrangement with a man, probably through marriage—for Agnes almost certainly through marriage. Whatever the differences in their personalities, they have quite a bit in common. Educationally and socially they appear to be pretty well matched. They are both single girls, working for a living, and looking forward to finding some satisfactory man/woman relationship. They have a decent respect for each other's rights and privileges. Agnes gets some vicarious pleasure from Rachel's affairs, and she has some sympathy for the problems Rachel makes for herself. However, the repeated pattern of the quick romance and the sudden break-up, followed by a trauma of remorse and regret, is getting to be a bore. Agnes tries to be a comfort, but she is running out of ways to do it.

Of the two, Agnes is the better adjusted and essentially happier. Speaking of adjustment toward the end of the play she says to Rachel, "Well sleep it off. I don't know why you should worry about Joe any more than you did about whoever it was before. You've got to admit the pattern is evident there somewhere. Maybe you really should go to an analyst, you know? No joke. You probably have some kind of problem there somewhere. I mean no one's normal. He's bound to find something."

When and Where   The time is the present. The scene is the bedroom of the shared apartment, about midnight. As in most contemporary plays, the dramatist describes the setting: "Twin beds on one wall, a vanity dresser across the room. A desk with books. The room is neat and in good taste. On the table between the beds is a phone. On the desk, is a dictionary, among other books; on the vanity is, among the usual paraphernalia, a box of large hair rollers and a bottle of nail polish. One exit is to the bathroom, another to the living room. RACHEL wears a gown and robe; AGNES pajamas and robe."

The Actors' Work   Analyze the scene for intentions, obstacles, beats, physical and verbal actions, relationships, subtext, sensory tasks. Write the results of your analysis on your script, to provide you with a score for playing the role.

The Ground Plan   The playwright's description lists the exits, furniture, and properties for the play. They may not all be essential to this scene. Experiment with the selection and arrangement to find what will be most helpful in carrying out your actions and communicating the scene to an audience.

Ludlow Fair[1]

LANFORD WILSON

RACHEL *onstage alone. She lights a cigarette, takes a puff, exhales. Goes to the mirror on the vanity and examines herself intently.*

AGNES *(offstage)*: I'm out. What are you up to?

Agnes means she is out of the bathtub, and Rachel can have her turn.

RACHEL *(without paying any attention. To herself)*: Oh, God. *(Sees herself in the mirror.)* Girl, you are a mess. Just a mess. *(Pause.)*
AGNES *enters. Without looking directly at* RACHEL, *she goes to her bed, picking up the dictionary on her way and tossing it on her bed.* AGNES *has a cold. She is carrying a box of Kleenex, a section of the* Times *folded open to the crossword, a brush and comb, and anything else she can find. Her hair is wet, combed straight down.*

Recalling the experience of having a cold and using physical actions to relieve it is one of Agnes' tasks.

AGNES *(without looking up, goes to her bed)*: Are you going to take a bath or what?
RACHEL: Take a bath? When did you start saying, "take a bath"? Take a bath, take a haircut, take a shower—I don't know what you're coming to.
AGNES: I got a cold.
RACHEL: What's that got to do with anything?
AGNES: Well, I abbreviate when I got a cold.
She situates herself on the bed with the paraphernalia about her, including a dish of peanut brittle.

Creating the cold is one of Agnes' sensory tasks.

RACHEL *(musing sadly)*: Four hundred and thirty-six dollars.
AGNES *(without looking up from the paper and brushing her hair)*: And thirty-eight cents.

Reprinted with the permission of Hill & Wang, a division of Farrar, Straus & Giroux, Inc., from "Ludlow Fair" from *Balm in Gilead and Other Plays* by Lanford Wilson. Copyright © 1965 by Lanford Wilson.

[1]To shape this excerpt into a unified scene a few speeches have been omitted.

RACHEL: I just wish I knew if I did the right thing.

AGNES: Look. A guy robs a store. If you turn him in, are you doing the right thing?

She states this as if it were an entirely hypothetical case.

RACHEL: Do I know this guy or not?

AGNES: What guy?

RACHEL: Who robbed the store. In your hypothesis.

AGNES: Leave my hypothesis out of it. What difference does it make? He robbed a store —you turn him in.

Agnes is working a crossword puzzle during this part of the scene; she's also eating peanut brittle. These are physical activities supplied by the dramatist for the creation of character.

RACHEL: He didn't rob a store.

AGNES: Are you going to take a bath or what?

RACHEL: I don't think so.

AGNES: You going to stay up and read all night or what?

RACHEL: Four hundred bucks. God.

AGNES: If you're going to start brooding I'm going to bed.

RACHEL: If just once we'd say to ourselves —you do that, girl, and you'll be sorry for it later.

Rachel means if "we girls would only think about the consequences before we get ourselves into such messes, we would be much better off."

AGNES: Yeah. Not bloody likely. *(Blowing her nose.)* Jesus, I'm coming down with something.

RACHEL *(studying her)*:   You know what you are?

AGNES: Yeah? Make it good.

RACHEL: Susceptible.

AGNES: Susceptible. You hook the dud and I'm susceptible. I got a lousy job in lousy Kew Gardens and a lousy date tomorrow for lunch and a lousy dentist appointment and a lousy boss and a lousy love life and a roommate who takes out her aggressions on me. And all you can say is I'm susceptible. I'm dying. Face it, Agnes, you got a lousy life.

RACHEL: I meant susceptible to colds. Or drafts.

AGNES: "Agnes Mulligan: This Is Your Life!" And the TV screen goes blank for thirty minutes.

RACHEL: Why do you always have a cold? You've had a cold since I've known you.

AGNES: Maybe I'm allergic to you. I wear low-cut dresses is why. I knew when I was nine, with a name like Agnes, I was in for a dumpy figure and a big bust and low-cut dresses and susceptibility to drafts.

RACHEL: Well, don't wear them.

AGNES (*almost always speaks as if she is talking to herself*): If I'da had any brains I'd have changed my name.

RACHEL: Why don't you?

AGNES: What's the point of having a big bust if you don't wear low-cut dresses. (*She puts the crossword on her lap, picks up the dictionary. Then, almost dreamily.*) What I can't wait for is a big house and about six handmaids and a big bed to sprawl all over. You know . . . I want to keep my figure—what there is of it. After I'm married, I mean. I really do. I want to look as nice as possible. God, I think that's important.

RACHEL: Oh, would you shut up? I thought you'd never get out of that tub. Don't you know not to leave a screwed-up girl alone with herself for three-quarters of an hour?

She has said it comically, but suddenly feels sad, puts her head in her hands again.

AGNES: Well, I was soaking. (*Notices her.*) Aw, come on, for Christ's sake.

RACHEL: I only want to know if I did the right thing.

AGNES: Look, a hundred of that was mine. He was a bum, what can I tell you? He was a bum and a thief and you turned him into the Secret Service and now what are you conjuring up? Lonely Joe in a cell? Well, forget it.

RACHEL: You're not funny.

AGNES: He was a bum. (*Aside.*) Damn, I'm all over peanut brittle.

RACHEL: He was. Of course he was. But I had no idea he'd done any of that other.

AGNES: · How long had you known him?

RACHEL: Three months.

AGNES: Well in three months you're supposed to know everything about the guy? Every bank he's robbed, for Christ's sake?

RACHEL: He hadn't robbed any banks.

AGNES: Federal bank notes passed totaling into the hundreds; you want to get technical, he's robbed a bank. A Federal bank at that. So you had fun; it wasn't worth it.

This stage direction that Agnes speaks as if talking to herself is significant in developing her character. Why does she have this habit?

Agnes needs to have specific images in her mind.

Within the confines of their characters, actors need to find a way to make expository information clear to the audience.

RACHEL: You're a lot of help. I think I'm going over the edge and you sit there complacently sticking to the blanket.

AGNES *(trying to wipe the blanket and Kleenex off her hands)*:   This damn stuff. I'm growing fuzz.

She sets the dish of candy on the table.

RACHEL: What will they do to him, do you think?

AGNES *(quickly, disgruntled)*:   I think they'll hang him.

RACHEL *(getting up)*:   Stop it! Now you just stop it!

AGNES: Hey, come on. He'll go to jail. He stole my dough and your dough and the Federal government's dough and God knows whose else's dough and he'll go to jail.

RACHEL: I just couldn't believe it.

AGNES: Yeah, me too.

RACHEL: We really had fun, too.

AGNES: Well, don't think about it, okay?

RACHEL: We really did.

AGNES: She says we really had fun, I tell her don't think about it, she says we really had fun. Jesus. Listen. You know what happened to the fag bookkeeper sits next to me at work? He picked up this guy. . . .

RACHEL: Agnes, I do not care what happened to the fag bookkeeper out at Standard Universal Plumbing.

AGNES: Standard Universal Fixtures. *(Pause. Firmly.)* There is no such thing as plumbing any more. *(Pause. Continuing.)* He took this guy he'd met up to—

RACHEL: Really! I don't—

AGNES: Look, do you think I'd trouble you if it wasn't pertinent? I'm not in the habit of telling you bedtime stories for the hell of it, am I? He picked up, good Lord, this guy! Apparently they just wander around till they see eye to eye with someone and then run right off the street and hit the sack, which, if you want to know my opinion, sounds a little capricious but not altogether impractical. Anyway, this big lug went home with him and "Stars Fell on

Notice how this speech is constructed. Agnes digresses from the story by making comments on it; then she brings herself back to the point.

Alabama,'' I suppose, or whatever the hell happens. Anyway, the next morning Henry waves good-by and two days later he sees this doll's picture in the paper—he'd been picked up for murder, my dear, of four or five fairies out in California and God knows how many more between here and there. Poor Henry almost died. He'd spent the night with this guy.

RACHEL *(pause)*: Fine! I'm sorry, I don't see the connection.

AGNES: You said you really had fun and you couldn't believe that Joe could possibly be—

RACHEL: —We happened to have been going together for three months!—

AGNES: —And you didn't know a damn thing about him—

RACHEL: You think a one night fling is the same—

AGNES: And you'd had some fun and you didn't know beans about him—

RACHEL: I didn't just pass him on the street!

AGNES: No, you didn't just meet him on a street—

RACHEL: Like your bookkeeper—

AGNES: You met him at Bickford's.

Bickford's is a chain of cafeterias catering to many people off the street; Longchamps' restaurants are quite expensive.
Build this beat to a climax with ''Bickford's. Longchamps.''

RACHEL *(defiantly)*: Longchamps! Honestly. I happen to be in love with him. That's why I'm wandering around this damn stupid —wondering—why the hell. Oh, Christ.

She sits back on the bed, stretches out, rolls over on her stomach, sobs once.

AGNES *(getting up)*: Oh, come on. Have a box of Kleenex.

RACHEL *(her face buried in the pillow)*: I don't want them.

AGNES: They pop up.

RACHEL: Go away. Why did I say anything? What had it cost me really? Nothing.

AGNES goes to the desk, gets a bottle of liquor out of the bottom drawer, fixes two drinks—just liquor, no mix.

This physical action is a transition.

AGNES: Honestly. Here. Have a shot. Me too,

''Honestly'' begins a new beat.

it's good for a cold. If I'm going to be running around nursing a roommate all night. Me? I'm always nursing someone else's broken heart. Just once I'd like a broken heart of my own.

RACHEL *(sitting up, takes the drink)*:   You're great.

AGNES: I snore actually. Why don't you go to bed?

RACHEL: I can't. I don't think. You go on. . . . It isn't late, is it?

AGNES: No. I hate you like this, I pass up more good cracks.

RACHEL: I think maybe I should call in the morning.

AGNES: And tell them what? That he really didn't do it? Not here or in Denver or in Tucson? They knew twice what you did about him. *(Moving toward her purse on the vanity.)* I got a hangnail. Damn that typewriter.

RACHEL: I could drop the charges.

AGNES *(looking through her purse for a file)*:   I doubt if they'd let him out for you. Besides, I don't know about you, but I'd be scared to death if he got out now.

RACHEL: I don't know what I should have done.

AGNES: Please don't worry about it. It's done. It's over; that's it.

RACHEL *(long sigh, not looking at AGNES)*:   Yeah.

RACHEL *is sitting gloomily, looking off into space.*

A Note on *Ludlow Fair*

The seeming simplicity is deceptive. The play is a searching study of two modern girls attempting, in their different ways, to find themselves in the sexual permissiveness of today's society. Establishing the contrast between their different ways is important. Agnes attempts to fill her empty life with crossword puzzles, peanut brittle, and dreams of handmaidens (she must have remembered the word from Sunday School) to wait on her. Rachel realizes that after each of her promiscuous affairs "the world it is the old world yet," and she is faced with the same old problems. The parts call for three-dimensional characterization, both physical and psychological, and provide an opportunity to make a statement about a common contemporary lifestyle.

The Subject Was Roses

FRANK GILROY

Exploratory Analysis of a Scene from Act I, Scene 3: 2 men, 1 woman

Background *The Subject Was Roses,* designated as a comedy-drama, won the Pulitzer Prize for the best American play in 1965, and in the same season was chosen by the New York Drama Critics as the "Best Play of the Year." A son, raised by indulgent parents, returns home after several years of army service. The family wants to have a good life together, but each comes to recognize that such a life is impossible. The mother (Nettie) is shattered to find that Timmy is no longer "her boy." The father (John) is indignant to find Timmy has ideas of his own. Jealousies erupt between the father and mother over the boy's affections. Valiant celebrations of the son's return begin in high spirits, but end in bitterness between husband and wife as they come face to face with their own unhappy relationship.

In the scene for exploration the three are coming home after an extravagant night on the town, including dinner, dancing and night-clubbing. That afternoon the father has given up an important business appointment to take Timmy to a ball game. They have had a good time. On returning John has brought Nettie a bouquet of roses, a gesture that has touched her deeply and has led her to hope she and John might regain the love they once shared.

Who JOHN CLEARY is a self-made man having stopped school at the age of ten to provide for himself and help his impoverished family. He is now able to provide a good life, including a comfortable apartment and a summer cottage, for his wife and son. He takes pride in the fact, or at least he frequently mentions the fact, that he was not pampered or spoiled as a boy as Timmy has been. He is Irish, Catholic, a firm believer in God and country but with a rather flexible set of moral standards. With no education beyond the first years of grade school, he has little interest in intellectual or cultural pursuits.

NETTIE is a few years younger than John, a trim good-looking woman. Strictly brought up in a middle-class home, she has never broken away from her mother. Sunday dinner at "mamma's" is still a regular event, and she is adamant about being on time. Enough better educated than John that she was once offered a job as a clerk in a law office, she feels superior to him. For some years her principal interest has been in being a mother rather than in being a wife.

TIMMY is twenty-one, having gone into the army at eighteen. He is a nice-looking, unexceptional fellow, cheerful and good-natured. He has a satisfactory army record including combat duty in which he conducted himself well. Being away has given him some objectivity about his parents. He sees his mother more clearly and his father more sympathetically.

Character Relationships The rancor between John and Nettie is long standing. When Timmy asks his mother what drew them together, she says: ". . . a certain wildness. He was not like my father at all . . . I was attracted and I was afraid. Twenty-four when I met him and making well over a hundred dollars a week. Great money in those days and his prospects were unlimited. The way he was going he would have been a millionaire. . . . That was his dream. . . . Nineteen twenty-nine took care of that. He was never quite the same afterwards. But when I met him he was cock of the walk. Good looking witty young Irishman. Everyone liked him . . . He was immediately at home on a ship, a train . . . in any bar. Strangers thought he was magnificent. And he *was* . . . as long as the situation was impersonal. . . . But that doesn't include the home, the family. . . ."

It turns out that John's failure to realize his dream was due in part to Nettie's unwillingness to break away from her mother and go with him where opportunity offered. Then came her almost fanatical devotion to Timmy, constituting an "alliance" between them which excluded John and prevented any close relationship between father and son. Timmy felt the estrangement keenly and blamed his father for it. In a later scene he tells John of a dream he used to have: "I'd be told you were dead and I'd run crying into the street. . . . Someone would stop me and ask me why I was crying and I'd say, 'My father's dead and he never said he loved me.' " Then

came John's sexual permissiveness and Nettie's righteous indignation.

Returning home, Timmy is caught in this bitter situation. He tries to do his best for both his parents. Toward the end of the play he says to Nettie: "When I left this house three years ago, I blamed *him* for everything that was wrong here. When I came home, I blamed *you*. . . . Now I suspect that no one's to blame. . . . Not even me."

Where and When The dramatist says that the action takes place in May, 1946. He describes the scene as "the kitchen and living room of a middle-class apartment in the West Bronx. A doorway Upstage links the two rooms. An invisible wall divides them. The living room is furnished with heavy upholstered pieces (replete with antimacassars) considered fashionable in the late twenties and early thirties."

The characters are "very American" and the environment is familiar to anyone who knows middle-class life in an urban setting. The year 1946 means that Timmy has returned from active duty in World War II. The characters and situation, however, are not peculiar to this period; the time could be the sixties or early seventies, with Timmy returning from the war in Viet Nam, without sacrificing the values of the play. A few references would have to be updated.

The Actors' Work Analyze the scene for intentions, obstacles, beats, physical and verbal actions, subtext, relationships, sensory tasks. Write the results of your analysis in your script to provide you with a score in rehearsing the role. Make a ground plan supplying what is necessary for effectively carrying out the physical actions.

The Subject Was Roses

FRANK GILROY

TIME: *Two A.M. Sunday morning.*

AT RISE: *The apartment is in darkness. From the hallway outside, we hear* TIMMY *and* JOHN *in loud but dubious harmony.*

TIMMY *and* JOHN *(Offstage):*   "Farewell Piccadilly . . . Hello Leicester Square . . . It's a long, long way to Tipperary . . . But my heart's right there."

This offstage scene should be worked the same as if it were in view of the audience.

NETTIE *(Offstage):*   You'll wake the Feldmans.

JOHN *(Offstage):*   Nothing could wake the Feldmans.

*(*TIMMY *and* JOHN *laugh.)*

The Feldmans are frequently mentioned neighbors who never appear in the play. "What the Feldmans will think" is a matter of concern to John and Nettie.

NETTIE *(Offstage):*   Open the door.

JOHN *(Offstage):*   Can't find my keys.

TIMMY *(Offstage—giggling):*   I can't find the door.

NETTIE *(Offstage):*   Honestly.

JOHN *(Offstage):*   Where would you be if you were my keys?

NETTIE *(Offstage):*   Here—I'll do it.

JOHN *(Offstage):*   Did you ever see such pretty hair?

The celebration, involving considerable drinking, has stimulated John's sexual desire for Nettie. What physical action is inherent in these lines?

NETTIE *(Offstage):*   Stop.

TIMMY *(Offstage):*   Beautiful hair.

NETTIE *(Offstage):*   Will you please let me open this door?

(A KEY *turns. The door opens.* NETTIE, *followed by* JOHN *and* TIMMY, *enters;* TURNS *on lights.)*

JOHN *(He is wearing* TIMMY'S *hat.):*   Home to wife and mother. *(Crosses D. R. of couch)*

NETTIE *(To* JOHN*):*   Someday we'll break our necks because you refuse to leave a light.

Timmy is still in uniform. This would be an overseas cap.

From *About Those Roses and The Subject Was Roses* by Frank D. Gilroy. Copyright © 1965 by Frank D. Gilroy. Reprinted by permission of Random House, Inc.

TIMMY (*Crosses to R. of* JOHN, *singing*):   "By the light . . ." (JOHN *joins in:*) "Of the silvery moon—"

NETTIE: —That's just enough. (*Taking coat off rear chair.*)
JOHN: Whatever you say, Antoinette.
(TIMMY *tosses* JOHN's *hat on* U. S. *table.*)
NETTIE: I say to bed. (*She turns L.*)
JOHN (*Crossing R. of* NETTIE):   Shank of the evening. (*He grabs her around the waist and manages a squeeze before she breaks away to L. with an indignant exclamation. Ignoring the look of censure she directs at him, he turns to* TIMMY.) No sir, you can't beat a law degree. Springboard for anything.

TIMMY: So they say.
NETTIE (*To* JOHN):   Anyone can be a lawyer. How many people become writers?
JOHN (*To her*):   That's my point.
NETTIE: You should be proud to have a son who wants to try something different.
JOHN: Did I say I wasn't proud of him?
TIMMY: Abra ka dabra ka deedra slatter-in. (*They regard him.*) The fellow in the red jacket says that when they reach the starting gate. Abra ka dabra ka deedra slatter-in. And here are your horses for the fifth race. . . . Long as you can say it, you're not drunk. . . . *Abra ka dabra ka deedra slatter-in.*
JOHN (*Crossing to R. of* TIMMY):   Abra ka dabra . . .
TIMMY: Ka deedra slatter-in.
NETTIE: Honestly. (*Puts her hat and coat and* JOHN's *jacket in closet.*)
JOHN: Ka zebra—
TIMMY: —Not zebra. Deedra . . . Ka deedra slatter-in . . . Abra ka dabra ka deedra slatter-in.
JOHN: Abra . . . ka dabra . . . ka deedra . . . slatter-in.
TIMMY: Faster.
JOHN (*Dancing jig*):   Abra, ka dabra, ka deedra, slatter-in.

John and Timmy are inebriated, a state that by definition is an hilarious and noisy phase of insobriety. Creating this state in the appropriate degree is one of the major sensory tasks.

This line revives a recurring conflict. Timmy has said he wants to be a writer and, of course, Nettie supports him. John wants his son to be a lawyer.

Abra ka dabra. . . . What is Timmy's intention here?

TIMMY: Faster.

JOHN: Abra ka dabra ka deedra slatter-in.

NETTIE (Crosses D. to L. of couch):   Have you both lost your minds?

JOHN: Nothing wrong with us that a little nightcap wouldn't cure. (He enters the kitchen, hides D. S. of door.)

NETTIE (Following him):   I'll nightcap you. (JOHN grabs her around waist. She breaks and crosses below table R.)

TIMMY (Crossing D.):   I can't bear to hear married people fight.

JOHN (To NETTIE):   We ought to go dancing more.

NETTIE (Crosses D. R. of table):   Now I know you're drunk.

TIMMY (Calling from the living room):   Who was it that used to call us The Four Mortons?

The Four Mortons. Here and several times later, Timmy and John recall popular vaudeville and radio performers of the thirties and forties.

JOHN (Calling back, crossing D. to chair):   Harold Bowen.

TIMMY (Staring at the audience):   I wish we were.

JOHN (To NETTIE):   Remember the first dance I took you to?

NETTIE: Of course.

JOHN: I'll bet you don't.

NETTIE: Of course I do.

TIMMY (Lost in contemplation of an imaginary audience):   I have this magical feeling about vaudeville.

Timmy, in the living room, is unrelated to John and Nettie in the kitchen.

JOHN (To NETTIE):   Where was it then?

NETTIE (Crosses U. L. of table):   The Crystal Terrace.

JOHN (Crosses R. of table):   What was the first song?

NETTIE: It's too late for quiz games.

TIMMY (D. C. in living room):   It doesn't matter how cheap and tinny the show is. . . . Soon as the house lights go down and the band starts up, I could cry.

JOHN (To NETTIE):   The first song we ever danced to was "Pretty Baby." (He hums a bit of the melody.) A blond guy crooned it.

Pretty Baby: a song popular in the twenties.

NETTIE: Through a gold megaphone.

JOHN: You *do* remember.

NETTIE: Of course. *(She crosses into living room.* JOHN *crosses to her. To escape his overtures, she sits on couch arm.)*

TIMMY *(To the audience—a la Smith and Dale):*   "I've got snew in my blood." . . . "What's snew?" . . . "Nothing. What's snew with you?" *(Crosses* L.*)*

> Smith and Dale were a popular comedy team noted for their gags and patter.

NETTIE *(To* JOHN—*indicating* TIMMY*):*   What's he doing?

JOHN: Playing the Palace. *(Crosses* D. R.*)*

NETTIE *(To* TIMMY*):*   Will you please go to bed?

TIMMY *(To the audience):*   In closing I would like to do a dance made famous by the inimitable Pat Rooney. *(Nods to* JOHN.*)* Maestro, if you please.

> Pat Rooney was a soft-shoe dancer. One of the tasks of this scene is to learn a few steps of a soft-shoe routine.

*(*JOHN *begins to hum "The Daughter of Rosie O'Grady" as both he and* TIMMY *dance in the manner of Pat Rooney.)*

NETTIE: John! Timmy! *(They stop dancing.)* Mama expects us at twelve.

TIMMY *(To the audience):*   We're running a bit long folks: No dance tonight. My mother thanks you. My father thanks you. My sister thanks you. And the Feldmans thank you. *(He goes into Jimmy Durante's closing song.)* "Good night . . . Good night . . . Good night—"

> Timmy uses the real audience as his imaginary audience. Since the style is essentially realistic, care must be taken not to break the illusion of the fourth wall.
>
> George M. Cohan, as a young entertainer appearing with his family, made a curtain speech in which he said: "My father thanks you. My mother thanks you. My sister thanks you. And I thank you."

NETTIE: —*Good night!*

TIMMY *(Kisses* NETTIE*):*   Good night, Mrs. Cleary—whoever you are.

NETTIE: Good night, dear.

> Jimmy Durante used to close his radio show with "Goodnight, Mrs. Calabash, wherever you are."

TIMMY *(To* JOHN—*indicating the audience):*   Tough house but I warmed them up for you.

JOHN *(Shakes hand):*   Thanks.

TIMMY: Don't look now, but your leg's broken.

JOHN *(Limps* L. *as* NETTIE *crosses to coffee table):*   The show must go on.

TIMMY *(To* NETTIE—*indicating* JOHN*):*   Plucky lad. *(Extends his hand to* JOHN.*)* Honor to share the bill with you.

> They are now pretending to be two vaudeville performers appearing on the same bill.

JOHN (*Shaking with him*): Likewise.

TIMMY: Sleep well, chaps.

JOHN: Night, Champ.

NETTIE: Sure you don't want an alka seltzer?

TIMMY: Abra ka dabra ka deedra slatter-in . . . see you in the morning.

JOHN: With the help of God.

TIMMY (*Moving toward his room*): Abra ka dabra ka deedra slatter-in . . . Abra ka dabra ka deedra slatter-in. . . . And here are your horses for . . . (*Enters his room; closes the door.*)

NETTIE: Home two days and both nights to bed like that.

On his first night home Timmy got drunk at a welcoming party.

JOHN: He's entitled. You should hear some of the things he's been through. They overran one of those concentration camps—

NETTIE: —I don't want to hear about it now.

JOHN (*Crosses to her* L.): You're right. It's no way to end a happy evening.

NETTIE: I think we have some aspirin in the kitchen. (*She moves into the kitchen. He follows; watches her take a bottle of aspirin from counter drawer.*)

JOHN (*Crossing to kitchen table*): You didn't say anything before about a headache.

NETTIE: I don't have a headache.

JOHN: Then what—

NETTIE: —I read that if you put an aspirin in cut flowers they keep longer. (*She drops an aspirin in the vase; regards the roses.*) I wonder what made you get them?

Nettie's relationship to the roses is an important task.

JOHN: I don't know.

NETTIE: There must have been some reason. (*Smells them.*)

JOHN: I just thought it would be nice to do.

NETTIE (*She turns to him.*): It was.

(*They regard each other a moment.*)

JOHN: I like your dress.

The relationship between John and Nettie needs to be established by each actor's supplying from his imagination specific details of their past life together.

NETTIE (*Crosses to counter with aspirin bottle*): You've seen it before.

JOHN (*Crossing to above her*): It looks different. . . . Everything about you looks different.

NETTIE (*Turns to him*): What mass are you going to?

JOHN: Ten o'clock.

NETTIE (*Picking up the vase of roses and starting toward the living room*):   I better set the alarm.

JOHN: Nettie? (*She turns to him.*) I had a good time tonight.

NETTIE: So did I. (NETTIE *enters the living room and places the roses on coffee table; arranges them.*)

JOHN (*Following her into the living room, to L. of phone*):   Did you really? Or were you putting it on for his sake?

NETTIE: I really did.

JOHN (*Crosses to her R.*):   So did I.

NETTIE (*Crosses to chair and picks up* TIMMY'S *jacket*):   I'll set the alarm for nine-fifteen. (*She starts away again.*)

JOHN: Now that he's back we'll have lots of good times.

NETTIE (*She stops*):   What's wrong between you and I has nothing to do with him.

JOHN (*Crosses to her L.*):   I didn't say it did.

NETTIE: We have to solve our own problems.

JOHN (*Crosses to her R.*):   Of course.

NETTIE: They can't be solved in one night.

JOHN (*Takes jacket from her and puts it on chair*):   I know.

NETTIE (*She crosses to C.*):   One nice evening doesn't make everything different.

JOHN (*Crosses with her and puts his arms around her waist*):   Did I say it did? (*His lips brush the nape of her neck.*)

NETTIE: I guess you don't understand.

JOHN (*Kisses her neck*):   I forgot how nice you smelled.

NETTIE: You'll spoil everything.

JOHN (*Squeezes her waist*):   I want things right between us.

NETTIE: You think this is going to make them right?

JOHN (*His hands moving to her breasts*):   We have to start someplace.

NETTIE (*Breaking away R.*):   Start?

JOHN: Bless us and save us.

NETTIE: *That's not my idea of a start.*

JOHN: Nettie, I want you . . . I want you like I

Give special attention to beginning this new beat. What is John's intention?

Nettie is providing a strong obstacle to John's intention.

never wanted anything in my life.

NETTIE *(Covering her ears):*   Stop.

JOHN *(Crosses to her L.):*   Please?

NETTIE *(Crosses to chair, picks up* TIMMY's *jacket and crosses L. of couch):*   You're drunk.

JOHN *(Turns L.):*   Do you think I could ask again if I wasn't?

NETTIE: I'm not one of your hotel lobby whores.

JOHN: If you were I wouldn't have to ask.

NETTIE: A couple of drinks, a couple of jokes, and let's jump in bed.

JOHN: Maybe that's my mistake.

NETTIE: How do you suppose Ruskin managed without you today? *(Crosses U.)*

JOHN *(Follows to her L.):*   Maybe you don't want to be asked! *(He seizes her.)*

NETTIE: Let me alone.

JOHN *(As they struggle at couch):*   You've had the drinks! You've had the jokes!

NETTIE: *Stop! (She breaks free of him, regards him for a moment, then picks up the vase of roses and hurls them against the floor. The impact is shattering. They both freeze. For a moment there is silence. Now* TIMMY's *door opens.)*

TIMMY *(Entering):*   What happened?

NETTIE: The roses . . . I knocked them over.

TIMMY: Sounded like a bomb.

NETTIE: I'm sorry I woke you. *(*TIMMY *bends to pick up a piece of the vase)* Don't . . . I'll clean up. You go back to bed. *(He hesitates.)* Please.

TIMMY *(Puts pieces of vase on coffee table):*   All right. . . . Good night.

NETTIE: Good night.

TIMMY: Good night, Pop.

*(*JOHN, *his back to* TIMMY, *remains silent.* TIMMY *hesitates a moment then goes off to his room: closes his door.)*

NETTIE *(To* JOHN*):*   You moved me this afternoon. . . . When you brought the roses, I felt something stir I thought was dead forever. *(Regards the roses on the floor.)* And now this. . . . I don't understand.

JOHN *(Without turning):*   I had nothing to do with the roses. . . . They were *his* idea.

(She bends and starts to pick up the roses.)

Ruskin is the business associate with whom John broke an appointment to take Timmy to the ball game.

Desire Under the Elms

EUGENE O'NEILL

Exploratory Analysis of Three Related Scenes from Part II: 1 man, 1 woman

Background Termed a "farmhouse tragedy" and considered a representative example of naturalistic drama, *Desire Under the Elms* has been frequently performed since its original production in 1924 and has been made into a motion picture with Sophia Loren and Anthony Perkins as Abbie and Eben. The story tells what happens when tyrannical old Ephriam Cabot brings to his rocky New England farm a young wife, Abbie Putnam, who has married him solely for the security she expects to find there. Ephriam's grown sons from two earlier marriages bitterly resent the new wife's presence. The two older sons desert the farm to seek gold in California. Eben, the youngest, stays with the land because the farm rightly belonged to his mother, and he is determined it will not pass out of his hands. To secure her own claim by producing an heir, as well as to satisfy her own physical needs, Abbie seduces Eben. Her greed and desire, however, turn to love. To prove her devotion to Eben she smothers their child to convince him that her love is greater than her greed for the farm. When the sheriff comes to arrest her, Eben proves his love by going with her as a partner in crime.

In a naturalistic play the actors are called upon to perform with the greatest possible attention to details observed from everyday life. Toward this end, Abbie and Eben speak in a dialect typifying the speech of uneducated New England farm people in the 1850s. O'Neill consistently misspells words to guide the actors toward pronunciations that vary from standard American speech. It is one of the actors' tasks to master this dialect and speak it in a convincing natural manner.

Another characteristic of this genre is that the behavior of the characters is motivated by their natural—and usually baser—instincts. Fully realizing these motivating drives is another challenge in this scene. O'Neill's confidence in an essential human dignity, however, distinguishes the play from the works of some other naturalistic dramatists in which the characters throughout exhibit only animalistic behavior. The sacrifices that Abbie and Eben make at the end lift them to a tragic nobility.

Who EBEN CABOT is twenty-five years old, a New England farmer, generally uneducated, although under his mother's influence he has acquired a sensitivity that distinguishes him from his older, coarser-grained half-brothers. O'Neill says that he is "tall and sinewy. His face is well-formed, good-looking, but its expression is resentful and defensive. His defiant dark eyes remind one of a wild animal's in captivity. . . . There is a fierce repressed vitality about him. . . . He is dressed in rough farm clothes." His actions are largely governed by his hatred of his Puritanical father, a religious fanatic, whose driving urge to conquer the land has made slaves of his family and has been responsible for the early death of Eben's mother. In spite of this hatred, he possesses some of his father's qualities as shown in his relentless desire to hold onto the farm and in some measure to avenge his mother's death.

ABBIE PUTNAM is a few years older than Eben. Like him she is driven by a relentless desire—to provide a security that has always been denied her. O'Neill describes her as "full of vitality. Her round face is pretty but marred by its rather gross sensuality. There is strength and obstinacy in her jaw, a hard determination in her eyes, and about her whole personality the same unsettled, untamed, desperate quality which is so apparent in Eben." Abbie tells about her past in an earlier scene in which she tries to win Eben's friendship and to overcome his resentment at someone's attempting to take his mother's place. "Yew must've cared a lot fur yewr Maw, didn't ye? My Maw died afore I'd growed. I don't remember her none. . . . Waal—I've had a hard life, too —oceans of trouble an' nuthin' but wuk fur reward. I was a orphan early an' had t' wuk fur others in other folks' hums. Then I married an' he turned out a drunken spreer an' so he had to wuk fur others an' me too agen in other folks' hums, an' the baby died, an' my husband got sick an' died too, an' I was glad sayin' now I'm free fur once, on'y I diskivered right away all I was free fur was t' wuk agen in other folks' hums, doin' other folks' wuk till I'd most give up hope o' ever doin' my own wuk in my own hum, an' then your Paw come. . . ."

Character Relationships   It is said that O'Neill's characters are bedeviled from within and from without. Abbie and Eben are victims of such bedevilment. They are enemies engaged in a tenacious struggle to possess the same piece of land. Eben sees Abbie's presence as a threat to his inheritance and as a sacrilege to the memory of his mother. Abbie sees Eben as a rival for the security she is determined to attain. At the same time they are desperately attracted to each other. The scenes for exploration reveal Eben's hostility, Abbie's determination and her successful attempt to seduce him for her own purposes. Through their physical union Abbie feels that she is assuring her claim to the farm, and Eben feels that he is avenging himself against his father by possessing his father's wife. We must remember, though, that by the end of the play their greed and desire have been transmuted into genuine love, a fact that must not be overlooked in playing these earlier scenes.

Where and When   A New England farm in the 1850s. The rocky soil from which the crops must be extracted, the weather-beaten farmhouse set among brooding elms, the loneliness, the bleakness of life there—all create an environment that is a major force in determining the behavior of the characters.

The Actors' Work   Analyze the scene for intentions, obstacles, beats, physical and verbal actions, relationships, subtext, sensory tasks. Write the results of your analysis in your script to provide you with a score in rehearsing the role.

The Ground Plan   The setting for the entire play requires both the exterior and interior of the farmhouse. The exterior shows the yard, and porch and the entrance to the kitchen. The interior shows the kitchen and the parlor on the ground floor, and two bedrooms upstairs. The scenes for exploration take place on the porch, in the two bedrooms simultaneously, and in the parlor. Plan your setting so that all locations are arranged beforehand, permitting you to move from one scene to the next without interruption. This is a device frequently used in staging plays that require several different locations. You need provide only furniture and properties essential to carrying out the physical actions.

Desire Under the Elms

EUGENE O'NEILL

PART TWO—SCENE ONE

The exterior of the farmhouse—a hot Sunday afternoon. ABBIE, *dressed in her best, is discovered sitting in a rocker at the end of the porch. She rocks listlessly, enervated by the heat, staring in front of her with bored, half-closed eyes.*

EBEN *sticks his head out of his bedroom window. He looks around furtively and tries to see—or hear—if anyone is on the porch, but although he has been careful to make no noise,* ABBIE *has sensed his movement. She stops rocking, her face grows animated and eager, she waits attentively.* EBEN *seems to feel her presence, he scowls back his thought of her and spits with exaggerated disdain—then withdraws back into the room.* ABBIE *waits, holding her breath as she listens with passionate eagerness for every sound within the house.*

EBEN *comes out. Their eyes meet; his falter. He is confused, he turns away and slams the door resentfully. At this gesture,* ABBIE *laughs tantalizingly, amused but at the same time piqued and irritated. He scowls, strides off the porch to the path and starts to walk past her to the road with a grand swagger of ignoring her existence. He is dressed in his store suit, spruced up, his face shines from soap and water.* ABBIE *leans forward on her chair, her eyes hard and angry now, and, as he passes her, gives a sneering, taunting chuckle.*

EBEN (*stung—turns on her furiously*):   What air yew cacklin' 'bout?

O'Neill, like some other modern dramatists, gives detailed directions for physical actions. Examine each direction to discover how it serves the character in accomplishing his overall situation. Do not perform any action until you know why *you are doing it.*

Copyright 1924 and renewed 1952 by Eugene O'Neill. Reprinted from *Selected Plays of Eugene O'Neill* by permission of Random House, Inc.

ABBIE (*triumphant*):   Yew!

EBEN: What about me?

ABBIE: Ye look all slicked up like a prize bull.

EBEN *(with a sneer)*:   Waal—ye hain't so durned purty yerself, be ye? *(They stare into each other's eyes, his held by hers in spite of himself, hers glowingly possessive. Their physical attraction becomes a palpable force quivering in the hot air.)*

ABBIE *(softly)*:   Ye don't mean that, Eben. Ye may think ye mean it, mebbe, but ye don't. Ye can't. It's agin nature, Eben. Ye been fightin' yer nature ever since the day I come—tryin' t' tell yerself I hain't purty t' ye. *(She laughs a low humid laugh without taking her eyes from his. A pause—her body squirms desirously—she murmers languorously)* Hain't the sun strong an' hot? Ye kin feel it burnin' into the earth —Nature—makin' thin's grow—bigger 'n bigger—burnin' inside ye—makin' ye want t' grow—into somethin' else—till ye're jined with it—an' it's your'n—but it owns ye, too —an' makes ye grow bigger—like a tree—like them elums— *(She laughs again softly, holding his eyes. He takes a step toward her, compelled against his will)* Nature'll beat ye, Eben. Ye might's well own up t' it fust 's last.

EBEN *(trying to break her spell—confusedly)*:   If Paw'd hear ye goin' on. . . . *(Resentfully)* But ye've made such a damned idjit out o' the old devil. . . ! (ABBIE *laughs*.)

ABBIE: Waal—hain't it easier fur yew with him changed softer?

EBEN *(defiantly)*:   No. I'm fightin' him—fightin' yew—fightin' fur Maw's rights t' her hum! *(This breaks her spell for him. He glowers at her)* An' I'm onto ye. Ye hain't foolin' me a mite. Ye're aimin' t' swaller up everythin' an' make it your'n. Waal, you'll find I'm a heap sight bigger hunk nor ye kin chew! *(He turns from her with a sneer.)*

ABBIE   *(trying to regain her ascendancy—seductively)*:   Eben!

EBEN: Leave me be! *(He starts to walk away.)*

ABBIE *(more commandingly)*:   Eben!

The stage directions contain many adverbs like languorously *and* resentfully. *These words describe effects, and the actor must concern himself with causes. You need in each case to discover what intention you can play that will* cause *the* effect *of languor or resentment.*

EBEN (*stops—resentfully*):   What d'ye want?

ABBIE (*trying to conceal a growing excitement*):   Whar air ye goin'?

EBEN (*with malicious nonchalance*):   Oh—up the road a spell.

ABBIE: T' the village?

EBEN (*airily*):   Mebbe.

ABBIE (*excitedly*):   T' see that Min, I s'pose?

EBEN: Mebbe.

ABBIE (*weakly*):   What d'ye want t' waste time on her fur?

EBEN (*revenging himself—grinning at her*):   Ye can't beat Nature, didn't ye say? (*He laughs and again starts to walk away.*)

ABBIE (*bursting out*):   An ugly old hake!

EBEN (*with a tantalizing sneer*):   She's purtier'n yew be!

ABBIE: That every wuthless drunk in the country has. . . .

EBEN (*tauntingly*):   Mebbe—but she's better'n yew. She owns up fa'r'n' square't' her doin's.

ABBIE (*furiously*):   Don't ye dare compare. . . .

EBEN: She don't go sneakin' an' stealin'—what's mine.

ABBIE (*savagely seizing on his weak point*):   Your'n? Yew mean—my farm?

EBEN: I mean the farm yew sold yerself fur like any other old whore—my farm!

ABBIE (*stung—fiercely*):   Ye'll never live t' see the day when even a stinkin' weed on it'll belong t' ye! (*Then in a scream*) Git out o' my sight! Go on t' yer slut—disgracin' yer Paw 'n' me! I'll git yer Paw t' horsewhip ye off the place if I want t'! Ye're only livin' here 'cause I tolerate ye! Git along! I hate the sight o' ye! (*She stops, panting and glaring at him.*)

EBEN (*returning her glance in kind*):   An' I hate the sight o' yew! (*He turns and strides off up the road. She follows his retreating figure with concentrated hate.*)

SCENE TWO

About eight in the evening. The interior of the two bedrooms on the top floor is shown. EBEN is sitting on the side of his bed in the room on the

(with malicious nonchalance) *What is Eben's intention?*

Hake (pronounced hāk): a variety of codfish.

*left. On account of the heat he has taken off
everything but his undershirt and pants. His feet
are bare. He faces front, brooding moodily, his
chin propped on his hands, a desperate
expression on his face.*

In the other room ABBIE *is sitting on the edge of
the bed, an old four-poster with feather mattress.
She is in her nightdress. Both rooms are lighted
dimly and flickeringly by tallow candles.*

EBEN and ABBIE *stare at each other through the
wall.* EBEN *sighs heavily and* ABBIE *echoes it. Both
become terribly nervous, uneasy. Finally* ABBIE
*gets up and listens, her ear to the wall. He acts as
if he saw every move she was making, he
becomes resolutely still. She seems driven into a
decision—goes out the door in rear
determinedly. His eyes follow her. Then as the
door of his room is opened softly, he turns away,
waits in an attitude of strained fixity.* ABBIE *stands
for a second staring at him, her eyes burning with
desire. Then with a little cry she runs over and
throws her arms about his neck, she pulls his
head back and covers his mouth with kisses. At
first, he submits dumbly; then he puts his arms
about her neck and returns her kisses, but finally,
suddenly aware of his hatred, he hurls her away
from him, springing to his feet. They stand
speechless and breathless, panting like two
animals.)*

ABBIE (at last—painfully):   Ye shouldn't,
Eben—ye shouldn't—I'd make ye happy!

EBEN (harshly):   I don't want t' be happy—from
yew!

ABBIE (helplessly):   Ye do, Eben! Ye do! Why
d'ye lie?

EBEN (viciously):   I don't take t'ye, I tell ye! I
hate the sight o' ye!

ABBIE (with an uncertain troubled laugh):
Waal, I kissed ye anyways—an' ye kissed
back—yer lips was burnin'—ye can't lie 'bout
that! (Intensely) If ye don't care, why did ye
kiss me back—why was yer lips burnin'?

EBEN (wiping his mouth):   It was like pizen on
'em. (Then tauntingly) When I kissed ye back,
mebbe I thought 'twas someone else.

*Be sure to state a specific intention for each of these
lines.*

ABBIE *(wildly)*: Min?

EBEN: Mebbe.

ABBIE *(torturedly)*: Did ye go t' see her? Did ye r'ally go? I thought ye mightn't. Is that why ye throwed me off jest now?

EBEN *(sneeringly)*: What if it be?

ABBIE *(raging)*: Then ye're a dog, Eben Cabot!

EBEN *(threateningly)*: Ye can't talk that way t' me!

ABBIE *(with a shrill laugh)*: Can't I? Did ye think I was in love with ye—a weak thin' like yew? Not much! I on'y wanted ye fur a purpose o' my own—an' I'll hev ye fur it yet 'cause I'm stronger'n yew be!

EBEN *(resentfully)*: I knowed well it was on'y part o' yer plan t' swaller everythin'!

ABBIE *(tauntingly)*: Mebbe!

EBEN *(furious)*: Get out o' my room!

ABBIE: This air my room an' ye're on'y hired help!

EBEN *(threateningly)*: Get out afore I murder ye!

ABBIE *(quite confident now)*: I hain't a mite afeerd. Ye want me, don't ye? Yes, ye do! An' yer Paw's son'll never kill what he wants! Look at yer eyes! They's lust fur me in 'em , burnin' 'em up! Look at yer lips now! They're tremblin' an' longin' t' kiss me, an' yer teeth t' bite! *(He is watching her now with a horrible fascination. She laughs a crazy triumphant laugh)* I'm a-goin' t' make all o' this hum my hum! They's one room hain't mine yet, but it's a-goin t' be tonight. I'm a-goin' down now an' light up! *(She makes him a mocking bow)* Won't ye come courtin' me in the best parlor, Mister Cabot?

EBEN *(staring at her—horribly confused —dully)*: Don't ye dare! It hain't been opened since Maw died an' was laid out thar! Don't ye. . . ! *(But her eyes are fixed on his so burningly that his will seems to wither before hers. He stands swaying toward her helplessly.)*

ABBIE *(holding his eyes and putting all her will into her words as she backs out the door)*: I'll expect ye afore long, Eben.

Don't try to be wild; play the intention.

EBEN *(stares after her for a while, walking toward the door. He murmurs):*   In the parlor? *(This seems to arouse connotations, for he comes back and puts on his white shirt, collar, half ties the tie mechanically, puts on coat, takes his hat, stands barefooted looking about him in bewilderment, mutters wonderingly)* Maw! Whar air yew? *(Then goes slowly toward the door in rear.)*

SCENE THREE

A few minutes later. The interior of the parlor is shown. A grim, repressed room like a tomb in which the family has been interred alive. ABBIE *sits on the edge of the horsehair sofa. She has lighted all the candles and the room is revealed in all its preserved ugliness. A change has come over the woman. She looks awed and frightened now, ready to run away.*

The door is opened and EBEN *appears. His face wears an expression of obsessed confusion. He stands staring at her, his arms hanging disjointedly from his shoulders, his feet bare, his hat in his hand.*

A positive relationship to the room is one of the major tasks.

ABBIE *(after a pause—with a nervous, formal politeness):*   Won't ye set?
EBEN *(dully):*   Ay-eh. *(Mechanically he places his hat carefully on the floor near the door and sits stiffly beside her on the edge of the sofa. A pause. They both remain rigid, looking straight ahead with eyes full of fear.)*
ABBIE: When I fust come in—in the dark—they seemed somethin' here.
EBEN *(simply):*   Maw.
ABBIE: I kin still feel—somethin'. . . .
EBEN: It's Maw.

Eben should work with specific images of his mother.

ABBIE: At fust I was feered o' it. I wanted t' yell an' run. Now—since yew come—seems like it's growin' soft an' kind t' me. *(Addressing the air—queerly)* Thank yew.
EBEN: Maw allus loved me.
ABBIE: Mebbe it knows I love yew, too. Mebbe that makes it kind t' me.

EBEN (*dully*):   I dunno. I should think she'd hate ye.

ABBIE (*with certainty*):   No. I kin feel it don't—not no more.

EBEN: Hate ye fur stealin' her place—here in her hum—settin' in her parlor whar she was laid— (*He suddenly stops, staring stupidly before him.*)

ABBIE: What is it, Eben?

EBEN (*in a whisper*):   Seems like Maw didn't want me t' remind ye.

Both Eben and Abbie need to establish a clear relationship to the invisible presence.

ABBIE (*excitedly*):   I knowed, Eben! It's kind t' me! It don't b'ar me no grudges fur what I never knowed an' couldn't help!

EBEN: Maw b'ars him a grudge.

ABBIE: Waal, so does all o' us.

EBEN: Ay-eh. (*With passion*) I does, by God!

ABBIE (*taking one of his hands in hers and patting it*):   Thar! Don't git riled thinkin' o' him. Think o' yer Maw who's kind t' us. Tell me about yer Maw, Eben.

EBEN: They hain't nothin' much. She was kind. She was good.

ABBIE (*putting one arm over his shoulder. He does not seem to notice—passionately*):   I'll be kind an' good t' ye!

EBEN: Sometimes she used t' sing fur me.

ABBIE: I'll sing fŭr ye!

EBEN: This was her hum. This was her farm.

ABBIE: This is my hum! This is my farm!

EBEN: He married her t' steal 'em. She was soft an' easy. He couldn't 'preciate her.

ABBIE: He can't 'preciate me!

EBEN: He murdered her with his hardness.

ABBIE: He's murderin' me!

EBEN: She died. (*A pause*) Sometimes she used to sing fur me. (*He bursts into a fit of sobbing.*)

ABBIE (*both her arms around him—with wild passion*):   I'll sing fur ye! I'll die fur ye! (*In spite of her overwhelming desire for him, there is a sincere maternal love in her manner and voice—a horribly frank mixture of lust and mother love*) Don't cry, Eben! I'll take yer Maw's place! I'll be everythin' she was t' ye! Let me kiss ye, Eben! (*She pulls his head *around. He makes a bewildered pretense of resistance. She is tender)* Don't be afeered! I'll kiss ye pure, Eben—same 's if I was a Maw t' ye—an' ye kin kiss me back 's if yew was my son—my boy—sayin' good-night t' me! Kiss me, Eben. *(They kiss in restrained fashion. Then suddenly wild passion overcomes her. She kisses him lustfully again and again and he flings his arms about her and returns her kisses. Suddenly, as in the bedroom, he frees himself from her violently and springs to his feet. He is trembling all over, in a strange state of terror.* ABBIE *strains her arms toward him with fierce pleading)* Don't ye leave me, Eben! Can't ye see it hain't enuf—lovin' ye like a Maw—can't ye see it's got t' be that an' more—much more—a hundred times more—fur me t' be happy—fur yew t' be happy?

EBEN *(to the presence he feels in the room):*   Maw! Maw! What d'ye want? What air ye tellin' me?

ABBIE: She's tellin' ye t' love me. She knows I love ye an' I'll be good t' ye. Can't ye feel it? Don't ye know? She's tellin' ye t' love me, Eben!

EBEN: Ay-eh. I feel—mebbe she—but—I can't figger out—why—when ye've stole her place—here in her hum—in the parlor whar she was—

ABBIE *(fiercely):*   She knows I love ye!

EBEN *(his face suddenly lighting up with a fierce, triumphant grin):*   I see it! I sees why. It's her vengeance on him—so's she kin rest quiet in her grave!

ABBIE *(wildly):*   Vengeance o' God on the hull o' us! What d'we give a durn? I love ye, Eben! God knows I love ye! *(She stretches out her arms for him.)*

EBEN *(throws himself on his knees beside the sofa and grabs her in his arms—releasing all his pent-up passion):*   An' I love ye, Abbie!—now I kin say it! I been dyin' fur want o' ye—every hour since ye come! I love ye! *(Their lips meet in a fierce, bruising kiss.)*

Realize Eben's intense inner conflict to be true to his mother's memory and to satisfy his desire for Abbie.

Small Craft Warnings

TENNESSEE WILLIAMS

Exploratory Analysis of a Scene from Act II: 1 man, 2 women

Background   The characters are people holding onto the remnants of their lives, trying with desperation and a certain courage to retain something that will make their lives meaningful. They are definitely "small craft" in a foggy sea. Despite their weaknesses and indulgences, they have a kind of seedy honesty, and Williams writes of them with the understanding and respect he has always shown for social misfits.

This is the final scene when only two of Monk's regular customers are still hanging around his bar, and he is ready to close for the night. Leona, having thrown her stud Bill out of her trailer, is ready to take off again in her "home on wheels." Violet, in part responsible for Leona's leaving because of rather outrageous liberties she has taken with Bill, has brought her battered suitcase over to Monk's place because she has nowhere else to go.

Who   VIOLET is in her twenties or early thirties. Her eyes are too large for her face, and they are usually moist: she cries a lot. Her appearance suggests a derelict existence. Her red nail polish is badly peeled, showing traces of dirt underneath. Still, she has a pale, bizarre sort of beauty. There is a not-quite-with-it appearance, something more like a possibility than a completed creature. She lives in a room, which Leona describes as "a Goddam rathole," over an amusement arcade. She has no closet, no bureau, so she hangs her dresses on a piece of rope stretched across a corner between two nails, and her other things she keeps on the floor in boxes. Her arrangements are always temporary.

LEONA. Late twenties or early thirties. She is a beauty operator, good enough that she can depend on getting a job in almost any town. She travels about the country in her house-trailer, which she has furnished with silver, crystal and Irish lace—to her an important means of maintaining self-respect. A job, a bar to hang out in, and her trailer with a man in it are her life requirements. Williams says she is "wearing white clam-digger slacks and a wooly pink sweater. On her head of dyed corkscrew curls is a sailor's hat which she occasionally whips off her head to slap something with—the bar, a tabletop, somebody's back—to emphasize a point." She likes to look after people, but she can be mean and violent when she feels they have not been sufficiently grateful. When angered, she comes on like a small bull making his charge into the ring.

MONK. Middle-aged. The bar-owner, "running a place of refuge for vulnerable human vessels." The bar is his life and, for the most part, he likes it. His liquor and his tolerance are needed by his customers and he is happy he can fulfill this need. He lives alone above the bar, and he expects to die there. He has had one or two mild heart attacks, he occasionally feels pain in his heart, and is aware that death is always nearby.

Character Relationships   Relationships among floaters in and out of a bar are not likely to be lasting, but they may be very intense. Leona, in a mean mood, has been abusing Violet all evening, not even stopping short of physical violence, and causing Violet to run for safety into the ladies' lavatory. She is contemptuous of everything about Violet's life, and in her drunken state she is in a rage about Violet's advances to Bill. Now, late at night, she is sobered and mellowed, and more compassionate in her attitude. Violet is afraid of Leona and tries to protect herself. But in her never-quite-with-it manner she responds like a cowering child who doesn't quite understand why she is being attacked and is incapable of making a defense. Both look at Monk as a refuge, for him at times a difficult position because he doesn't want to offend nor make trouble for anyone.

When and Where   The time is the present. The place is a bar along the California coast. Williams' description is as follows: ''The scene is a somewhat nonrealistic evocation of a bar on the beach-front in one of those coastal towns be-

tween Los Angeles and San Diego. It attracts a group of regular patrons who are nearly all so well known to each other that it is like a community club, and most of these regulars spend the whole evening there. Ideally, the walls of the bar, on all three sides, should have the effect of fog rolling in from the ocean. A blue neon outside the door says: 'Monk's Place.' The bar runs diagonally from upstage to down; over it is suspended a large varnished sailfish, whose gaping bill and goggle-eyes give it a constant look of amazement. There are about three tables with red-checked tablecloths. Stage right there is a juke box, and in the wall at right there are doors to the ladies' and gents' lavatories. A flight of stairs ascends to the bar-owner's living quarters.''

The Actors' Work   Analyze the scene for intentions, obstacles, beats, physical and verbal actions, relationships, subtext, sensory tasks. Write the results of your analysis on your script, to provide you with a score for playing your role.

The Ground Plan   The playwright describes a setting for the play. All details may not be essential to this scene. Experiment with the selection and arrangement to find out what will be most helpful in carrying out your actions and communicating the scene to an audience.

Small Craft Warnings

TENNESSEE WILLIAMS

NOTE: *At times in the course of the play, a character disengages himself from the action and speaks as if to himself, sharing his thoughts with*

Reprinted by permission of Tennessee Williams. Permission for performance of this work must be authorized by Bill Barnes, agent for Tennessee Williams, c/o ICM, 40 West 57th Street, New York, New York 10019.

the audience, but not seeming actually to do so. This scene is arranged to begin with the three characters onstage "disengaged" from each other, each in turn speaking his thoughts. If lights are used the speaking character would be lighted, the other two in semi-darkness.

LEONA *(sharing her thoughts):* . . . as for being lonely, that applies to every mother's son and daughter of us alive, we were given warning of that before we were born almost, and yet . . . When I come to a new place, it takes me two or three weeks, that's all it takes me, to find somebody to live with in my home on wheels and to find a night spot to hang out in. Those first two or three weeks are rough, sometimes I wish I'd stayed where I was before, but I know from experience that I'll find somebody and locate a night spot to booze in, and get acquainted with . . . friends . . . *(She moves downstage with her hands in her pockets, her face and voice very grave as if she were less confident that things will be as she says.)* And then all at once something wonderful happens. All the past disappointments in people I left behind me just disappear, evaporate from my mind, and I just remember the good things, such as their sleeping faces, and . . . Life! Life! I never just said, "Oh, well," I've always said "Life!" to life, like a song to God, too, because I've lived in my lifetime and not been afraid of . . . changes . . . *(She goes back to the shadows.)*

VIOLET *(sharing her thoughts):* It's perfectly true that I have a room over an amusement arcade facing the pier. But it wasn't like Leona describes it. It took me awhile to get it in shipshape condition because I was not a well girl when I moved in there, but I got it clean and attractive and had an atmosphere to it. I don't see anything wrong with living upstairs from the amusement arcade, facing the pier. I don't have a bath or a toilet but I keep myself clean with a sponge bath at the wash basin and use

In these monologues, the actors' task is to use their imagination and to recall experience which will keep specific images in their minds of what they are saying. This is a definite technique and should be practiced at each rehearsal. The non-speaking actors should provide from their imaginations an "inner monologue," which will lead directly into their speaking and which will continue after they have finished. These monologues should be written in the score.

Violet needs to see these details specifically and vividly as she recalls them, keeping a picture in front of her as if she were seeing it on a television screen.

the toilet in the amusement arcade. Anyhow it was a temporary arrangement, that's all it was, a temporary arrangement . . .

MONK (*behind the bar*): I'm fond of, I've got affection for, a sincere interest in my regular customers here. They send me postcards from wherever they go and tell me what's new in their lives and I am interested in it. Just last month one of them I hadn't seen in about five years, he died in Mexico City and I was notified of his death and that he'd willed me all he owned in the world, his personal effects and a two-hundred-fifty-dollar savings account in a bank. A thing like that is beautiful as music. These things, these people, take the place of a family in my life. I love to come down those steps from my room to open the place for the evening, and when I've closed for the night, I love climbing back up those steps with my can of Ballantine's ale, and the stories, the jokes, the confidences and confessions I've heard that night, it makes me feel not alone . . . I've had heart attacks, and I'd be a liar to say they didn't scare me and don't still scare me. I'll die some night up those steps, I'll die in the night alone, and I hope it don't wake me up, that I just slip away, quietly.

Using his imagination and recalling from his own experience whatever may be helpful, Monk needs to re-create what he is describing, including the frightening heart attacks and the fear of death.

(*He crosses to downstage table with a bottle and calls out.*) Come, sit down, Leona. (*She and Monk sit at the table. Violet comes out of the shadows. She sees Leona at the table and starts to retreat.*)

LEONA: Aw, hell, Violet. Come over and sit down with us, we're having a nightcap, all of us, my brother's death-day is over.

Leona's mean mood has been due in part to the fact that this is her brother's death-day. He was a homosexual who died some years ago when he was very young.

VIOLET: Why does everyone hate me? (*She sits at the table; drinks are poured from the bottle. Violet hitches her chair close to Monk's. In a few moments she will deliberately drop a matchbook under the table, bend to retrieve it, and the hand on Monk's side will not return to the table surface.*)

Feeling men under the table is Violet's habit whenever she has an opportunity. It was this behavior with Bill that angered Leona.

LEONA: Nobody hates you, Violet. It would be a compliment to you if they did.

VIOLET: I'd hate to think that I'd come between you and Bill.

LEONA: Don't torture yourself with an awful thought like that. Two people living together is something you don't understand, and since you don't understand it you don't respect it, but, Violet, this being our last conversation, I want to advise something to you. I think you need medical help in the mental department and I think this because you remind me of a . . . a . . . of a plant of some kind . . .

VIOLET: Because my name is Violet?

LEONA: No, I wasn't thinking of violets, I was thinking of water plants, yeah, plants that don't grow in the ground but float on water. With you everything is such a . . . such a . . . well, you know what I mean, don't you?

This description of Violet should be helpful in creating her character.

VIOLET: Temporary arrangement?

LEONA: Yes, you could put it that way. Do you know how you got into that place upstairs from the amusement arcade?

VIOLET: . . . How?

LEONA: Yes, *how* or *why* or *when*?

VIOLET: . . . Why, I . . . *(She obviously is uncertain on all three points.)*

A task of trying to see past events through a heavy fog might help Violet here.

LEONA: Take your time. And *think*. How, why, when?

VIOLET: Why, I was . . . in L.A., and . . .

LEONA: Are you sure you were in L.A.? Are you sure about even that? Or is everything foggy to you, is your mind in a cloud?

VIOLET: Yes, I was . . .

A technique of not focusing her eyes might help Violet to realize the "floating quality."

LEONA: I said take your time, don't push it. Can you come out of the fog?

MONK: Leona, take it easy, we all know Violet's got problems.

LEONA: Her problems are mental problems and I want her to face them, now, in our last conversation. Violet? Can you come out of the fog and tell us how, when, and why you're living out of a suitcase upstairs from the amusement arcade, can you just . . .

MONK *(cutting in)*:   She's left the amusement arcade, she left it tonight, she came here with her suitcase.

LEONA: Yeah, she's a water plant, with roots in water, drifting the way it takes her.

(Violet weeps.)

And she cries too easy, the water works are back on. I'll give her some music to cry to before I go back to my home on wheels and get it cracking up the Old Spanish Trail. *(She rises from the table.)*

MONK: Not tonight, Leona. You have to sleep off your liquor before you get on the highway in this fog.

Leona has been drinking throughout the evening, but she is habitually a heavy drinker who holds her liquor well, and she is beginning to sober up. This state of intoxication is one of the sensory tasks. Remember the intention is not to be drunk; it is to behave as soberly as possible.

LEONA: That's what you think, not what I think, Monk. My time's run out in this place. *(She has walked to the juke box and started the violin piece.)* . . . How, when, and why, and her only answer is tears. Couldn't say how, couldn't say when, couldn't say why. And I don't think she's sure where she was before she come here, any more sure than she is where she'll go when she leaves here. She don't dare remember and she don't dare look forward, neither. Her mind floats on a cloud and her body floats on water. And her dirty fingernail hands reach out to hold onto something she hopes can hold her together. *(She starts back toward the table, stops; the bar dims and light is focused on her.)* . . . Oh, my God, she's at it again, she got a hand under the table. *(Leona laughs sadly.)* Well, I guess she can't help it. It's sad, though. It's a pitiful thing to have to reach under a table to find some reason to live. You know, she's worshipping her idea of God Almighty in her personal church. Why the hell should I care she done it to a nowhere person that I put up in my trailer for a few months? I wish that kid from I-oh-a with eyes like my lost brother had been willing to travel with me, but I guess I scared him. What I think I'll do is turn back to a faggot's moll when I haul up to

The violin piece is Souvenir *by Franz Drdla, arranged by Albert Franz.*

The kid is a homosexual from Iowa who had been in the bar that evening and whom Leona had invited to travel with her in the trailer.

Sausalito or San Francisco. You always find
one in the gay bars that needs a big sister with
him, to camp with and laugh and cry with, and
I hope I'll find one soon . . . it scares me to be
alone in my home on wheels built for two . . .
*(She turns as the bar is lighted and goes back to
the table.)* Monk, HEY, MONK! What's my tab
here t'night?

MONK: Forget it, don't think about it, go home
and sleep, Leona. *(He and Violet appear to be
in a state of trance together.)*

LEONA: I'm not going to sleep and I never leave
debts behind me. This twenty ought to do it.
(She places a bill on the table.)

MONK: Uh-huh, sure, keep in touch . . .

LEONA: Tell Bill he'll find his effects in the
trailer-court office, and when he's hustled
himself a new meal ticket, he'd better try and
respect her, at least in public . . . Well . . . *(She
extends her hand slightly. Monk and Violet are
sitting with closed eyes.)* . . . I guess I've already gone.

VIOLET: G'bye, Leona.

MONK: G'bye . . .

LEONA: "Meglior solo," huh, ducks? *(Leona
lets herself out of the bar.)*

*Earlier in the play Leona has said: "I had an Italian
boy friend that taught me a saying, 'Meglior solo
que mal accompanota,' which means you're better alone than in the company of a bad companion."
It is part of the actor's job to learn to pronounce
correctly any foreign words that occur in his lines.*

MONK: . . . G'bye, Leona.

VIOLET: . . . Monk?

MONK *(correctly suspecting her intent)*: You
want your suitcase, it's . . .

VIOLET: I don't mean my suitcase, nothing
valuable's in it but my . . . undies and . . .

MONK: Then what've you got in mind?

VIOLET: . . . In *what?*

MONK: Sorry. No offense meant. But there's
taverns licensed for rooms, and taverns
licensed for liquor and food and liquor, and I
am a tavern only licensed for . . .

VIOLET *(overlapping with a tone and gesture of
such ultimate supplication that it would break
the heart of a stone)*: I just meant . . . let's go

upstairs. Huh? Monk? *(Monk stares at her reflectively for a while, considering all the potential complications of her taking up semi- or permanent residence up there.)* Why're you looking at me that way? I just want a tempor- ary, a night, a . . .

MONK: . . . Yeah, go on up and make yourself at home. Take a shower up there while I lock up the bar.

VIOLET: God love you, Monk, like me. *(She crosses, with a touch of "labyrinthitis," to the stairs and mounts two steps.)* Monk! . . . I'm scared of these stairs, they're almost steep as a ladder. I better take off my slippers. Take my slippers off for me. *(There is a tone in her voice that implies she has already "moved in" . . . She holds out one leg from the steps, then the other. Monk removes her slippers and she goes on up, calling down to him:)* Bring up some beer, sweetheart.

The "labyrinthine walk" further indicates the lack of direction in Violet's life.

MONK: Yeh, I'll bring some beer up. Don't forget your shower. *(Alone in the bar, Monk crosses downstage.)* I'm going to stay down here till I hear that shower running. I am not going up there till she's took a shower. *(He sniffs the ratty slipper.)* Dirty, worn-out slipper still being worn, sour-smelling with sweat from being worn too long, but still set by the bed to be worn again the next day, walked on here and there on—pointless—errands till the sole's worn through, and even then not thrown away, still put on to walk on till it's . . . past all repair . . . *(He has been, during this, turning out lamps in the bar.)* Hey, Violet, will you for Chrissake take a . . . *(This shouted appeal breaks off with a disgusted laugh. He drops the slipper, then grins sadly.)* She probably thinks she'd dissolve in water. I shouldn't of let her stay here. Well, I won't touch her, I'll have no contact with her, maybe I won't even go up there tonight. *(He crosses to open the door. We hear the boom of the ocean outside.)* I always leave the door open for a few minutes to clear the smoke and liquor smell out of the place, the human odors, and to hear the

Monk's speech is another example of Williams' technique of having characters share their thoughts with the audience without seeming actually to do so.

ocean. Y'know, it sounds different this late than it does with the crowd on the beach-front. It has a private sound to it, a sound that's just for itself and me. *(Monk switches off the blue neon sign. It goes dark outside. He closes the door.)*

(Sound of water running above. He slowly looks toward the sound.)

That ain't rain.

(Tired from the hectic night, maybe feeling a stitch of pain in his heart (but he's used to that), Monk starts to the stairs. In the spill of light beneath them, he glances up with a slow smile, wry, but not bitter. A smile that's old too early, but it grows a bit warmer as he starts up the stairs.)

CURTAIN

A Note on *Small Craft Warnings*

In his description of the setting Tennessee Williams asks for a "somewhat nonrealistic evocation of a bar." In his notes he stresses the need in performance of "that lyricism—which is, as always, what I must chiefly rely on as a playwright." He wrote in an article for the New York *Times* that serves as a preface for the published play: "It is the responsibility of the writer to put his experience as a being into work that refines and elevates it and that makes of it an essence that a wide audience can somehow manage to feel in themselves: 'This is true.'

"In all human experience, there are parallels which permit common understanding in the telling and hearing, and it is the frightening responsibility of an artist to make it directly or allusively close to his own being communicable and understandable, however disturbingly, to the hearts and minds of all whom he addresses."

Evocation, lyricism, essence, experience as a being are words that may help the actor find a direction here, as well as in other of Williams' plays.

Cowboys #2

SAM SHEPARD

Exploratory Analysis of a Scene from a One-Act Play: 2 men

Background   Sam Shepard is probably the most original of the younger American playwrights, and perhaps ultimately the most significant. He is a keen and sympathetic observer of the American scene, especially of those subcultures that remain either by choice or necessity outside of the establishment. He has a sensitive ear for the rhythms and patterns of colloquial American speech, and for the sound of American life. And he sharply observes the things that people do. He disregards the standard elements of drama. There is no careful plotting, as in Ibsen. The plot of *Cowboys #2* is that two cowboys, idle as cowboys often are, are passing the time in conversation and coping with the elements. Early in the play they are caught in the rain; at the end they are seeking shade to protect them from a blistering sun. There are no three-dimensionally developed characters, as in Chekhov. No theme, as in Shaw. Locale and atmosphere are not important. The place is really a stage although the lines, the physical actions and the sensory work of the actors make it outdoors, by a stream, near a highway. The play is funny and moving and real. And it provides splendid opportunities for actors.

Who   The two characters are STU and CHET. They are stereotypes, possibly travesties, of cowboys. They are buddies. They look after each other. They are drifters—washing in streams and sleeping on the ground. They are lonesome, reminiscing about the past and dreaming of what they would like to have —mostly food. Chet's recital of what he would like for breakfast encompasses the morning menu of every roadside diner in America: "Some scrambled eggs and hot chocolate and toast. Rye toast. . . . Some farina. Hot farina with cold milk and prune juice. Maybe some pancakes, with butter and maple syrup and powdered sugar. About ten pancakes on top of each other. You know, they have all kinds of cereal there. Cold and hot. Cornflakes, Rice Crispies, Oat Meal, Sugar Corn Pops, farina, Malto-Meal, Purina and many others." This is only the beginning.

There is some character differentiation. Stu is more of a leader, Chet a follower. There is little conflict between them except petty arguments and irritations that are soon forgotten. Their distinguishing feature is their frequent shifting into the characters of old men when they become MEL and CLEM. The shift may be interpreted realistically as a game they play to amuse themselves in passing the time. It is, however, an application of an acting exercise called *transformation* originated at Chicago's Second City Workshop and described by a member of the group as an improvisation in which the given circumstances of a scene change several times during the course of the action. What may change are character and/or situation and/or time and/or intentions. Whatever realities are established at the beginning are destroyed after a few minutes and replaced by others. Basic acting techniques do not change. Within each situation the actor can, and should, be as real as the circumstances permit. Transformations, of course, are demanding because there is little time to prepare and develop a character. Their success depends upon the actors' being able immediately to establish character, situation, and relationship.

Where and When The time is now. The setting, as described by the playwright is "a bare stage, very dimly lit. Upstage center is a sawhorse with a yellow caution light mounted on it.

The light blinks on and off throughout the play. On each side of the sawhorse is a young man seated against the upstage wall. They both wear black pants, black shirts and vests and black hats. They seem to be sleeping. Offstage is the sound of a single cricket which lasts throughout the play. As the curtain rises there is a long pause, then a saw is heard offstage, then a hammer, then the saw again." So the ground plan is simple; it's a bare stage. For this scene the young men, who are background characters, may be eliminated.

The Actors' Work Analyze the scene for intentions, obstacles, beats, physical and verbal actions, subtext, relationships, sensory tasks. Write the results of your analysis in your script to provide you with a score in rehearsing the role. Notice that the transformations tend to determine the beginning and the end of the beats.

Cowboys #2[1]

SAM SHEPARD

CHET (*Off left*): It's going to rain.
STU: Do you think so?
CHET: What?
STU: Uh, rain?

CHET: Oh . . . sure. Maybe.
STU: Could be.
CHET: Let's see.
(*A pause*)
STU: It wouldn't be bad for my clothes?
CHET: Clothes?
STU: It'd be good for my clothes, I said. It'd be like taking a bath with my clothes on.

The personal experience on which you draw for the scene will doubtless be largely from movies and television. The play, in fact, is a travesty on screen cowboys. But don't merely imitate. Carefully play your intentions and perform your sensory tasks.

Both need to establish a relationship to their clothes.

Reprinted with permission of Urizen Books, Inc., New York, N.Y. Copyright © 1976 by Sam Shepard.

[1]For purposes of scene study a few lines have been omitted.

CHET: Sure. It'd be the same for me, I guess.

STU: Sure. Why don't you go over there and see if you can see any cloud formations?

(HE *points downstage;* CHET *gets up and crosses downstage like an old man; he stands center and looks up at the sky, then speaks like an old man)*

This is the first transformation. You need to make an immediate change—physically and vocally—into old men. Don't do easy imitations; discover what causes old men to move and speak differently from young men.

CHET: Well, well, well, well. I tell ya, boy. I tell ya. Them's some dark ones, Mel. Them's really some dark ones.

STU *(Talking like an old man):*   Dark, eh? How long's it been since ya seen 'em dark as that?

Give attention to the speech rhythms.

CHET: How longs's it been? Long? How long?

STU: Yeah. How long a time, Clem?

CHET: Long a time? Well, it's been a piece. A piece o' time. Say maybe, off a year or so. Maybe that.

STU: A year, eh?

CHET: Yep. Could be longer.

STU: Longer?

CHET: Yep. Could be two or three year since I seen 'em all dark like that.

STU: That's a piece o' time, Clem. That's for sure.

CHET: Yep! Yep!

(He whistles loudly and starts doing a dance like an old man)

Find an appropriate dance. Adjust to an old man's physical limitations.

STU *(Normal voice):*   Hey! Come back! (CHET *stops short; he walks back upstage like an old man and and sits in his original position)* You know what?

They both change the circumstances and become Stu and Chet.

CHET: What?

STU: I think I'll take a look.

CHET: Okay.

(STU *stands and walks downstage like an old man; he looks up at the sky and speaks like an old man)*

Notice that Stu "transforms," but Chet doesn't. Chet is like a child refusing to play a make-believe game that another child initiates.

STU: By jingo! Them really is some dark ones.

CHET: Sure.

STU: Them's really dark like ya said, Mel.

CHET: Dark as they come.

STU: All dark and puckery like—like—
CHET: Like what?
STU: Well . . .
CHET: Like what?

(STU *turns to* CHET *and speaks in a normal voice*)

STU: Would you give me a chance?
CHET: Like what?
STU: Give me a chance to figure like what. I haven't even thought of it yet. So give me a chance.
CHET: Okay. (STU *turns back and looks at the sky; he looks for a while*) Have you decided? (STU *turns back to* CHET) I'm sorry.
STU: Are you going to give me a chance or aren't you?
CHET: I said I'm sorry. So go ahead.

(STU *turns back and looks at the sky again*)

STU *(Old man)*:   By jingo, them's really some dark ones, eh, Mel?
CHET: Fuck.

(STU *turns suddenly to* CHET)

STU: Goddamn you!
CHET: Well, shit, why don't you say it? I'm not going to sit here all day.
STU: *All right! (He turns back very fast to the audience and looks at the sky; he says the lines rapidly)* By jingo, them's really some dark ones, eh, Mel? I haven't probably seen clouds as dark as them myself.
CHET *(Stands and yells at* STU): *So!*
STU *(Still facing the audience)*:   So it's important! Ya got to notice things like that! It's important!
CHET: *So!*
STU: So ya can stay alive or something. Ya got to notice things like that.
CHET: Why?
STU: So ya can tell when it's gonna rain! So ya can tell when it's gonna snow. So ya can tell when—when—so ya can tell!
CHET: I seen 'em already!

The conflict in this part of the scene comes from Chet's annoyance that Stu can't say how dark the clouds are. Find the several beats in this conflict.

Note that in the transformations Stu and Clem frequently reverse their old men characters.

Build the conflict to a climax.

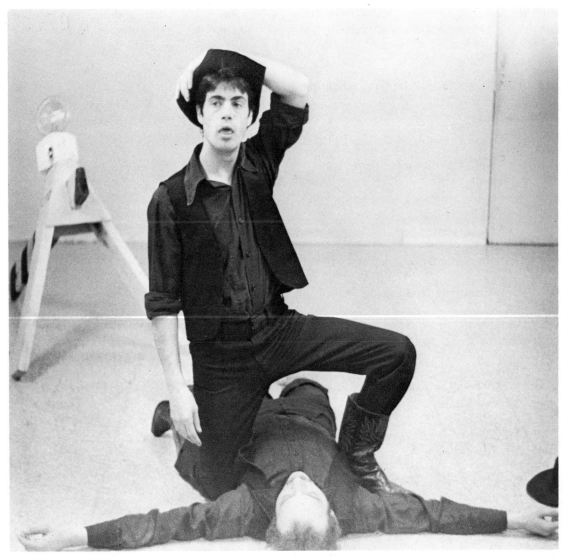

Students Vinnie Guastaferro and Marty Levy in a classroom rehearsal of *Cowboys #2* by Sam Shepard. (Photograph: Goodman School of Drama)

STU: Good!

CHET: I seen 'em lots o' times in Utah and other
  places.

STU *(Turns to* CHET): So?

CHET: So I already seen 'em. If I already seen
  'em, there ain't no point in me lookin' agin'.

(CHET *sits abruptly. There is a pause, then* STU *starts doing jumping calisthenics, clapping his hands over his head. He faces* CHET *as he does this*)

STU: Clap, clap, clap. Clapping, clapping. Clap.

CHET: What are you doing?

STU: This?

CHET: That.

STU: Oh. Well, you remember yesterday?

CHET: Yesterday what?

STU: Remember yesterday when I was sitting and my feet fell asleep?

CHET: Yeah.

STU: Well, this is for that.

CHET: Oh. To get the blood going and circulating?

STU: Yes. To get the blood going the way it should.

CHET: So it runs.

STU: So it runs.

CHET: So it doesn't stop and get clogged up?

STU: Right.

CHET: You know, you may have something like, uh, diabetes.

STU (*Stops and looks at* CHET): Diabetes?

CHET: Yes. It may be a low sugar content.

STU: No. That's diabetes.

CHET: Yes.

STU: Well, that's what I don't have. (*He starts jumping again*)

CHET: You don't know. You can't really tell. (CHET *gets up and crosses to* STU. *He walks around* STU *in a circle, talking to him as* STU *continues jumping*) Diabetes is a strange thing. Very strange. It's known to lie dormant for years, then one day it just pops up. And there you are.

(STU *stops jumping as* CHET *continues to walk around him*)

STU: Where?

CHET: There you are, lying in bed or sitting on a subway or walking down the street or eating a

Chet's line and his sitting abruptly are a terminal point to the beat. The pause makes transition, and the calisthenics begin a new beat.

Make the most of these repetitions and rhythmic variations.

Mock serious medical commentary, included for its own sake, often occurs in Shepard's plays. The verbal action to convince Stu that, if he has diabetes, he's in a bad way.

hamburger or drinking a Coke or smoking a
cigarette.

STU: There I am.

CHET: Oh. Shh!

STU: What?

CHET: Shh! Listen.

(CHET *stands slowly. They both stand facing the
audience and listening; the sound of rain is heard
faintly offstage; the sound builds as they
continue the scene)*

*For scene work, developing your sensory memory by
hearing sounds in your imagination is an excellent
exercise. Later you are going to imagine rain, mud,
rifles, and so on. The purpose is actually to hear the
sounds in your imagination, not merely to behave
as if you were hearing them. If you show the scene
before a group, you may want to improvise simple
sound effects.*

STU: Is it?

CHET: Sounds like it.

(Smiling, they look up at the sky)

STU: I think it is.

*(They start doing a dance and laughing, slowly
building and getting more hysterical)*

CHET: It's them clouds!

STU: Rain! Rain, mother!

*(They take off their hats and wave them over their
heads)*

CHET: It's comin' down.

STU: Here we go!

CHET: Look at it!

STU: Rain, bitch! Rain!

Response to the imaginary rain is a sensory task.

(They laugh hysterically)

CHET: My clothes!

STU: You could tell by them fuckin' clouds!

CHET: Rain on me!

STU: Come on, baby!

CHET: It's like the great flood of 1683!

STU: Everything's wet!

CHET: Wet all over!

STU: Look at the mud!

CHET: Mud!

(They fall on the floor and roll around in the imaginary mud)

STU: Mud! You're beautiful!
CHET: All this mud!
STU: Mud all over!
CHET: Kiss me, mud!
STU: Dirty mud!
CHET: *Aaah!*
STU: Muddy, muddy!
CHET: Dirty gook!

(They kiss the floor and throw mud on each other)

STU: Muck and slime!
CHET: *Aaah, mud!*
STU: Fucky, fuck!
CHET: Muck and guck!

(The rain sound stops suddenly)

STU: Oh, mud.
CHET: Mud.

(They slowly stop laughing and roll over on their backs. They stare at the ceiling)

CHET: You know, some girl asked me about the Big Dipper and I couldn't tell her.
STU: You couldn't tell her what?
CHET: I couldn't tell her anything about it. The big one.
STU: Is that the big one?

(He points to the ceiling)

CHET: That's what she asked me and I couldn't tell her, so how can I tell you?
STU: Is that the big one or the little one? *(A pause)* Is that the big one or the little one?
CHET: It looks like the little one to me.
STU: Can't you tell? *(A pause)* Can't you tell? (CHET *stands suddenly and walks upstage looking at the ceiling)* You don't know?
CHET: I said before that it looks like the little one. I said that. Now what?
STU: Then it is the little one, isn't it?
CHET: I guess! Yes! Why not?

A good opportunity for committing yourself fully to a sensory task.

This is a time transformation—from rain to a starry night.

Focus your eyes on infinity. See the stars.

(STU *stands and walks up to* CHET; CHET *walks around the stage looking up at the ceiling as* STU *follows close behind him;* CHET *turns suddenly to* STU; *they stare at each other*)

CHET: *(The old man's voice)* Clem, I thought we was in the Red Valley.
STU: *(The old man's voice)* Red Valley? That's right, Mel. This here's the Red Valley area.
CHET: Is that right?
STU: That's right, boy. Come on down here.

(STU *leads* CHET *downstage center; they look out over the audience*)

CHET: What?
STU: Come on. Now see that?

(He points off in the distance)

CHET: What?
STU: See all that out there? That area all out in there?
CHET: Yep.
STU: That's it, Clem.
CHET: This whole area's the Red Valley?

(The sound of horses running can be heard offstage faintly)

STU: That's right, Mel.
CHET: This here's the same Red Valley you was referrin' to back in Des Moines?
STU: This here's the very same area.

(The horses get louder)

CHET: The very same place? Clem, I think you was either lyin' to me or you was misinformed somehow.
STU: How's that, Mel?
CHET: Listen.

(The horses get louder)

STU: What's that?
CHET: Well, that's what I mean.
STU: What?
CHET: That.

(He points in the distance; the sound of Indians

The movement provides a transition.

screaming joins in with the horses and becomes very loud)

STU: Damn.

CHET: We got to do somethin', boy.

STU: Get down behind them barrels and get out yer rifle.

(They kneel down and hold imaginary rifles)

In early rehearsals it will be helpful to work with actual rifles; then transfer the memory of that experience to handling imaginary rifles. All of your senses except taste should be involved.

CHET: Sure is a lot of 'em, Clem.

STU: Well, we can hold 'em for a while.

CHET: Don't have much ammo . . .

STU: We'll fight 'em with our rifle butts after that.

(The sound offstage gets very loud and is joined by gunfire)

CHET: Wait till they get up close.

STU: Okay.

CHET: Okay. Fire!

(They make gun noises and fire at imaginary Indians)

Don't make this a general fight. See the Indians specifically. Handle the imaginary rifles properly. Take accurate aim before you fire.

STU: Fire!

CHET: Fire!

STU: Damn! Look like Apaches!

CHET: Some of 'em's Comanches, Clem!

STU: Fire!

CHET: Good boy, ya got him!

STU: Fire!

CHET: Got him again. One shot apiece, Clem.

STU: Get 'em, Mel.

CHET: Fire! Got me a brave! Got me a brave!

STU: Good boy!

CHET: Thought he was fancy, ridin' a pinto.

STU: Your left, Clem. Got him! Tore him up!

CHET: Good boy. Got him in the head that time. Right in the head. Watch it!

STU: Fire!

CHET: 'Atta baby! (STU *grabs his shoulder, screams and falls back;* CHET *stands and yells out at the audience, firing his rifle)* You lousy red-skinned punks! Think you can injure my buddy? Lousy red assholes! Come back and fight!

(The sound fades out; CHET *pulls* STU *upstage and props him up against the wall)*

STU: My arm . . .
CHET: Ya okay, boy?
STU: Got me in the arm.
CHET: Take it easy. Easy. I'll take care o' ya, boy. Take it easy.
STU: Redskins all over.
CHET: Red Valley area. (CHET *rolls* STU's *sleeve up and breaks off an imaginary arrow)* Easy, boy.

A Note on *Cowboys #2*

1. Transformation was an essential exercise at Joseph Chaikin's Open Theatre, and some of the work materialized in plays by Megan Terry. Four such plays—*Viet Rock, Comings and Goings, Keep Tightly Closed in a Cool Dry Place,* and *The Gloaming, Oh My Darling*—are published together in one volume (New York: Simon and Schuster, 1966). They provide good material for actors, and reading them will help you understand transformation as an acting exercise. Another play that uses transformation in a realistic context is *Green Julia* by Paul Abelman (New York: Grove Press, Inc., 1966). It contains excellent material for two actors.

2. Work on improvisational exercises involving transformations. For example:

You are having breakfast with your roommate. Your intention is to borrow money from him. The obstacle is that he does not want to lend you money and says he doesn't have any. You say that he could get some from the *bank.* The word *bank* triggers a transformation. Your partner says:

"This is a holdup. Put the money in this bag."

The situation has changed. Your partner is a bank-robber. You are a bank-teller. As you improvise this situation, your partner says:

"Don't call for help, unless you want to end up a *stiff* in the morgue."

Free association with the word *stiff* evokes another set of circumstances. You say:

"Doctor, I've had this stiff leg for almost a week."

You are now a patient in a doctor's office, and your partner is a physician.

During the improvisation, transformations may occur whenever an action or a word by one of the actors suggests a new situation to his partner. The new situation must be clearly established in just a few words and the other actor (or actors—more than two may work together in this kind of exercise) must make an immediate adjustment.

The Gloaming, Oh My Darling

MEGAN TERRY

Exploratory Analysis of a Scene from a One-Act Play: 2 women

Background Megan Terry is an innovative playwright whose work has emerged from a playwright's workshop sponsored by Joseph Chaikin's improvisational group, the Open Theatre. Her method of working, as described by Richard Schechner in his introduction to a collection of her plays, is different from that of other dramatists: "Miss Terry's plays are made with her actors. They begin as 'notions,' move through a chrysalis stage of improvisation, become 'solidified' in a text, and are produced. . . . Miss Terry's plays in print do not have the same authority as, say, the texts of Arthur Miller; and this lack of authority is to the plays' advantage. The texts, as Gide would say, remain 'pretexts' for productions; their staging should not be a re-creation so much as a reconstruction."

In this play two old women, long confined to a nursing home, spend their time berating each other and recalling events from the past. They also have kidnapped from the men's ward an elderly patient named Mr. Birdsong and hidden him in one of their beds. Although Mr. Birdsong is currently in a coma, the two women are fierce rivals in a fantasy romance they have created around him.

In dramatizing past events, the play makes use of a device called *transformation*. For a description of it please refer to the introductory material to the scene from *Cowboys #2*. See also the suggestion for transformation exercises at the end of the scene.

Who The two women are alike in that both are old, facing death in a nursing home to which they have been committed by uncaring sons and daughters. Although they recognize the realities of their situation, they want to spend their time *living* instead of *dying*. Both are still interested in amatory experience. Megan Terry says "the backbone of the play is the embrace of life —however little of it may be left."

The women's names tell us something about them and suggest character contrasts.

MRS. TWEED is physically the stronger of the two. She used to work in a wire factory and at the time she received her retirement pension she "could still run up and down the ladders as good as the men." Although twice married, her life does not seem to have provided romantic excitement.

MRS. WATERMELLON is referred to as a tub, a term

that does not belie the image evoked by her name. Her life's ambition was to "found a great family." We realize the irony of this ambition when we witness at the end of the play the callous indifference with which she is treated by her son and grandchildren.

Character Relationship   The two women have been "roommates" for a long time. They quarrel, they call each other names. They threaten each other. They declare they are going to ask to be separated. At the same time they are quite dependent upon each other physically and emotionally. In moments of objectivity they recognize that all they have left is each other. MRS. WATERMELLON is the dominant partner. MRS. TWEED'S attitude is more conventional; she is more respectful of rules and regulations.

Where and When   The time is now. The scenery can be just two cots and two chairs, or a complete nursing-home room. The situation dictates that the characters wear hospital gowns, robes, and slippers.

The Actors' Work   Analyze the scene for intentions, obstacles, beats, physical and verbal actions, relationships, subtext, sensory tasks. Write the results of your analysis in your script to provide you with a score in rehearsing the role. Plan an arrangement of necessary furniture that will help you in carrying out the physical actions. The author has this advice: "There is no need for the actresses to be old. Any age will do. If the actresses cannot do a successful Irish accent, they should use whatever they are successful at. The accents of their mothers or grandmothers, or the accent of their native regions. No agony or time should be spent on the technical aspect of this—dwell on the relationships in the play—the relationships of the women to one another, to themselves, to their families, their country, to the past and future. . . .

"The transitions should flow one into the other without pause or marking of any kind. The time slides in and out, and the final result should be that it is all the same time. . . . The intent is to see two lifetimes and certain aspects of the life of a country in one concentrated look."

The Gloaming, Oh My Darling

MEGAN TERRY

(Two women sit on two chairs in a nursing home. There are two beds in the small sunny room. One of the beds is occupied, but the sheet and blanket are drawn up over the head of the occupant. The two old women speak in Irish accents.)

MRS. TWEED: Ah yes, Mrs. Watermellon, and the days go by and the days go by and the days

The occupant is Mr. Birdsong. Establishing a relationship to the figure in the bed is an important task.

From *Viet Rock and Other Plays* by Megan Terry. Copyright © 1966, 1967, by Megan Terry. Reprinted by permission of Simon & Schuster, Inc. For performing rights to *The Gloaming, Oh My Darling* by Megan Terry, apply to Elisabeth Marton, 96 Fifth Avenue, New York, N.Y. 10011.

go by and the days go by, and by and by the days go by. My God, how the days go by!

MRS. WATERMELLON: From where I sit . . . I have to agree with you. But they don't go fast enough by, Mrs. Tweed, not by a half sight, not by a full sight. The world is waiting for the sunrise, and I'm the only one who knows where it begins.

MRS. TWEED: Why do you keep it a secret?

MRS. WATERMELLON: No secret. I've told everyone. I've told and told and told everyone.

MRS. TWEED: Where does it begin then?

MRS. WATERMELLON *(Slapping her breast)*: Here. Right here. Right here it starts! From the old ticker it starts and pumps around and thumps around, coagulates in my belly and once a month bursts out onto the ground . . . but all the color's gone . . . all but one . . . all but . . . one . . .

MRS. TWEED: So that's where the sunrise went.

MRS. WATERMELLON: You three-minute egg. You runny, puny twelve week's old, three-minute egg. You're underdone and overripe. What do you know? You only learned to speak when you got mad enough . . . I'm going to sleep. I'd as soon live in the mud with turtles as to have to converse with the likes of you.

MRS. TWEED: Don't talk like that. That hurts me.

MRS. WATERMELLON: Nothing can hurt you if your mind is on a high plain.

MRS. TWEED: If you go to sleep on me, then I'll let him go.

MRS. WATERMELLON: If you let him go, Mrs. Tweed, then I'll tell you where your daughter is.

"Him" is Mr. Birdsong.

Laura, Mrs. Tweed's favorite daughter, always finds some excuse for not coming to visit her mother. "Where she is" is never revealed in the play.

MRS. TWEED: I won't listen.

MRS. WATERMELLON: Oh yes, you'll listen. You'll listen to me tell you where she is. It makes you cry and you hate to cry. But once you get started crying you wake up everyone, and then they'll give you an enema.

MRS. TWEED: I don't care if they do. There's nothing more to come out. They've tubed, and they've squirted, and they've radiated and they've intravened . . . There's nothing more to come out of me. I haven't had reason to pick my nose in two years.

MRS. WATERMELLON: Do you think he's awake yet?

MRS. TWEED: Mrs. Watermellon, what if someone comes to visit him?

MRS. WATERMELLON: I won't let them see him.

MRS. TWEED: You have to let them see him if they're his folks.

MRS. WATERMELLON: Nope, you dope, I don't.

MRS. TWEED: You do have to let folks see him. What else would folks be coming up here for, if not to see him.

MRS. WATERMELLON: Perhaps he's passed on—passed over. I'll say he's gone West. ANYWAY, Mrs. Tweed, he's mine now.

MRS. TWEED: Why, he's ours, Mrs. Watermellon. You can't have him all to yourself!

MRS. WATERMELLON: That's what I did in the night. I DIDN'T want you to find out, but since I see what a busybody you finally are, after all these bygone days, I'll tell you once and for all. He's mine!

MRS. TWEED: But we got him together. I carried the bottom end. You weak old tub, you couldn't even have lifted him from his bed by yourself. You'd have dropped and broken him. They'd have put us in jail for stealing and murder. They'd have electrocuted and hung us . . . they'd have . . .

MRS. WATERMELLON: Hush your mouth! Hush up. I won't have him disturbed by your temper.

MRS. TWEED: I'm going to give him back. Tonight I'll carry him back to the men's ward and tuck him in his crib.

MRS. WATERMELLON: No, you won't. He's mine.

MRS. TWEED: Ours.

MRS. WATERMELLON: Mine.

MRS. TWEED: Ours . . .

MRS. WATERMELLON: All right. All right, you pukey squashed robins egg, all right! All right, all right, you leftover maggot mangy mop rag.

This last sentence provides a climax for this speech.

Notice the character contrasts suggested in this speech.

All right! All right, you dried-up, old snot rag, I'm going to tell you, I'M GOING TO TELL you right here and now. Do you hear me? I'm going to tell you right here and now.

MRS. TWEED: I don't want to hear. Not here. Not now.

VOICE (A recorded voice of a young woman sings.

WATERMELLON and TWEED freeze in their places during the song:

If the recording presents a problem, for purposes of scene study the two women could suspend the action and sing the song themselves— preferably in harmony, in young voices without accent.

"In the gloaming, oh my darling,
When the lights are soft and low,
Will you think of me and love me
As you did once long ago?"

MRS. WATERMELLON (Coming back to life):   I'm hungry for canned rhubarb! Never did get enough. My greedy little sister used to get up in the night when we's all asleep and sneak down to the fruit cellar and eat two quarts of rhubarb, every single night.

MRS. TWEED: She must a had the cleanest bowels in the whole country.

MRS. WATERMELLON: My mother had the best dinner. For her last birthday two days before she died my brother asked her what she wanted. She knew it was her last supper.

MRS. TWEED: Chicken baked in cream in the oven?

MRS. WATERMELLON: Nope, you dope. Pheasant she wanted. Cherrystone clams, six of them, roast pheasant and wild-blackberry pie. She ate every bit of it. We watched her. She ate it all up, every speck of it. Cherrystone clams, six of them, roast pheasant, and wild-blackberry pie. Licked her lips.

Use specific images in recalling past events.

MRS. TWEED: That rings a bell. I had pheasant once. Pheasant under glass. Looked so pretty, I didn't eat it. Where was that?

MRS. WATERMELLON: You had it at the old Biltmore. She licked her lips and closed her eyes. She never opened them again.

MRS. TWEED: That rings a bell. Who'd I have it with? Did I taste it? Under a lovely glass bell. Who was I with?

MRS. WATERMELLON: You were with your husband, Mrs. Tweed. Your second husband. You did that on your anniversary. On your wedding anniversary, you dope. You've told me every one of your anniversary stories five hundred times a year.

MRS. TWEED *(Laughs)*:   It's gone from me. All gone from me. Fancy that, but it does ring a bell.

MRS. WATERMELLON: You can eat mushrooms under glass too. Don't you know?

MRS. TWEED: Myrtle Classen used to serve them at her bridge lucheons. Mushrooms, under glass. I didn't eat any of those either.

MRS. WATERMELLON: What have you done with him, Mrs. Tweed?

MRS. TWEED: I made him even.

MRS. WATERMELLON: WHAT have you done with him?

MRS. TWEED: What'll you give me if I tell, Mrs. Watermellon?

MRS. WATERMELLON: Tell.

MRS. TWEED: Give.

MRS. WATERMELLON: Tell.

MRS. TWEED: Give.

MRS. WATERMELLON: Tell, tell.

MRS. TWEED: Give, give.

MRS. WATERMELLON: Tell, tell, tell!

MRS. TWEED: Give, give, give!

MRS. WATERMELLON *(Melting)*:   I give.

MRS. TWEED: All up?

MRS. WATERMELLON: All.

MRS. TWEED: Say it. Say it all, Mrs. Watermellon.

MRS. WATERMELLON: I give it all up. I give it all up to my uncle. My uncle. Uncle.

MRS. TWEED: Who is he? Who is he, your uncle, uncle?

MRS. WATERMELLON *(Exhausted)*:   You are. You . . . are . . . Mrs. Tweed.

MRS. TWEED: Then you've got to tell me what you did to Mr. Birdsong in the night.

MRS. WATERMELLON: Now?

MRS. TWEED: Not a moment too late.

This is the familiar game of making someone cry "Uncle." What is the inherent physical action?

MRS. WATERMELLON: I . . . I married him. I married Mr. Birdsong.

MRS. TWEED: No.

MRS. WATERMELLON: In the night, I lifted the covers from his body and I married him. Mrs. Birdsong. Mrs.

MRS. TWEED: But he was ours. We brought him here together.

The operative words are "ours" and "together."

MRS. WATERMELLON: In the night . . .

MRS. TWEED: It isn't fair. You didn't do it fair. He was . . .

MRS. WATERMELLON: I didn't want to do it, because we've been such good, such only friends. But I didn't want to tell you 'cause I don't want you to stop rubbing my back on rainy days. I didn't want to tell you because I didn't want you to stop cleaning my nails on Sunday mornings. I didn't want to tell you because you eat those hardcooked carrots for me on Wednesday nights. I didn't want to tell you 'cause you rub a nipple and make me feel sweet sixteen when we play boy friends. I didn't want to tell you because you're all I've got . . . you're all I've been given in this last twenty years. You're all I've seen in this never-never. I didn't want to tell you because you're the only one who can see *me*. I didn't want to tell you because you were all I had. But now I've got Mr. Birdsong. Mr. and Mrs. Birdsong.

This speech tells something about the relationship between the two women.

MRS. TWEED: Don't tell me that. You shouldn't have told me that.

MRS. WATERMELLON: And you don't even know any good lifetime stories. I've been shut up with a life that never moved at all. The only thing you can remember is how . . .

MRS. TWEED: . . . Is how I rode out in the Maine snow night with my DOCTOR Father and he held his fur-coat arms around me on his horse and I sat in front of him with his fur-coat arms around me and I held his scratched and leather smelly doctor's bag. Held it tight so's not to drop it in the Maine snow night.

MRS. WATERMELLON: That's what I mean, just one sentimental perversion after another.

MRS. TWEED: There's nothing perverted about father love.

MRS. WATERMELLON: There is if there's something perverted about Father.

MRS. TWEED: Who?

MRS. WATERMELLON: You. You. You, Mrs. Tweed.

MRS. TWEED *(Trying to rise)*:   That did it. That did it. That just about did it in, all right.

MRS. WATERMELLON: Sit down, you old windbag.

MRS. TWEED: That did it. That did it, Mrs. Watermellon. That just about did it in, all right.

MRS. WATERMELLON: Sit down, you old battle-ax.

MRS. TWEED *(On a rising scale)*:   That did it. That did it. That just about did it. That did it all right.

MRS. WATERMELLON: Sit down, you old blister.

MRS. TWEED *(She bursts)*:   THAT DID IT! *(She explodes into a convulsive dance. She sings. As she sings her accent disappears):*

Find a tune for the words and suggestive movement for the dance.

That's done it, that's better.
That's done it,
What ease.
That's done it,
That's better.
What took you so long,
You tease?

MRS. WATERMELLON: Don't leave me. I forbid you to go. Don't leave me, Tweed. Come back. Don't leave me here alone with a man.

MRS. TWEED *(She dances herself down to the age of sixteen)*:   I'm so tired. I'm so tired and so done in. We drank and drank so much grape punch and then that gentle Keith Lewiston took me behind the schoolhouse and you know what he did?

Mrs. Tweed transforms to a sixteen-year-old girl sharing confidences with her girlfriend.

MRS. WATERMELLON: He hitched you to his buggy and drove you round the yard.

Mrs. Watermellon does not transform immediately.

MRS. TWEED *(Embracing her)*:   He soul kissed me. He kissed my soul. Like this.

MRS. WATERMELLON *(Dodges)*:   Don't start that mush again.

MRS. TWEED *(Still sixteen)*:   He kissed my soul. Like this. *(She plants a kiss finally on* MRS. WATERMELLON'S *neck.)*

MRS. WATERMELLON *(She starts to howl in pain, but the howl changes to a kind of gargle and then to a girlish laugh. Her accent leaves also)*:   Did it make a strawberry? Did you make me a strawberry on my neck? *(Now* MRS. WATERMELLON *is also sixteen.)* Do it again and make a big red strawberry mark. Then we'll have to wear long scarves around our necks, to school, but everyone will know why. They'll think the boys kissed us behind the schoolhouse. Is it red yet? Is it strawberry red yet?

Mrs. Watermellon makes her transformation here.

MRS. TWEED *(Coming back to old age, she knots an imaginary scarf around* MRS. WATERMELLON'S *neck and her Irish accent returns)*:   No—not—yet.

MRS. WATERMELLON *(Chokes and laughs as if strangling)*:   Don't. We're friends. We're best friends. We're girl friends. *(Her Irish accent returns.)* Don't kill me. I'm your mother.

MRS. TWEED: Save all that for Doctor. I'm on to you. Your smart-assed psycho—hology won't work on me any more. Save it for Mr. Birdsong. *If* you can find him.

MRS. WATERMELLON: What have you done with him?

MRS. TWEED: Wouldn't you like to know.

MRS. WATERMELLON: What have you done with him? What have you done with my . . .

MRS. TWEED: *Your* what?

Catch-22

JOSEPH HELLER

Exploratory Analysis of a Scene from Act I: 3 men

Background Joseph Heller's novel *Catch-22* has been called "wild, moving, shocking, hilarious, raging, exhilarating . . . and the best American novel to come out of World War II . . . the best American novel to come out of anywhere in years." Joseph Heller has dramatized his best-selling book for the stage retaining its comedy, its sharp satire, and its assemblage of fascinating characters. The principal action takes place at an air force base on a tight little island off the Italian coast. The officers in charge are comically ridiculous in their incompetency, their pettiness, their personal ambition, their determination to make the war pay off for *them*. One of their annoying problems is Yossarian, a bombadier who has flown the required number of missions and wants to go home. Each time he requests a discharge the commanding officer raises the required number. To accomplish his purpose Yossarian declares himself insane, but here he comes up against Catch-22: he does not want to fly more missions because he is insane, but no sane man wants to fly more missions; therefore the fact that he does not want to fly proves that he is not insane.

In the scene for exploration the Chaplain has come to Colonel Cathcart's office to intercede for Yossarian. He finds Cathcart and his associate, Lieutenant Colonel Korn, occupied with other concerns, none of them having to do with the good conduct of the war.

Who COLONEL CATHCART, in his thirties is described by Joseph Heller as "dashing and dejected, poised and chagrined. . . . He was complacent and insecure, daring in the administrative stratagems he employed to bring himself to the attention of his superiors and craven in his concern that his schemes might all backfire. Colonel Cathcart was conceited because he was a full colonel with a combat command at the age of only thirty-six; and Colonel Cathcart was dejected because although he was already thirty-six he was still only a full colonel. . . . The fact that there were men of his age and younger who were already generals contaminated him with an agonizing sense of failure and made him gnaw at his fingernails with an unappeasable anxiety.

". . . He displayed an ornate cigarette holder grandly on every occasion and had learned to manipulate it adroitly. . . . As far as he could tell, his was the only cigarette holder in the whole Mediterranean theatre of operations, and the thought was both flattering and disquieting. He had no doubts at all that someone as debonair and intellectual as General Peckem approved of his smoking with a cigarette holder, even though the two were in each other's presence rather seldom, which in a way was lucky, Colonel Cathcart recognized with relief, since General Peckem might not have approved of his cigarette holder at all. When such misgivings assailed Colonel Cathcart, he choked back a sob and wanted to throw the damned thing away, but he was restrained by his unswerving conviction that the cigarette holder never failed to embellish his masculine, martial physique with a high gloss of sophisticated heroism. . . . Although how could he be sure?''

LIEUTENANT COLONEL KORN is a few years older than Cathcart, intelligent, shrewd, scheming, but not personally ambitious. He is not a particularly attractive man, tending to be overweight and underheight. He is sweaty and untidy, his shirt-tails forever ''bunching up from inside his sagging belt and ballooning down over his waist.'' Heller tells us that Colonel Korn has a ''curt, derisive tongue and knowing, cynical eyes''; that he wears rimless icy glasses and that he is always sensitively touching his domelike pate with the tips of his splayed fingers. He is a lawyer graduated from a state university and makes no pretensions of being Ivy league. He satisfies his ego through his disdainful treatment of his associates.

THE CHAPLAIN is younger than the others. According to Heller, he is slightly built with a narrow, rather pale face and ''brown diffident eyes.'' It is not required that an actor have the exact physical appearance described by the author; however, the author's descriptions often suggest basic character traits that the actor should attempt to realize. The *diffident eyes* suggest that the Chaplain is a timid person lacking confidence in his ability to stand up to his associates and to deal with the problems incumbent upon his military assignment. Since he is a captain he is outranked by both Korn and Cathcart, which accounts in part for his reticent unimpressive manner.

Character Relationships   Colonel Cathcart's desperate ambition to become a general determines his relationship to everyone around him. He is abnormally concerned with making a favorable impression upon his superiors, ridiculously attempting to interpret their every word and gesture as an indication of approval or disapproval. He is suspicious of everyone's motives whether or not they could have any influence upon his future. Lieutenant Colonel Korn is an indispensable aide because he furnishes the brains for Cathcart's schemes. They are very close and do not like each other at all. Cathcart is jealous of Korn's intelligence and is able to tolerate it only by reminding himself that, although older than he, Korn is just a lieutenant colonel. Korn tolerates the situation by reminding himself that, although Cathcart is superior in rank, he is inferior in brains.

They both treat the Chaplain with complete disdain. He cowers fearfully in their presence and hates himself for his cowardice.

Where and When   The fact that the characters are air force officers requires attention to military deportment and the gestures of respect paid to rank. Some semblance of uniforms may be helpful in realizing the characters. The scene takes place on a hot August morning. None of the officers would be wearing jackets. Cathcart and Korn would probably have their shirts open at the neck; the Chaplain would wear a necktie. Setting a sensory task of adjusting to the heat will aid in establishing the reality of the scene.

The Actors' Work   Analyze the scene for intentions, obstacles, beats, physical and verbal actions, relationships, subtext, sensory tasks. Write the results in your script to provide you with a score for playing the role. Formulate a ground plan that will enable you effectively to carry out the physical actions; include in your plan only absolute essentials.

Catch-22

JOSEPH HELLER

(COLONEL CATHCART *enters wearing a black circle around one eye and an Indian headdress with several feathers. He has a long cigarette holder in his mouth and carries a small box of tomatoes in one hand and a large bell in the other. He removes his black eye and his headdress as he reaches the desk and rings his bell furiously.*)

CATHCART: Korn! Colonel Korn!

(COLONEL KORN *enters with a dry expression. His manner throughout is one of leisurely, thinly-veiled derision.*)

KORN: You rang, sir?

CATHCART: Come in, Korn. I need your advice. What do you think of this cigarette holder?

KORN: It's imitation black onyx with inlaid chips of imitation ivory.

CATHCART: That's not what I mean. Will it help me become a general?

KORN: It might. With someone like General Dreedle, it could be a terrible black eye . . . (CATHCART's *face falls.*) . . . while with someone like General Peckem . . .

CATHCART: It could be another feather in my cap! I think I'll take that risk. Now what about that farmhouse of mine in the hills?

KORN: A feather in your cap. But only if you use it.

CATHCART: I hate it there. I've got nothing to do. I'm not even sure where that farmhouse came from or who's paying for it. How'd I get it, anyway?

In his anxiety about pleasing his superiors, Colonel Cathcart sees everything he does either as a feather in his cap (approval) or a black eye (disapproval). This anxiety is broadly satirized by his Indian headdress and the black circle. The bell satirizes his insistent demand for attention and his love of browbeating everyone he isn't afraid of.

Cathcart keeps a list of "feathers" and "black eyes" arranged in parallel columns. This detail can provide a physical action.

Through some finagling, Korn has got Cathcart a house in the hills. He had planned it as a scene of wild parties that would enhance Cathcart's reputation among fellow officers. The plan never came off.

Six pages from Act 1 excerpted from *Catch-22: A Dramatization* by Joseph Heller. Copyright © 1973 by Scapegoat Productions, Inc. Reprinted with the permission of Delacorte Press.

KORN: You stole it.

CATHCART: Is that legal?

KORN: Sure.

CATHCART: Well, you're the lawyer and you ought to know. How about these black market tomatoes we're buying up and selling to Milo illegally?

Milo Minderbinder is the mess officer, an operator who buys tomatoes from Korn and Cathcart at outrageous prices for a three-way split of the profits.

KORN: That's legal, too.

CATHCART: Currency manipulation?

KORN: Legal.

CATHCART: Income tax evasion?

KORN: That's legal also.

CATHCART: Well, if you say so. I wish you'd gone to Harvard or Yale, though, instead of a state university. It's very degrading for someone like me to have to depend on someone like you.

It rankles Cathcart that he is dependent upon a lawyer who was not educated at one of the Eastern prestige schools.

KORN: I understand. That's why I always try to be so helpful.

CATHCART: I appreciate that. Get the Chaplain up here. There's something I want to discuss with him.

KORN: He's already here. There's something he wants to discuss with you.

The Chaplain has promised Yossarian he will talk to the Colonel.

CATHCART: That's what I call a real meeting of the minds, eh? Send him in. (KORN *exits. The* CHAPLAIN *enters.*) Come on in, Chaplain.

The Chaplain would come to attention and salute. In the novel Cathcart forgets to put the Chaplain "at ease," so he remains at attention throughout the scene. In rehearsal explore this possibility. Cathcart could put the Chaplain "at ease" at whatever point seems to work best.

What does the Chaplain intend to say? Always write in your score how a "cut speech" would have concluded. When you start speaking, don't anticipate the interruption.

CHAPLAIN: Thank you, sir. Sir, I want to speak—

CATHCART: Take a look at this copy of *Life* magazine. Here's a big photograph of a colonel in England who has his chaplain say prayers in the briefing room before each mission. Do you think that prayers will work as well here as they do for these people in England?

CHAPLAIN: Yes, sir. I should think they would.

CATHCART: Then I'd like to give it a try. Maybe if we say prayers, they'll put *my* picture in *Life* magazine. What are you staring at?

CHAPLAIN: Tomatoes—I think.

CATHCART: Wanna buy some?

CHAPLAIN: No, sir. I don't think so.

CATHCART: That's all right. Milo is glad to snap up all we can produce. What was it you wanted to speak to me about?

CHAPLAIN: Sir, I—

CATHCART: We'll begin with the next mission. Now, I don't want any of this Kingdom of God or Valley of Death stuff. That's all too negative. What are you making such a face for?

Note that Cathcart does not allow the Chaplain to answer.

CHAPLAIN: I'm sorry, sir. I happened to be thinking of the Twenty-third Psalm as you said that.

CATHCART: How does that one go?

CHAPLAIN: That's the one you were just referring to, sir. "The Lord is my shepherd; I—"

CATHCART: That's the one I was just referring to. It's out. What else have you got?

CHAPLAIN: "Save me, O God; for the waters are come in unto—"

CATHCART: No waters. I don't like waters. Why don't we try something musical? How about the harps on the willows?

CHAPLAIN: That has the rivers of Babylon in it, sir. ". . . there we sat down, yea, we wept, when we remembered Zion."

CATHCART: Zion? Let's forget *that* one right now. I wonder how it even got in there. I'd like to keep away from the subject of religion altogether if we can.

CHAPLAIN: I'm sorry, sir. But just about all the prayers I know make at least some passing reference to God.

CATHCART: Then let's get some new ones. Why can't we take a more positive approach? Why can't we all pray for something good, like a direct hit with all our bombs? Couldn't we pray for a direct hit with all our bombs?

Try making "Then let's get some new ones" a terminal point, beginning a new beat with "Why can't we take a more positive approach?"

CHAPLAIN: Well, yes, sir, I suppose so.

CATHCART: Then that's what we'll do. It will be a feather in our cap if we pray for a direct hit with all our bombs—even if we get a direct miss. We can slip you in while we're synchronizing the watches. I don't think there's anything secret about the right time. Will a minute and a half be enough?

CHAPLAIN: Yes, sir. If it doesn't include the time necessary to excuse the atheists and admit the enlisted men.

CATHCART: What atheists? There are no atheists in my outfit. Atheism is against the law, isn't it?

CHAPLAIN: No, sir.

CATHCART: Then it's un-American, isn't it?

CHAPLAIN: I'm not sure, sir.

CATHCART: Well, I am! I'm not going to disrupt our religious services just to accommodate a bunch of lousy atheists. They can stay right where they are and pray with the rest of us. And what's all this about enlisted men? Just how do they get into this act?

Cathcart is paranoid about enlisted men.

CHAPLAIN: I'm sorry, sir. I just assumed you would want the enlisted men to be present.

CATHCART: Well, I don't. They've got a God and a chaplain of their own, haven't they?

CHAPLAIN: No, sir.

CATHCART: You mean they pray to the same God we do?

CHAPLAIN: Yes, sir.

CATHCART: And he *listens?*

CHAPLAIN: I think so, sir.

CATHCART: Well, I'll be damned. I'd like to keep them out anyway. Honestly, Chaplain, you wouldn't want your sister to marry an enlisted man, would you?

CHAPLAIN: My sister *is* an enlisted man.

CATHCART: Are you trying to be funny?

CHAPLAIN: Oh, no, sir. She's a master sergeant in the Marines.

CATHCART: I see. Well, now that I think about it, having the men pray to God probably wasn't such a hot idea anyway. The editors of *Life* might not cooperate.

CHAPLAIN: Will that be all, sir?

CATHCART: Yeah. Unless you've got something else to say.

CHAPLAIN: Yes, sir, I have. Sir, some of the men are very upset since you raised the number of missions to sixty. They've asked me to speak to you about it.

CATHCART: Well, you just spoke to me about it.

CHAPLAIN: They wonder why they have to keep flying more and more missions.

CATHCART: That's an administrative matter, Chaplain. Tell them it's none of their business.

CHAPLAIN: Yes, sir.

CATHCART: Help yourself to a tomato, Chaplain. Go ahead, it's on me. That's an order.

CHAPLAIN *(Takes a tomato)*:   Thank you, sir. Sir—

CATHCART: Thanks for dropping around.

CHAPLAIN: Yes, sir. *(Bracing himself.)* Sir, I'm particularly concerned about one of the bombardiers. Captain Yossarian.

CATHCART: Who?

CHAPLAIN: Yossarian, sir. A man was killed in his plane recently and—

CATHCART: That's a funny name.

CHAPLAIN: He's in a very bad way, sir. I'm afraid he won't be able to take it much longer without doing something desperate.

CATHCART: Is that a fact, Chaplain?

CHAPLAIN: Yes, sir. I'm afraid it is.

CATHCART *(Ponders)*:   Tell him it's God's will. That's all now. (CHAPLAIN *gives up and exits.* CATHCART *broods nervously. Wailing suddenly:)* I want to be a general! *(Rings his bell.)* Korn! Korn!

KORN *(Entering)*:   You rang, sir?

CATHCART: We may have a big problem. There's a captain named Yossarian who doesn't want to fly the sixty missions.

KORN: Yossarian? That's a funny name.

CATHCART: It's a terrible name, isn't it? There are too many esses in it, like . . .

KORN: Odious, and insidious.

CATHCART: Subversive. It's not one of those good, crisp, clean-cut American names like—

KORN *(Getting it in first)*:   Korn.

CATHCART *(Eyeing him resentfully)*:   Or Cathcart. I wonder how he ever got to be a captain, anyway.

Before coming to see Cathcart, the Chaplain had resolved to take a strong stand on this matter.

Later the Chaplain is accused of stealing the tomato from the Colonel.

He braces himself to begin a new beat.

"I want to be a general." What is his subtext? It relates to Yossarian.

Emphasize the "s" sounds.

KORN: You probably promoted him.

CATHCART: You probably told me to.

KORN: I probably told you not to. But you wouldn't listen.

Emphasize listen.

CATHCART: I should have listened.

Emphasize should.

KORN: You never listen.

Emphasize never.

CATHCART: From now on, I'll listen. Stop picking on me, will you? Maybe sixty missions are too many. Should I lower them?

Emphasize listen. *Pick up cues fast.*

KORN: Raise them. You won't impress anybody by fighting *less.*

CATHCART: A man was killed in his plane.

KORN: One man? Colonel, if we're going to start waxing sentimental about every man who might be killed . . . we might just as well not have a war.

CATHCART: Korn, you're right! I'll raise them . . . to seventy.

KORN: Put another feather in your cap.

CATHCART: It certainly won't be a black eye, will it? *(Handing* KORN *a feather.)* Here— have one for your cap. And do you know what else? I'm going to volunteer for Bologna.

Bologna had the reputation of being a very dangerous mission.

KORN: Bologna? That's very brave of you.

CATHCART: Yes, it is. But I have confidence in my men. And I believe that no target in the world is too dangerous for them to attack. Tell Captain Black the good news. And let's get these damn tomatoes over to Milo. Before the Chaplain snatches another one.

The Chairs

EUGENE IONESCO
Translated by Donald M. Allen

Exploratory Analysis of a Scene from a One-Act Play: 1 man, 1 woman

Background   *The Chairs* is the story of an old man and his wife, aged 95 and 94, who live in a tower on a lonely island. They have invited a crowd of important people to hear a message in which the old man will pass the wisdom he has acquired during his long life onto posterity. Because he has difficulty expressing his thoughts, he has engaged a professional orator to speak for him. The guests, all invisible, arrive one by one. The old couple greet them graciously and bring chairs for them to sit on. Finally the stage is filled with chairs occupied by the invisible guests. After the Orator arrives and the old man is certain the crowd will hear his message, he jumps from a tower window into the sea, followed by his wife. When the Orator tries to speak, he can make only gurgling meaningless sounds and he writes on a blackboard only a meaningless confusion of letters. The old man's message will never be known.

Ionesco does not write plays in which life is represented onstage as if it were actually taking place. He attempts, in his own words, to "exteriorize the anxiety" of modern living. He uses words, physical actions, and relationships, not to create an illusion of reality, but directly to create feelings of futility, fear, and our inability to communicate with each other. His plays are bet-

ter experienced than explained. *The Chairs* says something about the futility of existence, a life's experience going to waste; the necessity of illusion to maintain one's ego; the impossibility of communication; the inanity of polite social conversation. Ionesco sees the human condition as both tragic and ridiculous, and he designates this play as a "tragic farce."

The invisibility of the guests is a dramatic image of the illusory quality of life; it is also a striking theatrical device. Responding and establishing relationships to the imaginary characters is a challenging task for the actors, and it must be performed with meticulous attention to detail.

The scene for exploration occurs near the beginning of the play when the old couple are receiving their first guest.

Who   The OLD MAN (he is given no name) exhibits some characteristics of senility. He has difficulty remembering past events, his sensory perception is not always clear (he mistakes nighttime for daytime), he is frequently shorttempered with his wife, sometimes childish, sometimes self-pitying. He seems always to have been irascible; we learn early in the play that he habitually quarreled with his friends and associates, a habit that seems to have been at least partly responsible for his present isolation. He strives, however, to maintain his self-importance, taking pride in the fact that he is a general. He is, of course, only a general factotum, which we may construe as being a general handyman. In the original French, he is called a concierge, which would mean a combination doorman, porter, and janitor. In this isolated tower, his responsibilities as doorman and porter could not be very demanding. His ego is further fed by his sense of mission, the urgency of bringing his important message to the world.

The OLD WOMAN, though only a year younger than her husband, has retained greater agility —both mental and physical. Like most doting wives, she makes her husband the center of her existence. Her importance lies in her relationship to him. In spite of her age and isolation, she takes pride in her appearance as evidenced by her concern over her hair and dress when the guests begin to arrive.

Character Relationships The OLD MAN is completely dependent upon his wife, although in her devotion she is sensitive enough to his ego to keep him unaware of his dependence. She excuses his long life of unaccomplishment and accepts the image he has of himself. She protects him from danger; she tends to his needs. She caresses him as she must have done when they were young. She cuddles him like a child. She cheerfully tolerates his choleric disposition. And, finally, she goes with him to their death. They have been married eighty years, and their relationship reflects these many decades of loyalty, devotion, and dependence.

Where and When Ionesco provides some details about the room in which the play takes place. It is circular with several doors leading to adjoining rooms. There is a doorway Up Center that provides access to the outside, apparently by means of stairs to a seawall where the boats land. Near this doorway is a window that looks out over the water. The place is sparsely furnished. It is evening, and the room is lighted by a gas lamp. Ionesco lives in France; there are references to a Paris that existed at sometime in the past, but we do not know to what country the island belongs. Similarly there is no mention of when the events take place. It seems to have been a few years ago, but the play is definitely related to the contemporary absurdist theatre.

The Actors' Work Analyze the scene for intentions, obstacles, beats, physical and verbal actions, relationships, subtext, sensory tasks. Write the results of your analysis in your script to provide you with a score for rehearsing your role.

The Ground Plan The playwright provides a drawing and describes the ground plan as follows: "Circular walls with a recess upstage center. A large very sparsely furnished room. To the right going upstage from the proscenium, three doors. Then a window with a stool in front of it; then another door. In the center of the back wall of the recess, a large double door, and two other doors facing each other and bracketing the main door: these last two doors, or at least one of them, are almost hidden from the audience. To the left, going upstage from the proscenium, there are three doors, a window with a stool in front of it, opposite the window on the right. . . . A gas lamp hangs from the ceiling."

Consider this description and provide as many elements of it as are necessary for carrying out the physical actions.

The Chairs

EUGENE IONESCO

Translated by Donald M. Allen

(Two straight-backed chairs placed stage center.)

Consider beginning with a physical action given in a stage direction earlier in the play: The Old Man seats himself quite naturally in the lap of the Old Woman. *This physical relationship would immediately establish a character relationship.*

OLD MAN: It's too far away, I can no longer . . . recall it . . . where was this?

OLD WOMAN: But what?

OLD MAN: What I . . . what I . . . where was this? And who?

OLD WOMAN: No matter where it is—I will follow you anywhere, I'll follow you, my darling.

OLD MAN: Ah! I have so much difficulty expressing myself . . . but I must tell it all.

OLD WOMAN: It's a sacred duty. You've no right to keep your message from the world. You must reveal it to mankind, they're waiting for it . . . the universe waits only for you.

OLD MAN: Yes, yes, I will speak.

OLD WOMAN: Have you really decided? You must.

OLD MAN: Drink your tea.

OLD WOMAN: You could have been head orator, if you'd had more will power in life . . . I'm proud, I'm happy that you have at last decided to speak to every country, to Europe, to every continent!

Several times earlier in the play the Old Woman has bolstered the Old Man's ego by assuring him he could have been "head president, head king, head doctor," in fact, "head anything" he wanted to be.

OLD MAN: Unfortunately, I have so much difficulty expressing myself, it isn't easy for me.

OLD WOMAN: It's easy once you begin, like life and death . . . it's enough to have your mind made up. It's in speaking that ideas come to us, words, and then we, in our own words, we

Extract from *The Chairs* taken from *Three Plays* published by Calder and Boyars Ltd., London. Reprinted by permission of Grove Press, Inc. Copyright © 1958 by Grove Press, Inc.

find perhaps everything, the city too, the garden, and then we are orphans no longer.

OLD MAN: It's not I who's going to speak, I've hired a professional orator, he'll speak in my name, you'll see.

OLD WOMAN: Then, it really is for this evening? And have you invited everyone, all the characters, all the property owners, and all the intellectuals?

OLD MAN: Yes, all the owners and all the intellectuals. *(Silence.)*

OLD WOMAN: The janitors? the bishops? the chemists? the tinsmiths? the violinists? the delegates? the presidents? the police? the merchants? the buildings? the pen holders? the chromosomes?

OLD MAN: Yes, yes, and the post-office employees, the inn-keepers, and the artists, everybody who is a little intellectual, a little proprietary!

OLD WOMAN: And the bankers?

OLD MAN: Yes, invited.

OLD WOMAN: The proletarians? the functionaries? the militaries? the revolutionaries? the reactionaries? the alienists and their alienated?

OLD MAN: Of course, all of them, all of them, all of them, since actually everyone is either intellectual or proprietary.

OLD WOMAN: Don't get upset, my darling, I don't mean to annoy you, you are so very absent-minded, like all great geniuses. This meeting is important, they must all be here this evening. Can you count on them? Have they promised?

OLD MAN: Drink your tea, Semiramis. *(Silence.)*

OLD WOMAN: The papacy, the papayas, and the papers?

Ionesco's characters are occasionally haunted by memories of a distant and happier past. Earlier the Old Man has recalled a beautiful place, situated at the end of a garden and named Paris, of which nothing remains "except a song." In his loneliness and isolation the Old Man has insisted he is an orphan and has cried for his mamma.

Note that the invited guests range from bishops to janitors to low life forms.

Semiramis (pronounced sĕ-mĭr'-ȧ-mĭs) is a legendary queen of Assyria, wife of Ninus, noted for her beauty, wisdom, and voluptuousness.

This repetition of similar sounds without logical meaning is a kind of childish game the old couple play. Earlier the Old Woman has crooned "orphan, dworphan, worfan, morphan, orphan." Contradictions and illogicalities often occur in Ionesco's plays demonstrating his conviction that real communication through language is impossible.

OLD MAN: I've invited them. *(Silence.)* I'm going to communicate the message to them . . . All my life, I've felt that I was suffocating; and now, they will know all, thanks to you and to the Orator, you are the only ones who have understood me.

OLD WOMAN: I'm so proud of you . . .

OLD MAN: The meeting will take place in a few minutes.

OLD WOMAN: It's true then, they're going to come, this evening? You won't feel like crying any more, the intellectuals and the proprietors will take the place of papas and mammas? *(Silence.)* Couldn't you put off this meeting? It won't be too tiring for us?

(More violent agitation. For several moments the OLD MAN *has been turning around the* OLD WOMAN *with the short, hesitant steps of an old man or of a child. He takes a step or two towards one of the doors, then returns and walks around her again.)*

More violent agitation *refers to an earlier stage direction:* he gets off the Old Woman's lap and walks with short, agitated steps.

OLD MAN: You really think this might tire us?

OLD WOMAN: You have a slight cold.

OLD MAN: How can I call it off?

OLD WOMAN: Invite them for another evening. You could telephone.

OLD MAN: No, my God, I can't do that, it's too late. They've probably already embarked!

OLD WOMAN: You should have been more careful.

(We hear the sound of a boat gliding through the water.)

These sounds could be actual or they could be inaudible, just as the guests are invisible. Hearing imaginary sounds is a greater challenge.

OLD MAN: I think someone is coming already . . . *(The gliding sound of a boat is heard more clearly.)* . . . Yes, they're coming! . . .

(The OLD WOMAN *gets up also and walks with a hobble.)*

OLD WOMAN: Perhaps it's the Orator.

OLD MAN: He won't come so soon. This must be somebody else. *(We hear the doorbell ring.)* Ah!

OLD WOMAN: Ah!

(Nervously, the OLD MAN and the OLD WOMAN move towards the concealed door in the recess to the right. As they move upstage, they say:)

OLD MAN: Come on . . .

OLD WOMAN: My hair must look a sight . . . wait a moment . . .

(She arranges her hair and her dress as she hobbles along, pulling up her thick red stockings.)

OLD MAN: You should have gotten ready before . . . you had plenty of time.

OLD WOMAN: I'm so badly dressed . . . I'm wearing an old gown and it's all rumpled . . .

OLD MAN: All you had to do was to press it . . . hurry up! You're making our guests wait.

(The OLD MAN, followed by the OLD WOMAN still grumbling, reaches the door in the recess; we don't see them for a moment; we hear them open the door, then close it again after having shown someone in.)

VOICE OF OLD MAN: Good evening, madam, won't you please come in. We're delighted to see you. This is my wife.

VOICE OF OLD WOMAN: Good evening, madam, I am very happy to make your acquaintance. Take care, don't ruin your hat. You might take out the hat-pin, that will be more comfortable. Oh! no, no one will sit on it.

VOICE OF OLD MAN: Put your fur down there. Let me help you. No, nothing will happen to it.

VOICE OF OLD WOMAN: Oh! what a pretty suit . . . and such darling colors in your blouse . . . Won't you have some cookies . . . Oh, you're not fat at all . . . no . . . plump . . . Just leave your umbrella there.

Experiment to discover whether you want to follow the stage direction by greeting the guest offstage, or whether you want to play the action before the audience. In either case all the physical actions inherent in the lines should be carried out.

VOICE OF OLD MAN: Follow me, please.

OLD MAN *(back view)*:   I have only a modest position . . .

(The OLD MAN and OLD WOMAN re-enter together, leaving space between them for their guest. She is invisible. The OLD MAN and OLD WOMAN advance, downstage, facing the audience and speaking to the invisible Lady, who walks between them.)

OLD MAN *(to the invisible Lady)*:   You've had good weather?

OLD WOMAN *(to the Lady)*:   You're not too tired? . . . Yes, a little.

OLD MAN *(to the Lady)*:   At the edge of the water . . .

OLD WOMAN *(to the Lady)*:   It's kind of you to say so.

OLD MAN *(to the Lady)*:   Let me get you a chair.

(OLD MAN goes to the left, he exits by door Down Left.)

OLD WOMAN *(to the Lady)*:   Take this one, for the moment, please. *(She indicates one of the two chairs and seats herself on the other, to the right of the invisible Lady.)* It seems rather warm in here, doesn't it? *(She smiles at the Lady.)* What a charming fan you have! My husband . . . *(The OLD MAN re-enters, carrying a chair.)* . . . gave me one very like it, that must have been seventy-three years ago . . . and I still have it . . . *(The OLD MAN places the chair to the left of the invisible Lady.)* . . . it was for my birthday! . . .

(The OLD MAN sits on the chair that he has just brought onstage, so that the invisible Lady is between the old couple. The OLD MAN turns his face towards the Lady, smiles at her, nods his head, softly rubs his hands together, with the air of following what she says. The OLD WOMAN does the same business.)

OLD MAN: No, madam, life is never cheap.

OLD WOMAN *(to the Lady)*:   You are so right . . .

Creating the invisible guest and establishing relationships to her is a challenging task. Both actors and audience must realize her as a physical presence—see her move and hear her speak. It should be helpful to enlist the aid of another actor at some early rehearsals who would improvise lines and actions of the imaginary character.

(The Lady speaks.) As you say, it is about time all that changed . . . *(Changing her tone:)* Perhaps my husband can do something about it . . . he's going to tell you about it.

OLD MAN *(to the* OLD WOMAN*)*: Hush, hush, Semiramis, the time hasn't come to talk about that yet. *(To the Lady:)* Excuse me, madam, for having aroused your curiosity. *(The Lady reacts.)* Dear madam, don't insist . . .

(The OLD MAN *and* OLD WOMAN *smile. They even laugh. They appear to be very amused by the story the invisible Lady tells them. A pause, a moment of silence in the conversation. Their faces lose all expression.)*

OLD MAN *(to the invisible Lady)*: Yes, you're quite right . . .

OLD WOMAN: Yes, yes, yes . . . Oh! surely not.

OLD MAN: Yes, yes, yes. Not at all.

OLD WOMAN: Yes?

OLD MAN: No!?

OLD WOMAN: It's certainly true.

OLD MAN *(laughing)*: It isn't possible.

OLD WOMAN *(laughing)*: Oh! well. *(To the* OLD MAN*)*: She's charming.

OLD MAN *(to the* OLD WOMAN*)*: Madam has made a conquest. *(To the invisible Lady)*: my congratulations! . . .

OLD WOMAN *(to the invisible Lady)*: You're not like the young people today . . .

OLD MAN *(bending over painfully in order to re-cover an invisible object that the invisible Lady has dropped)*: Let me . . . don't disturb yourself . . . I'll get it . . . Oh! you're quicker than I . . . *(He straightens up again.)*

OLD WOMAN *(to the* OLD MAN*)*: She's younger than you!

OLD MAN *(to the invisible Lady)*: Old age is a heavy burden. I can only wish you an eternal youth.

OLD WOMAN *(to the invisible Lady)*: He's sincere, he speaks from the heart. *(To the* OLD MAN*)*: My darling!

(Several moments of silence. The OLD MAN *and* OLD WOMAN, *heads turned in profile, look at the*

In your score write lines for the Lady that will motivate indicated responses from the Old Couple. Listen to the Lady's line at each rehearsal.

Notice that the lines of the invisible Lady motivate new beats.

The Lady's lines here are especially important.

invisible Lady, smiling politely; they then turn their heads towards the audience, then look again at the invisible Lady, answering her smile with their smiles, and her questions with their replies.)

OLD WOMAN: It's very kind of you to take such an interest in us.

OLD MAN: We live a retired life.

OLD WOMAN: My husband's not really misanthropic, he just loves solitude.

OLD MAN: We have the radio, I get in some fishing, and then there's fairly regular boat service.

OLD WOMAN: On Sundays there are two boats in the morning, one in the evening, not to mention privately chartered trips.

OLD MAN *(to the invisible Lady)*:   When the weather's clear, there is a moon.

OLD WOMAN *(to the invisible Lady)*:   He's always concerned with his duties as general factotum . . . they keep him busy . . . On the other hand, at his age, he might very well take it easy.

OLD MAN *(to the invisible Lady)*:   I'll have plenty of time to take it easy in my grave.

OLD WOMAN *(to the OLD MAN)*:   Don't say that, my little darling . . . *(To the invisible Lady:)* Our family, what's left of it, my husband's friends, still came to see us, from time to time, ten years ago . . .

OLD MAN *(to the invisible Lady)*:   In the winter, a good book, beside the radiator, and the memories of a lifetime.

OLD WOMAN *(to the invisible Lady)*:   A modest life but a full one . . . he devotes two hours every day to work on his message.

(The doorbell rings. After a short pause, we hear the noise of a boat leaving.)

OLD WOMAN *(to the OLD MAN)*:   Someone has come. Go quickly.

OLD MAN *(to the invisible Lady)*:   Please excuse me, madam. Just a moment! *(To the OLD WOMAN:)* Hurry and bring some chairs!

The Old Couple must see vividly in their minds all the details of their "retired life."

These lines tell us much about the Old Couple's isolation.

(Loud ringing of the doorbell.)

OLD MAN *(hastening, all bent over, towards door up Right Center, while the* OLD WOMAN *goes towards the concealed door on the left, hurrying with difficulty, hobbling along)*:   It must be someone important. *(He hurries, opens door and the invisible Colonel enters. Perhaps it would be useful for us to hear discreetly several trumpet notes, several phrases, like "Hail the Chief." When he opens the door and sees the invisible Colonel, the* OLD MAN *stiffens into a respectful position of attention.)* Ah! . . . Colonel! *(He lifts his hand vaguely towards his forehead, so as to roughly sketch a salute.)* Good evening, my dear Colonel . . . This is a very great honor for me . . . I . . . I . . . I was not expecting it . . . although . . . indeed . . . in short, I am most proud to welcome you, a hero of your eminence, into my humble dwelling . . . *(He presses the invisible hand that the invisible Colonel gives him, bending forward ceremoniously, then straightens up again.)*

A Note on *The Chairs*

It is neither necessary nor desirable that the actors be old. The play is a comment on life, not a representation of it. Young actors skillfully creating old-aged characters will admirably realize the values of the scene. It provides a good opportunity for observing the physical and mental characteristics of old age and reproducing them onstage.

A Man for All Seasons

ROBERT BOLT

Exploratory Analysis of a Scene from Act I: 2 men

Background   Robert Bolt writes in his preface "the bit of English history which is the background to this play is pretty well known. Henry VIII, who started with everything and squandered it all, who had the physical and mental fortitude to ensure a lifetime of gratified greeds, . . . is one of the most popular figures in the whole procession. We recognize in him an archetype, one of the champions of our baser nature, and are in him vicariously indulged.

"Against him stood the whole edifice of medieval religion, founded on piety, but by then moneyed, elaborate, . . . which Henry brought down with such a satisfying and disgraceful crash.

"The collision came about like this: While yet a Prince, Henry did not expect to become a King, for he had an elder brother, Arthur. A marriage was made between this Arthur and a Spanish Princess, Catherine, but Arthur presently died. The Royal Houses of Spain and England wished to repair the connection, and the obvious way to do it was to marry the young widow to Henry, now heir in Arthur's place. But Spain and England were Christian monarchies and Christian law forbade a man to marry his brother's widow.

"To be a Christian was to be a Churchman and there was only one Church (though plagued with many heresies) and the Pope was its head. At the request of Christian Spain and Christian England the Pope dispensed with the Christian law forbidding a man to marry his brother's widow, and when in due course Prince Henry ascended to the English throne as Henry VIII, Catherine was his Queen.

"For some years the marriage was successful; they respected and liked one another, and Henry took his pleasures elsewhere but lightly. However, at length he wished to divorce her.

". . . Catherine had grown increasingly plain and intensely religious; Henry had fallen in love with Anne Boleyn; the Spanish alliance had become unpopular. None of these absolutely necessitated a divorce but there was a fourth motive that did. Catherine had not been able to provide Henry with a male child and was now presumed barren. There was a daughter, but competent statesmen were unanimous that a Queen on the throne of England was unthinkable. Anne and Henry were confident that between them they could produce a son; but if that son was to be Henry's heir, Anne would have to be Henry's wife.

"The Pope was once again approached, this time by England only, and asked to declare the marriage to Catherine null, on the grounds that it contravened the Christian law which forbade marriage with a brother's widow. But England's insistence that the marriage had been null was now balanced by Spain's insistence that it hadn't.

135

. . . After much ceremonious prevarication, while Henry waited with a rising temper, it became clear that so far as the Pope was concerned, the marriage with Catherine would stand.

"To the ferment of a lover and the anxieties of a sovereign Henry now added a bad conscience; and a serious matter it was, for him and those about him."

One of those about him was Sir Thomas More, recently appointed Lord Chancellor, which is to say principal advisor to the King. Because More was noted for his goodness and integrity, his public sanction of Henry's divorce and remarriage was important to Henry's reputation. More, a very orthodox Catholic, searched his soul for a way to support his monarch. He could not find it in his soul to do it; and, since for him the consequence of perjury was damnation, he lost his head to save his soul.

The play is a conflict between a man of conscience and a man of convenience. And when the man of convenience is a powerful king, he is almost sure to win. This scene comes early in the play, near the beginning of the conflict.

Who SIR THOMAS MORE when the events of this play begin is in his forties. Described by the dramatist as "pale, middle-sized, not robust. But the life of the mind is so abundant and debonair that it illuminates the body. His movements are open and swift but never wild, having a natural moderation. The face is intellectual and quickly delighted, the norm to which it returns serious and compassionate . . ." Again: "Respectably, not nobly born, he distinguished himself first as a scholar, then as a lawyer, was made an Ambassador, finally Lord Chancellor. . . . He corresponded with the greatest minds in Europe as the representative and acknowledged champion of the New Learning in England. He was a friend of the King, who would send for More when his social appetites took a turn in that direction . . . He adored and was adored by his own large family. He parted with more than most men when he parted with his life, for he accepted and

enjoyed his social context." While enjoying his life, his faith in God was absolute. In the last moments of the play, standing near the block, he says to the Headsman: "Friend, be not afraid of your office. You send me to God . . . He will not refuse one who is so blithe to go to him."

Robert Whittington, More's contemporary wrote, "More is a man of angel's wit and singular learning; I know not his fellow. For where is the man of that gentleness, lowliness, and affability? And as time requireth a man of marvellous mirth and pastimes; and sometimes of as sad gravity: a man for all seasons."

KING HENRY VIII is not the Henry of the famous Holbein portrait—double-jowled, gross, and corrupt. He is a man in his late thirties, clean-shaven, bright-eyed, graceful, and athletic. He is keen of intellect, learned, artistically gifted—a composer of music and a splendid dancer—the latter being a requisite for popularity at Court. He seeks adulation to feed his enormous vanity, but only the levity with which he handles his absolute power foreshadows his future corruption. He makes his entrance into Act I (a bit earlier than the scene we are going to explore) wearing a suit of cloth of gold and blowing on a pilot's whistle. He has just launched a ship appropriately named the *Great Harry*.

Character Relationships The relationship between Henry and Sir Thomas may have been quite clearly suggested in the above paragraphs. More was scrupulous in discharging any duty, and certainly not the least of his responsibilities were those connected with his position as Lord Chancellor. In addition, he and Henry shared a kind of mutual affection. Henry once walked around the garden of More's house in Chelsea with his arm around More's neck. Said More, "If my head would win him a castle in France, it should not fail to fall." More was not unmindful of the dangers in not yielding to Henry's desires. His predecessor in office, the great Cardinal Wolsey, had just been stripped of power and property (a circumstance that doubtless precipitated his death) because he had not been able to gain an annulment of Henry's marriage. Henry was quixotic, given to rages of temper, and his favors were an on-again-off-again thing. All this More knew. He knew also that even to please his King there were things he could not do.

When and Where   The time is 1531 during the reign of Henry VIII. The place is the garden of Sir Thomas More's house in Chelsea, along the River Thames. The King has come for supper, having arrived on the Royal Barge accompanied by servants and musicians. The time, place, and circumstances affect the behavior of the characters. At a meeting between a King and his Chan-

cellor, even a meeting designated as informal, proprieties must be observed.

The Actors' Work   Analyze the scene for intentions, obstacles, beats, physical and verbal actions, relationships, subtext, sensory tasks. Write the results of your analysis in your script, to provide you with a score for playing your role.

The Ground Plan   Study the lines and the stage directions to determine what items are needed to carry out the physical actions, and then arrange them in a way that will help you. The play is written to be done with simple staging. Don't provide more than is necessary.

A Man for All Seasons

ROBERT BOLT

HENRY VIII *and* SIR THOMAS MORE *standing in the garden of More's house. Music is heard without, stately and oversweet.*

HENRY *(Speaking as the music begins to recede)*:   Listen to this, Thomas. *(He walks about, the auditor, beating time)* Do you know it?
MORE: No, Your Grace, I—
HENRY: Sh! (MORE *is silent;* HENRY *goes on listening)* I launched a ship today, Thomas.
MORE: Yes, Your Grace, I—
HENRY: *Listen,* man, listen . . . *(A pause)* . . . The *Great Harry* . . . I steered her, Thomas, under sail.
MORE: You have many accomplishments, Your Grace.

The situation involves both actors in the sensory task of listening to music. Each character has a different relationship to the music.

From *A Man for All Seasons* by Robert Bolt. Copyright © 1960, 1962, by Robert Bolt. Reprinted by permission of Random House, Inc. Also reprinted by permission of Heinemann Educational Books Ltd.

HENRY (*Holds up a finger for silence. A pause*): A great experience. (MORE *keeps silent*) . . . A great experience, Thomas.

MORE: Yes, Your Grace.

(*The music is growing fainter*)

HENRY: I am a fool.

MORE: How so, Your Grace?

HENRY (*A pause, during which the music fades to silence*): What else but a fool to live in a Court, in a licentious mob—when I have friends, with gardens.

MORE: Your Grace—

HENRY: No courtship, no ceremony, Thomas. Be seated. You are my friend, are you not? (MORE *sits*)

MORE: Your Majesty.

HENRY (*Eyes lighting on the chain on the table by* MORE): And thank God I have a friend for my Chancellor. (*Laughingly, but implacably, he takes up the chain and lowers it over* MORE'S *head*) Readier to be friends, I trust, than he was to be Chancellor.

MORE: My own knowledge of my poor abilities—

HENRY: I will judge of your abilities, Thomas . . . Did you know that Wolsey named you for Chancellor?

MORE: Wolsey!

HENRY: Aye, before he died. Wolsey named you and Wolsey was no fool.

MORE: He was a statesman of incomparable ability, Your Grace.

HENRY: Was he? Was he so? (*He rises*) Then why did he fail me? Be seated—it was villainy then! Yes, villainy. I was right to break him; he was all pride, Thomas; a proud man; pride right through. And he failed me! (MORE *opens his mouth*) He failed me in the one thing that mattered! The one thing that matters, Thomas, then or now. And why? He wanted to be Pope! Yes, he wanted to be the Bishop of Rome. I'll tell you something, Thomas, and you can check this for yourself—it was never merry in England while we had Cardinals amongst us.

By court regulations no one could sit in the presence of the king until bidden to do so. Henry wants his visit to appear friendly and casual.

A great chain with a pendant medallion was the emblem of office of the Lord Chancellor. You can see it pictured in Holbein's frequently reproduced portrait of Sir Thomas.

Henry's "Be seated" indicates that More, according to protocol, stood up as soon as the King rose. Henry wants to maintain an aura of friendly informality.

(He nods significantly at MORE, *who lowers his eyes)* But look now—*(Walking away)*—I shall never forget the feel of that . . . great tiller under my hands . . . I took her down to Dogget's Bank, went about and brought her up in Tilbury Roads. A man could sail clean round the world in that ship.

MORE *(With affectionate admiration)*:   Some men could, Your Grace.

HENRY *(Offhand)*:   Touching this matter of my divorce, Thomas; have you thought of it since we last talked?

MORE: Of little else.

HENRY: Then you see your way clear to me?

MORE: That you should put away Queen Catherine, Sire? Oh, alas *(He thumps the table in distress)* as I think of it I see so clearly that I can *not* come with Your Grace that my endeavor is not to think of it at all.

HENRY: Then you have not thought enough! . . . *(With real appeal)* Great God, Thomas, why do you hold out against me in the desire of my heart—the very wick of my heart?

MORE *(Draws up his sleeve, baring his arm)*:   There is my right arm. *(A practical proposition)* Take your dagger and saw it from my shoulder, and I will laugh and be thankful, if by that means I can come with Your Grace with a clear conscience.

HENRY *(Uncomfortably pulls at the sleeve)*:   I know it, Thomas, I know . . .

MORE *(Rises, formally)*:   I crave pardon if I offend.

HENRY *(Suspiciously)*:   Speak then.

MORE: When I took the Great Seal your Majesty promised not to pursue me on this matter.

HENRY: Ha! So I break my word, Master More! No no, I'm joking . . . I joke roughly . . . *(He wanders away.)* I often think I'm a rough fellow . . . Yes, a rough young fellow. *(He shakes his head indulgently.)* Be seated . . . That's a rosebay. We have one like it at Hampton—not so red as that though. Ha—I'm in an excellent

Notice Henry's tactic of leading up to a discussion of the divorce and then changing the subject.

What is More's subtext?

The Lord Chancellor was the Keeper of the Great Seal. It had to be pressed on a draft of all laws and proclamations before they became official, thus indicating the king's approval.

Rosebay: a species of flowering shrub.

frame of mind. *(Glances at the rosebay.)* Beautiful. *(Reasonable, pleasant.)* You must consider, Thomas, that I stand in peril of my soul. It was no marriage; she was my brother's widow. Leviticus: "Thou shalt not uncover the nakedness of thy brother's wife." Leviticus, Chapter eighteen, Verse sixteen.

MORE: Yes, Your Grace. But Deuteronomy—

HENRY *(Triumphant):* Deuteronomy's ambiguous!

Deuteronomy 25:5. If brethren dwell together, and one of them die, and have no child, the wife of the dead shall not marry without unto a stranger: her husband's brother shall go in unto her, and take her to him to wife . . .

MORE *(Bursting out):* Your Grace, I'm not fit to meddle in these matters—to me it seems a matter for the Holy See—

HENRY *(Reprovingly):* Thomas, Thomas, does a man need a Pope to tell him when he's sinned? It was a sin, Thomas; I admit; I repent. And God has punished me; I have no son . . . Son after son she's borne me, Thomas, all dead at birth, or dead within the month; I never saw the hand of God so clear in anything . . . I have a daughter, she's a good child, a well-set child—But I have no son. *(He flares up)* it is my bounded *duty* to put away the Queen, and all the Popes back to St. Peter shall not come between me and my duty! How is it that you cannot see? Everyone else does.

Henry is using a strong verbal action to achieve his intention.

MORE *(Eagerly):* Then why does Your Grace need my poor support?

HENRY: Because you are honest. What's more to the purpose, you're known to be honest . . . There are those like Norfolk who follow me because I wear the crown, and there are those like Master Cromwell who follow me because they are jackals with sharp teeth and I am their lion, and there is a mass that follows me because it follows anything that moves—and there is you.

MORE: I am sick to think how much I must displease Your Grace.

HENRY: No, Thomas, I respect your sincerity. Respect? Oh, man, it's water in the desert . . . How did you like our music? That air they played, it had a certain—well, tell me what you thought of it.

Be sure to find and think the subtext in the image of "water in the desert."

MORE (*Relieved at this turn; smiling*):   Could it have been Your Grace's own?

HENRY (*Smiles back*):   Discovered! Now I'll never know your true opinion. And that's irksome, Thomas, for we artists, though we love praise, yet we love truth better.

MORE (*Mildly*):   Then I will tell Your Grace truly what I thought of it.

HENRY (*A little disconcerted*):   Speak then.

MORE: To me it seemed—delightful.

HENRY: Thomas—I chose the right man for Chancellor.

MORE: I must in fairness add that my taste in music is reputedly deplorable.

HENRY: Your taste in music is excellent. It exactly coincides with my own. Ah music! Music! Send them back without me, Thomas; I will live here in Chelsea and make music.

Them refers to the entourage that has accompanied Henry on his visit.

MORE: My house is at Your Grace's disposal.

HENRY: Thomas, you understand me; we will stay here together and make music.

MORE: Will Your Grace honor my roof after dinner?

HENRY (*Walking away, blowing moodily on his whistle*):   Mm? Yes, I expect I'll bellow for you . . .

MORE: My wife will be more—

HENRY: Yes, yes. (*He turns, his face set*) Touching this other business, mark you, Thomas, I'll have no opposition.

The conflict is reaching a climax.

MORE (*Sadly*):   Your Grace?

What is More's subtext?

HENRY: No opposition, I say! No opposition! Your conscience is your own affair; but you are my Chancellor! There, you have my word—I'll leave you out of it. But I don't take it kindly, Thomas, and I'll have no opposition! I see how it will be; the bishops will oppose me. The full-fed, hypocritical, "Princes of the *Church*"! Ha! As for the Pope! Am I to burn in Hell because the Bishop of Rome, with the King of Spain's knife to his throat, mouths me Deuteronomy? Hypocrites! They're all hypocrites! Mind they do not take you in, Thomas! Lie low if you will, but I'll brook no opposition—no noise! No words, no signs, no letters, no pamphlets—Mind that, Thomas —no writings against me!

MORE: Your Grace is unjust. I am Your Grace's loyal minister. If I cannot serve Your Grace in this great matter of the Queen—

More was a persuasive eloquent writer.

HENRY: I have no Queen! Catherine is not my wife and no priest can make her so, and they that say she is my wife are not only liars . . . but traitors! Mind it, Thomas!

How would More have completed this sentence if he had not been interrupted? Always know specifically what the end of a "cut speech" would have been, then don't anticipate the interruption.

MORE: Am I a babbler, Your Grace? (*But his voice is unsteady.*)

HENRY: You are stubborn . . . (*Wooingly.*) If you could come with me, you are the man I would soonest raise—yes, with my own hand.

MORE (*Covers his face*):   Oh, Your Grace overwhelms me! (*A complicated chiming of little bells is heard.*)

HENRY: What's that?

MORE: Eight o'clock, Your Grace.

HENRY (*Uneasily eyeing* MORE):   Oh, lift yourself up, man—have I not promised? (MORE *braces.*) Shall we eat?

MORE: If Your Grace pleases (*Recovering.*) What will Your Grace sing for us?

HENRY: Eight o'clock you said? Thomas, the tide will be changing. I was forgetting the tide. I'd better go.

Be sure to make clear the reason Henry does not stay for supper.

MORE (*Gravely*):   I'm sorry, Your Grace.

Think carefully about More's subtext.

HENRY: I must catch the tide or I'll not get back to Richmond till . . . No, don't come. (*He starts to go.*)

MORE (*Bowing*):   Good night, Your Grace. (*Exit* HENRY.)

Notes on *A Man for All Seasons*

1. Robert Bolt says that in this play he tried for a "bold and beautiful verbal architecture." The language is simple, but it is not the colloquial speech of *When You Comin Back, Red Ryder?* and of many contemporary American plays. The actors need to speak well, and they need to be

aware of the structure of the speeches and use it effectively. Notice, for example, Henry's speech beginning "Because you are honest"—how it builds through a series to a focal point at the end, "and there is you." Again notice his speech beginning "No opposition, I say"—how, when Henry is ready to tell More what he came to say, he uses repetition to build his speech to a strong climax.

2. An interesting sidelight on Henry's character is given earlier in the play by Thomas Cromwell in describing the preparation for the launching of the ship: ". . : next week at Deptford we are launching the *Great Harry*—one thousand tons, four masts, sixty-six guns, an overall length of one hundred and seventy-five feet; it's expected to be very effective—all this you probably know. However, you may not know that the King himself will guide her down the river; yes, the King himself will be her pilot. He will have some assistance, of course, but he himself will be her pilot. He will have a pilot's whistle upon which he will blow, and he will wear in every respect a common pilot's uniform. Except for the material, which will be cloth of gold. These innocent fancies require more preparation than you might suppose . . ."

3. Some reading about this period, as well as examining some reproductions of painting s and drawings, will provide additional historical background and a knowledge of dress, manners, and customs that will help in realizing the characters. It is a rewarding period for the actor to study because the English Renaissance—the periods of Henry VIII and Elizabeth I—is the setting for some of the world's greatest dramatic literature, including many of Shakespeare's major plays. These books are recommended:

John Farrow. *The Story of Thomas More*. New York: Sheed and Ward, 1954.

Albert H. Marvin. *The Divorce*. New York: Simon and Schuster, 1965.

John van Duyn Southworth. *Monarch and Conspiracy: The Wives and Woes of Henry VIII*. New York: Crown Publishers, 1973.

The Prodigal

JACK RICHARDSON

Exploratory Analysis of a Scene from Act II, Scene 1: 2 men, 1 woman

Background   The story of the house of Atreus, including the Orestes legend, has stimulated dramatists to some of their greatest work for over two thousand years. The most significant is the Oresteia trilogy of Aeschylus; the legend also provided material for Sophocles and Euripides. In modern times it has been made into an opera by Richard Strauss and into a motion picture starring Irene Pappas and Katharine Hepburn. It is the subject of Eugene O'Neill's trilogy *Mourning Becomes Electra* and of *The Flies* by Jean-Paul Sartre.

The story briefly is this: Agamemnon, King of Argos, returns home in triumph after a ten years' absence fighting the Trojan wars, bringing with him Cassandra, a Trojan princess and prophetess. He finds that during his absence his cousin Aegisthus has taken control of the kingdom and has become the lover of his wife Clytemnestra. In order to maintain their power, Aegisthus and Clytemnestra murder Agamemnon, exile his son Orestes, and relegate his daughter Electra to the position of a household servant because she vows to avenge her father's murder. Orestes returns from exile and, goaded by Electra, kills his mother and her lover. He is pursued by Furies for the crime of matricide, finally brought to trial by the goddess Athena, who mercifully declares that through suffering he has atoned for his crime and that he is free of guilt.

In *The Prodigal,* first produced in 1960, Jack Richardson brings us a startlingly modern Orestes and provides compelling variations of the themes of idealism, political opportunism, and the causes and nature of war. The play begins with the anticipated return of Agamemnon, tells us of Orestes' refusal to accept his father as a hero, of his attempt to keep himself uninvolved in the blood feud, and of his final return to the scene of action. Of his return he says at the end of the play: "I can resist . . . no longer. I will go back, murder, and say it's for a better world, for this must be said to prevent insanity. And when I'm standing, addressing the crowds of Argos, telling them what great things are to come because of my act, I will know it is nothing but weakness that brought me there in front of them. I will speak of the golden days to come and boast of my killing to achieve them; but . . . I will do so under protest. I will do so knowing I was not great enough to create something better."

Who   ORESTES is in his early twenties. He has a bright mocking mind, closer mentally than physically to the Greek ideal. He is not unattractive, although he refers to himself as underweight and obviously he never embraced the classic practice of body building. He has been close enough to the sources of power to know that humanitarian causes are likely to be a blind behind which people seek political advantage, and that idealistic goals are attained through willing disregard of individual rights. This insight has generated nothing but contempt for heroes and rulers, and has led him, with his companion Pylades, to lead a life of pleasure amounting to frivolity.

Early in the play Penelope, formerly Orestes' governess, taxes him with his seeming irresponsibility: "I find it peculiar that a prince should be indifferent to the reputation of his country; that he should allow jests and insults about his father and himself to pass unnoticed and unavenged; that he should be totally uncaring about the noble traditions and laws his father shed blood to establish; . . . that he should allow a weak charlatan . . . to usurp his power and degrade his mother—yes, all this I find strange in a prince." Ultimately he discovers that it is impossible to maintain this posture and accepts the inevitability of avenging the murder of a father whose principles and practices he despised. He finds he is subservient to the demands of society, that laws and conventions prevent him from doing as he pleases.

PYLADES is the same age as Orestes. Handsome, charming, witty—a fine companion for pleasurable pursuits. While superficially Pylades and Orestes are two of a kind, the contrasts between them are important. Pylades has an unoriginal mind, seeking pleasure in his youth and settling later into a life of conventional mediocrity. Contradictory as it may seem, Orestes' frivolity is a serious statement of principle—a principle that, though it may be admirable, he comes to find it impossible to live by.

CASSANDRA is middle-aged, described by the dramatist as "small, round, and comical-looking" but with a forceful manner. She is clear-sighted and outspoken with a wry humor and a rather tolerant good-nature. In classic mythology Cassandra was endowed with the gift of prophecy, but it was her fate that no one ever believed what she foretold.

Character Relationships   Orestes and Pylades are what may platitudinously be termed "boon companions." They share common interests and desires and find genuine pleasure in each other's company. Although Pylades occasionally refers to and addresses Orestes as Prince, his use of the title does not denote ceremonial respect. Indeed, such respect is not inherent in their relationship. The character contrasts mentioned above are not in this scene a part of their consciousness. However, toward the end of the play conventional Pylades deserts Orestes because he does not want to be associated with a prince who fails his responsibilities and with a son who does not follow custom by avenging a murdered father.

Cassandra sees Pylades as a callow youth who does not warrant serious attention. With her knowledge of Orestes' future, she is understanding of his youthful failure to grasp realities.

Where and When   Historically, or more aptly mythologically, the setting is the kingdom of Argos in ancient Greece, and it would not be wrong to conceive the play in classic costume with the action taking place in a large chamber of an ancient palace. The playwright, however, has blended legend with contemporary reality, and the flavor of both needs to be realized. The behavior of the characters is dignified but not ceremonious. Although the dialogue is not exalted speech, it is free of colloquialisms; and all of the characters are highly articulate. An appropriate blend of flavors might come in part from acting in modern dress with more formal behavior than is generally suitable in contemporary plays.

The Actors' Work   Analyze the scene for intentions, obstacles, beats, physical and verbal actions, relationships, subtext, sensory tasks. Devise a ground plan that will enable you effectively to carry out the actions. Write the results of your analysis in your script to provide you with a score in rehearsing the role.

This scene presents a problem somewhat different in degree from most of the others in this text. The stage directions provide a minimum of physical action, and very little physical action is inherent in the dialogue. It is a "language play" in which the verbal actions are paramount. Be sure you know specifically how you want each line to influence the character to whom it is spoken, and then speak it to accomplish this intention. At the same time you should invent physical actions suitable to your character that will help to create the reality of the situation both for you and for the audience.

The Prodigal

JACK RICHARDSON

A large chamber inside the palace. As curtain is raised, CASSANDRA, on stage, is engrossed in weaving a small wicker basket when Pylades enters.

Cassandra's basket weaving is an appropriate physical action of the kind you will need to invent.

PYLADES: Good morning, old woman. Have you, by chance, seen Prince Orestes about?

CASSANDRA *goes on with weaving.*

I say, have you seen the prince?

No reply.

Poor thing must be deaf.

CASSANDRA *(without looking up from work)*:   Do you expect a reply when you address a woman enjoying the noonday brightness of middle age as "old"?

PYLADES: Pardon, but if I knew your name I could salute you in a less personal manner.

CASSANDRA: As you are young, you should be

Reprinted by permission of Harold Freedman Brandt & Brandt Dramatic Department, Inc. Copyright © 1960 by Jack C. Richardson.
CAUTION: *The Prodigal* is the sole property of the Author and is fully protected by copyright. It may not be acted by professionals or amateurs without formal permission and the payment of a royalty. All rights, including professional, amateur, stock, radio and television broadcasting, motion picture, recitation, lecturing, public reading, and the rights of translation in foreign languages are reserved. All inquiries should be addressed to the author's agent: Harold Freedman Brandt & Brandt Dramatic Department, Inc., 101 Park Avenue, New York, N.Y. 10017. All inquiries concerning amateur rights should be addressed to Dramatists Play Service, Inc., 14 East 38th Street, New York, N.Y. 10016.

forced to undergo formality. However, you may call me Cassandra.

PYLADES (*somewhat taken aback*):   Cassandra? The Trojan prophetess?

CASSANDRA (*nodding and putting her work aside*):   There, enough of that. What one won't do to keep the mind busy.

PYLADES: If what I've heard of you is true, Cassandra, then I should imagine you would have little trouble keeping yourself amused.

CASSANDRA: I judge you think the future is amusing.

PYLADES: No, interesting is probably the better word.

CASSANDRA: In any case you overestimate it. What is your name?

PYLADES: Pylades.

Pronounced pĭl'ə-dēz.

CASSANDRA: Well, Pylades, the future, unfortunately for those with my gifts, is an unimaginable bore.

PYLADES (*laughing*):   That might be true in general, but I'm sure each man believes his own endowed with epic events.

CASSANDRA: Yes, I suppose, but when he stops believing and begins to know it's quite another matter.

PYLADES: Don't suspect me of seeking a free consultation, but I wish at times I knew mine.

CASSANDRA: Would you really, Pylades? Would you really wish to know that in five years an indiscretion with the daughter of a dangerously influential man will leave you an unwilling husband and the father of red-haired twins? Would you care to discover that the eight years following this unforeseen slip will be crowned with furtive adulteries, one summer cruise with your wife, and a physician's recommendation that you reduce your wine consumption? Would it please you to be told that the year following your wife's long-postponed death you will consider your life had enough unorthodox importance to embarrass the few friends left you with rather intimate memoirs? Shall I go on?

PYLADES: Is that really my life?

CASSANDRA: Perhaps. It is somebody's; I see the events clearly enough, but whose life they are a part of is still somewhat blurred. Still, Pylades, such is what one usually finds when he peeks over the present.

PYLADES *(happily relieved)*:   Cassandra, you are an old fraud—excuse me, I meant a middle-aged one.

CASSANDRA: In my profession, fraudulence is a necessary defense.

PYLADES: Still, you did give me a fright. Red-headed twins! Brr! Such a thought could spoil some very pleasant moments.

(Enter ORESTES.*)*

Ah, just in time, Orestes, to find out your dismal future. *(To Cassandra, under his breath.)* Tell him about the memoirs. He'll explode.

ORESTES: I know enough already, Pylades. That's why I asked you to meet me here. *(To* CASSANDRA.*)* Good morning, Cassandra. I hope you forgive me for my quick and rather awkward departure yesterday.

CASSANDRA: Knowing the life you will have, Orestes, it is easy to forgive you.

PYLADES *(egging her on)*:   You know what's in store for our prince?

CASSANDRA: Not the slightest idea. That's why I'm sure he will have a hard time of it. A comfortable life spiced with ordinary happiness is easily predictable.

ORESTES: Happy or no, I can tell you what mine will be for the next few years.

PYLADES: What, then?

ORESTES: Pylades, my friend, Aegisthus has informed me that, due to my poor and flippant behavior at yesterday's sacrifice, I am to be sent on a long, long voyage so I may deepen my mind, broaden my point of view, understand world problems, and . . . What else did he say? Ah, yes, assume the serious attitude necessary for a prince of Argos. In a word, he

Refusing to pay homage to Agamemnon as a conquering hero and to accept the role of a traditional Prince of Argos, Orestes had abruptly cut short his welcome to his father.

Aegisthus (pronounced ĭ-jĭs'thəs) has attempted to eliminate individual ambition and warring heroes as an ideal of manhood in favor of respect for the performance of menial tasks and acceptance of a simple life strictly prescribed by the gods to whom sacrifices must regularly be made.

has completely lost patience with me and has ordered this trip.

PYLADES: You lucky dog! Do you mean that your punishment for having dozed during the ritual Aegisthus prepared with such care is to be an indefinite voyage?

ORESTES: That it is, Pylades, and you are to come with me.

PYLADES (elated):   I, too?

ORESTES: Aegisthus almost choked with delight when I demanded you accompany me.

PYLADES: Oh, the advantages of unpopularity. But this is really beyond belief. When do we leave? When can I say good-by to this silly city?

ORESTES: Tomorrow.

PYLADES: Tomorrow! Is Aegisthus really so anxious?

ORESTES: He is. That's why I wanted to meet you as soon as possible. You must be ready by tomorrow noon at the latest. Can you do it?

PYLADES: With a day to spare. I'm off right now to tie ends together and bring this happy news to my family. Now, when asked, they can say their son is traveling. Why, I'll have an occupation. (Starts offstage.) You see, Cassandra, your prophecy was not for me at all.

CASSANDRA: Perhaps, Pylades; but at any event I wish you a happy trip.

(PYLADES exits.)

(To ORESTES.) And are you as overjoyed about leaving Argos?

ORESTES: Of course! Why shouldn't I be?

CASSANDRA (shrugging):   Some might consider it an insult to be told to leave their home and go broaden their point of view.

ORESTES: Some might were they prone to look for insults. I see only the pleasure of a well-financed, leisurely voyage, and this is enough to keep my small amount of pride standing erect.

CASSANDRA: Even when you know why Aegisthus is sending you?

ORESTES *(evenly)*:   Yes, Cassandra. Even when I know that. I'm aware of the grand issues I leave behind me, but that's exactly where I want them to be.

CASSANDRA: You're wiser then than I was. I knew what would happen at Troy and had a hundred opportunities to leave also, but I had to feel I might be able to convince others of the idiocy which was to occur and perhaps help to avert it. My reward? My countrymen thought me insane, I saw Troy burn to the ground, and just when all finally hailed me as the wisest of prophets, I was captured, turned into a slave, and my morals called into question.

ORESTES: And what do you think of the man who caused all this?

CASSANDRA: You think one man should be blamed?

ORESTES: I think one man contributed more than the ordinary share of responsibility to such things.

CASSANDRA: Your father? (ORESTES nods.) Perhaps; perhaps he was a great fool in many ways, but then there are so many fools who are small.

ORESTES: And harmless.

CASSANDRA: Not always. Paris, for example, was a small fool who placed overactive glands and twitching nerves above all else when he ran off with Helen. That was rather costly nonsense, wasn't it?

ORESTES: No one forced the Greeks to become the champions of virtue.

CASSANDRA: Nonsense! Do you think that is what sustained the Greek army for ten years in the field? Do you think the soldiers cared who crawled into Helen's bed? No, Orestes, Troy was a rich city, and if anyone had any ideals . . .

ORESTES: It was my father. My father, Cassandra, who led the whole affair. Paris might have slipped into the bushes with Helen and a hundred kings want Troy's gold, but it took

Cassandra had accurately foretold the defeat of the Trojans, but her predictions were not taken seriously until after they had come to pass. Captured as a slave of war, she was reputed to have become Agamemnon's mistress.

Paris, Prince of Troy, had abducted Helen, Queen of Sparta and wife of Agamemnon's brother Menelaus. To avenge this violation of Helen's chastity (earlier Orestes has called Helen's chastity a "contradiction of terms") was the ostensible though not the actual cause of the Trojan Wars.

someone with a keen moral sense to start and justify the war.

CASSANDRA: From what you're saying I can't understand why Aegisthus wants you to leave.

ORESTES: Don't be misled, Cassandra. Aegisthus may be less pretentious and a better psychologist than my father, but that's all that really separates them. He knows my feelings about his inverted philanthropy.

CASSANDRA: And if you had to choose between them?

ORESTES: But I don't have to. Between Aegisthus' creeping, crawling, microscopic figure who's buffeted by the gods and happy to be so, and my father's fumbling giant of the future who steps in everybody's garden and on everybody's toes with good intentions, the only choice is anger or laughter. I've taken the second.

CASSANDRA (as if a suspicion has been confirmed):   Orestes, you're going to be a hero, but it will cost you a great deal.

ORESTES (in amused amazement):   That's not only improbable but insulting.

CASSANDRA: Heroes may change, Orestes. You might find it suits you.

ORESTES: Oh, no, Cassandra, take a good look at me. I'm about to leave Argos and my father to be disposed of by my mother's lover. I have chosen as my sole friend and traveling companion a person whose only worth is his charming uselessness. I am sickened by state ethics, find religion, at its best, high comedy, and while having been tutored in wrestling since a boy, I can't remember having ever won a fight. How, Cassandra, can you fit those qualifications into a heroic pattern?

CASSANDRA: Hmm. I'll admit it wouldn't be easy, but I still feel you are marked for something. Perhaps standards will change.

ORESTES: Let's pray they won't. A world in which my attitudes would set a fashion!

CASSANDRA: In that case, Orestes, it will be up to you to change. Oh, don't scowl, I'm only trying to fit you into my premonitions.

Note that this speech has a very contemporary application.

ORESTES: Perhaps, then, they should be changed.

CASSANDRA: What, change the future?

ORESTES: Is it so eternally fixed?

CASSANDRA: It would seem so. Remember what I told you about Troy. It appears no matter how we squirm and invent happy alternatives there is only one future for us.

ORESTES: And you still think that in this I am to be a hero?

CASSANDRA: Give me time, Orestes. It's not easy to gather confirming details together. Let's just say it's a possibility.

ORESTES: Why do you bother me with possibilities? Their very infinity renders them meaningless.

CASSANDRA: Now don't be angry with me. I am trying to help you prepare in case you do find yourself acting a new part. I don't want you to be unnecessarily shocked by it, that's all.

ORESTES: There is nothing which could make me give up the role I have now.

CASSANDRA: Don't be certain, Orestes. It only takes one crashing moment to destroy the mind's labored perspective. The philosopher weeps at the pain of a dog even after he's decided that man and physics no longer deserve pity. The enemy of war, who describes brutality and death with such horrifying elegance, reaches for his sword and cries blood and vengeance when he discovers he's been made cuckold. The confirmed skeptic, who has never lost a logical argument, lets the death of a friend or a severe case of measles turn him into a fanatic worshipper of health foods and herbs. One time when the mind loses control, and who knows what acts you will commit, Orestes.

ORESTES: It will take then a moment greater than those you have just described.

CASSANDRA: Of course; but believe me, such exist.

Be sure to find specific verbal intentions and play them strongly. A sharp conflict of ideas is truly dramatic.

FOR READING AND STUDY

For a fuller understanding of *The Prodigal,* compare and contrast it with some of the other plays, both ancient and modern, about the same characters.

Aeschylus. *Agamemnon.*
———. *The Choephori (The Libation Bearers).*
———. *The Eumenides (The Furies).*
Sophocles. *Electra.*
Euripides. *Electra.*
———. *Orestes.*
Eugene O'Neill. *Mourning Becomes Electra.*
Jean Giraudoux. *Electra.*
Jean-Paul Sartre. *The Flies.*

The Devil's Disciple

GEORGE BERNARD SHAW

Exploratory Analysis of a Scene from Act III; 1 man, 1 woman

Background The story is about Richard Dudgeon, a young man who revolts against the rigid Puritanism and religious hypocrisy with which he was indoctrinated as a child. He believes the Puritans—self-appointed men and women of God—are uncharitable, inhumane, and dedicated to causing misery. Since he believes in human happiness, he calls himself the Devil's Disciple and has become an outcast in his native town of Westerbridge, New Hampshire. He is particularly repellent to Judith Anderson, the minister's young wife.

The time is 1777 and the British, pushing through the New England colonies, are hanging a leading citizen in every town as an example and a warning to the revolutionists. Nearby they have hanged Dick's Uncle Peter; in Westerbridge they come for Parson Anderson. But the Parson is out and, to Judith's distaste, Dick is there. Having taken off his coat because it is wet with rain, he is mistaken for the Reverend Anderson. He is arrested and, refusing to reveal his identity, is condemned to hang. When Anderson hears what has happened, he gallops off to safety. Judith is dismayed and disillusioned by her husband's cowardly behavior.

In the scene for exploration, Judith visits Dick in jail the morning after his arrest in an attempt to save him from what appears to be inevitable

death. She does not succeed and in the following scene Dick is placed on the gallows. We must take note that in the end all turns out well, although not in the way Judith believed she wanted. Reverend Anderson proves to be not a coward trying to save his life, but a revolutionist who gains a victory over the British and frees Dick Dudgeon. Judith discovers she loves her husband in his new role as a man of action; and the Devil's Disciple is carried on the shoulders of the townspeople as a hero. The play resembles a traditional melodrama—indeed Shaw consciously exploited that structure. But he used the melodramatic clichés in a fresh and realistic manner.

Who RICHARD DUDGEON is a mature young man, in his twenties or early thirties. He is described by Shaw as "certainly the best looking member of his family; but his expression is reckless and sardonic, his manner defiant and satirical, his dress picturesquely careless. Only his forehead and mouth betray an extraordinary steadfastness; and his eyes are the eyes of a fanatic." He is a man who believes in something and lives according to his beliefs. What he believes is that there is some natural goodness in man, that good deeds are performed spontaneously for their own sake, not for motives of gain,

154

and certainly not to assure eternal salvation. He never confuses the spirit of Christianity with church-going. He sees his act of sacrifice as natural. It is not done nobly to save another man's life, nor romantically to save the husband of a woman he loves. In fact, he does not love Judith at all and any suggestion that he does (as intimated in some portrayals) is contrary to Shaw's intention.

JUDITH ANDERSON is about twenty-five. Shaw says that "she is pretty and proper and ladylike, and has been admired and petted into an opinion of herself sufficiently favorable to give her a self-assurance which serves her instead of strength. She has a pretty taste in dress, and in her face the pretty lines of a sentimental character formed by dreams. Even her little self-complacency is pretty, like a child's vanity. Rather a pathetic creature to any sympathetic observer who knows how rough a place the world is." She begins with a traditional view of right and wrong and sees herself as the wife in an idyllic Christian home. She holds also a rather romantic notion of what motivates men's actions. Judith is disillusioned by the behavior of both Anderson and Dick, but by the end of the play she sees life more clearly and realistically.

Character Relationships   Among several appropriate titles for the Jail Scene between Richard and Judith, one might be *Dick Disillusions Judith*. Early in the play, as a "good Christian woman," Judith has resisted having any association with such a sinner as Dick. He has responded to her dislike with a kind of sardonic humor. When Anderson invited Dick to the par-

sonage, it was only because of her husband's insistence that she had served him tea. With the unexpected turn of events—Dick's apparently heroic act to save Anderson's life, and Anderson's apparent willingness to let him do it—Judith has developed romantic notions about Dick's intentions and has come to believe she loves him. When Richard discovers in this scene how her feelings have changed, he finds it necessary to make her understand why he behaved the way he did.

Where and When   It is winter in Westerbridge, New Hampshire, in 1777. While the time is the eighteenth century, the characters do not dress and behave as they would on the plantations of Virginia or in the fashionable watering town of Bath (see Introduction to the scene from *The Rivals*). They are common folk dealing with the hardships of life in a small New England town. They are neither wealthy, leisured, nor elegant. In other scenes, General Burgoyne, an urbane British officer, complains about the crudeness of his surroundings. Shaw says this scene takes place in "a little empty panelled waiting room" at the British headquarters in the Town Hall, which also contains the jail. The time is early morning. The atmosphere needs to suggest the grimness of the situation.

The Actors' Work   Analyze the scene for intentions, obstacles, beats, relationships, physical and verbal actions, subtext, sensory tasks. Make a ground plan that will enable you to carry out the physical actions effectively. Write the results of your analysis in your script to provide you with a score in playing the role.

The Devil's Disciple

GEORGE BERNARD SHAW

RICHARD: Mrs Anderson: this visit is very kind of you. And how are you after last night? I had to leave you before you recovered; but I sent word to Essie to go and look after you. Did she understand the message?

Essie is the illegitimate orphan child of Dick's recently hanged Uncle Peter. Dick is the only one in Westerbridge willing to befriend her.
Shaw was an advocate of simplified spelling and punctuation. He eliminated the apostrophe in contractions.

JUDITH *(breathless and urgent)*: Oh, dont think of me: I havnt come here to talk about myself. Are they going to—to—*(meaning "to hang you")?*

RICHARD *(whimsically)*:   At noon, punctually. At least, that was when they disposed of Uncle Peter. *(She shudders)*. Is your husband safe? Is he on the wing?

JUDITH: He is no longer my husband.

RICHARD *(opening his eyes wide)*:   Eh?

JUDITH: I disobeyed you. I told him everything. I expected him to come here and save you. I wanted him to come here and save you. He ran away instead.

Richard had entreated Judith not to tell Anderson what had happened.

RICHARD: Well, thats what I meant him to do. What good would his staying have done? Theyd only have hanged us both.

JUDITH *(with reproachful earnestness)*:   Richard Dudgeon: on your honour, what would you have done in his place?

RICHARD: Exactly what he has done, of course.

JUDITH: Oh, why will you not be simple with me—honest and straightforward? If you are so selfish as that, why did you let them take you last night?

RICHARD *(gaily)*:   Upon my life, Mrs Anderson, I dont know. Ive been asking myself that question ever since; and I can find no manner of reason for acting as I did.

Reprinted with the permission of The Society of Authors on behalf of the Bernard Shaw Estate.

JUDITH: You know you did it for his sake, believing he was a more worthy man than yourself.

RICHARD *(laughing)*:   Oho! No: thats a very pretty reason, I must say; but I'm not so modest as that. No: it wasnt for his sake.

JUDITH *(after a pause, during which she looks shamefacedly at him, blushing painfully)*: Was it for my sake?

RICHARD *(gallantly)*:   Well, you had a hand in it. It must have been a little for your sake. You let them take me, at all events.

JUDITH: Oh, do you think I have not been telling myself that all night? Your death will be at my door. *(Impulsively, she gives him her hand, and adds, with intense earnestness)* If I could save you as you saved him, I would do it, no matter how cruel the death was.

RICHARD *(holding her hand and smiling, but keeping her almost at arms length)*:   I am very sure I shouldnt let you.

JUDITH: Dont you see that I can save you?

RICHARD: How? By changing clothes with me, eh?

JUDITH *(disengaging her hand to touch his lips with it)*:   Dont *(meaning "dont jest")*. No: by telling the Court who you really are.

RICHARD *(frowning)*:   No use; they wouldnt spare me; and it would spoil half his chance of escaping. They are determined to cow us by making an example of somebody on that gallows today. Well, let us cow them by showing that we can stand by one another to the death. That is the only force that can send Burgoyne back across the Atlantic and make America a nation.

JUDITH *(impatiently)*:   Oh, what does all that matter?

RICHARD *(laughing)*:   True: What does it matter? What does anything matter? You see, men have these strange notions, Mrs Anderson; and women see the folly of them.

JUDITH: Women have to lose those they love through them.

RICHARD: They can easily get fresh lovers.

Burgoyne was commander of the British forces.

JUDITH (revolted):   Oh! (Vehemently) Do you realize that you are going to kill yourself?

RICHARD: The only man I have any right to kill, Mrs Anderson. Dont be concerned: no woman will lose her lover through my death. (Smiling) Bless you, nobody cares for me. Have you heard that my mother is dead?

JUDITH: Dead!

RICHARD: Of heart disease—in the night. Her last word to me was her curse: I dont think I could have borne her blessing. My other relatives will not grieve much on my account. Essie will cry for a day or two; but I have provided for her: I made my own will last night.

Richard's mother was an uncompromising Puritan of whom Shaw says, "Being exceedingly disagreeable, she was held to be exceedingly good." Her goodness consisted mainly in denying herself and others of any pleasure, a denial that provided her considerable satisfaction. In the first act, Richard, through his father's will, received substantially all of the Dudgeon property.

JUDITH (stonily, after a moment's silence):   And I!

RICHARD (surprised):   You?

JUDITH: Yes, I. Am I not to care at all?

RICHARD (gaily and bluntly):   Not a scrap. Oh, you expressed your feelings towards me very frankly yesterday. What happened may have softened you for the moment; but believe me, Mrs Anderson, you dont like a bone in my skin or a hair on my head. I shall be as good a riddance at 12 today as I should have been at 12 yesterday.

Judith had said to Dick: "I hate you and dread you."

JUDITH (her voice trembling):   What can I do to shew you that you are mistaken?

RICHARD: Dont trouble. I'll give you credit for liking me a little better than you did. All I say is that my death will not break your heart.

Shew: pronounce it show. Shaw chose to use an archaic spelling for this word.

JUDITH (almost in a whisper):   How do you know? (She puts her hands on his shoulders and looks intently at him).

RICHARD (amazed—divining the truth):   Mrs Anderson! (The bell of the town clock strikes the quarter. He collects himself, and removes her hands, saying rather coldly) Excuse me: they will be here for me presently. It is too late.

JUDITH: It is not too late. Call me as witness: they will never kill you when they know how heroically you have acted.

Allison Giglio and Kenneth Welsh as Judith Anderson and Richard Dudgeon in a Goodman Theatre Center production of *The Devil's Disciple* by George Bernard Shaw. Production directed by William Woodman. (Photograph: Terry Shapiro)

RICHARD (with some scorn): Indeed! But if I dont go through with it, where will the heroism be? I shall simply have tricked them; and theyll hang me for that like a dog. Serve me right too!

JUDITH (wildly): Oh, I believe you want to die.

RICHARD (obstinately): No I dont.

Wildly, obstinately. Don't try to be wild or obstinate. Play causes, not effects. Find intentions for these lines and attempt to realize the intentions through verbal actions.

JUDITH: Then why not try to save yourself? I implore you—listen. You said just now that you saved him for my sake—yes (clutching him as he recoils with a gesture of denial) a little for my sake. Well, save yourself for my sake. And I will go with you to the end of the world.

RICHARD (taking her by the wrists and holding her a little way from him, looking steadily at her): Judith.

JUDITH (breathless—delighted at the name): Yes.

RICHARD: If I said—to please you—that I did what I did ever so little for your sake, I lied as men always lie to women. You know how much I have lived with worthless men—aye, and worthless women too. Well, they could all rise to some sort of goodness and kindness when they were in love (the word love comes from him with true Puritan scorn). That has taught me to set very little store by the goodness that only comes out red hot. What I did last night, I did in cold blood, caring not half so much for your husband, or (ruthlessly) for you (she droops, stricken) as I do for myself. I had no motive and no interest; all I can tell you is that when it came to the point whether I would take my neck out of the noose and put another man's into it, I could not do it. I dont know why not: I see myself as a fool for my pains; but I could not and I cannot. I have been brought up standing by the law of my own nature; and I may not go against it, gallows or no gallows. (She has slowly raised her head and is now looking full at him). I should have done the same for any other man in town, or any other

This speech is of a kind that occurs regularly in Shaw's plays. A protagonist who embodies a vital life force helps another character whose views are conventional and sterile to grow up, to attain a clearer vision. This process of education constitutes the inner action—the real spine of the plays. The actor's task is strongly to play the intention of affecting another character; such speeches must not become only statements of theme unrelated to the action.

man's wife. *(Releasing her)* Do you understand that?

JUDITH: Yes: you mean that you do not love me.

RICHARD *(revolted—with fierce contempt)*: Is that all it means to you?

JUDITH: What more—what worse—can it mean to me? *(She throws herself on her knees)*. I pray to you—

RICHARD: Hush! The sergeant is coming for me.

JUDITH *(clinging to him)*: Only one thing more—I entreat, I implore you. Let me be present in the court. I have seen Major Swindon: he said I should be allowed if you asked it. You will ask it. It is my last request: I shall never ask you anything again. *(She clasps his knee)*. I beg and pray it of you.

RICHARD: If I do, will you be silent?

JUDITH: Yes.

RICHARD: You will keep faith?

JUDITH: I will keep—*(She breaks down, sobbing)*.

This is a climactic moment in the plot, bringing the characters into sharp conflict and revealing a major theme. Take care to understand the full significance of these lines.

Judith's throwing herself on the floor and clasping Richard around the knees are manifestations of melodrama, the form Shaw chose for the "outer action." The task of the actors is to realize both the inner and outer action at the same time.

The Wild Duck

HENRIK IBSEN

Exploratory Analysis of a Scene from Act III: 2 men

Background *The Wild Duck* (1884), written when Ibsen was in full control of his powers, is frequently cited as his finest work. As the last of his social problem plays, it combines realistic setting and psychologically motivated characters with poetic symbolism. The principal character is Hjalmar Ekdal, a poor photographer, living happily with his wife Gina and their daughter Hedvig. He allows them to do most of the work while he deludes himself that he is going to invent some wonderful mechanism. Gregers Werle, the idealistic son of a wealthy manufacturer, returns to town after a long absence, rejects his father for his compromises with truth (one of which resulted in the imprisonment of Hjalmar's father), and seeks in Hjalmar a man capable of living an ideal life free of all deceit and compromise. Despite objections from Dr. Relling, who knows that Hjalmar's "life illusions" are essential to his existence, Gregers decides that Hjalmar can face the truth. He tells him that Hedvig is probably the daughter of old Werle, for whom Gina was working at the time of her marriage, and that his happy home is supported by old Werle's contributions. Far from becoming stronger, Hjalmar is completely shattered. He rejects his wife and daughter, and Hedvig in an effort to prove her love shoots herself.

The title names the play's underlying symbol.

162

In the attic in a forest of old Christmas trees, Hedvig and Hjalmar's father keep, along with other fowls, a wild duck that has been wounded by a hunter. Although it is not the great forest in which old Ekdal as an army officer once shot bears, nor one of the exotic places Hedvig reads about, the attic provides the setting for many happy excursions into a world of dreams. Hjalmar enjoys it, too.

Who   HJALMAR EKDAL is a rather ordinary man. It is important that we see in him qualities that exist in most of us. He has failed to realize the promise he exhibited in his school days, and now he has reconciled himself to that failure by maintaining the fantasy that he is going to do something great. Those that love him—and he is not unlovable —never challenge him because they accept the fact that he cannot meet the challenge. He is essentially selfish in that he thinks always of his own well-being and is unconcerned about the demands he makes on others. His concern for himself is reflected in his happy, healthy, well-fed appearance. He is well-intentioned in that he does not want to do harm to anyone, but he has no strong convictions either moral or intellectual (Hedvig observes that he is "not much for reading"). He would not be likely to give up comfort for the sake of principle. He is an egotist, given to self-dramatization and constantly sees himself as the self-sacrificing son, husband, and father. The incongruity between his image of himself and the reality is often comic.

GREGERS WERLE is a direct contrast to Hjalmar. He is so uncompromising an idealist he believes that truth must be served at all costs, and that no man can realize himself unless he resolutely banishes all untruths and half-truths from his life. In this play Ibsen stacks the cards against such fanaticism, making clear that idealists who try to shape the lives of others do great damage. Gregers, indeed, mutilates the life of everyone he influences. Dr. Relling expresses Ibsen's meaning when he says: "Rob the average man of his life lie and you rob him of his happiness at the same stroke." Gregers, uncompromising to the last, answers: "If you are right and I am wrong, then life is not worth living."

The play implies that Greger's attitudes are derived from his mother, a sickly unhappy woman, who demanded from old Werle a strict observance of her code of morals. Although Gregers turns out to be a dangerous meddler, we must not suspect from the beginning that he is so. His intentions are sincere (he remembers the unhappiness old Werle caused his mother), and his initial arguments for truth are convincing. It is interesting to note that in other plays Ibsen defended the opposite side of the coin.

Character Relationships   Gregers and Hjalmar went to school together. At that time, before old Ekdal's imprisonment, their fathers were business partners. Popular and excelling in many activities, especially the reciting of dramatic verse, Hjalmar was a hero to the shy and introspective Gregers. Long separated because of Ekdal's reversal of fortune, Gregers wants Hjalmar again to embody his ideals. For Gregers is a hero-worshipper. He does not strive to realize his ideals within himself, but by urging them upon others. That Gregers fails to see clearly is evident in his mistaking Hjalmar for a superior being living a life of illusions (Gregers would say a life of lies) only because he has not had the opportunity to know the truth. Hjalmar finds

Gregers' renewal of their friendship flattering, especially since he thought Gregers had renounced him because of his father's disgrace. In the scene for exploration Hjalmar is still secure and happy with his illusions; he does not comprehend Gregers' intimating that there may be something wrong with his life.

When and Where   As written, the play takes place in a Norwegian city in the 1880s. Except for a few minor details, however, it is not restricted to a particular place or period. Of a recent English revival in modern dress the *London Times* reported: "Of all Ibsen's plays it is most likely to disturb the moral and intellectual complacency of a modern audience." And the *London Observer* stated: "Dr. Relling diagnosing 'rectitudinal fever' is a national necessity in any country." The play does not demand a recreation of the manners of the period in which it was written.

The setting is the photographic studio that serves also as a living room. It is on the top floor with a large studio window and double door at the back leading to the attic. It is comfortably and cheerfully furnished.

The Actors' Work   Analyze the scene for intentions, obstacles, beats, relationships, physical and verbal actions, subtext, sensory tasks. Make a ground plan that will enable you to carry out the physical actions effectively. Write the results of your analysis in your script to provide you with a score in playing the role.

You will note that after Hjalmar's first speech the text contains no stage directions; the characters' intentions are realized through verbal rather than physical actions. Yet physical activity is necessary to create character, to emphasize verbal actions, to maintain audience attention and, perhaps most important, to relax the actors. Use your imaginations to invent physical actions that will accomplish these objectives. Commenting upon a fine portrayal of Hjalmar, British critic Kenneth Tynan wrote that the actor used "every prop the stage affords" to help him accomplish his purpose.

The Wild Duck[1]

HENRIK IBSEN

GREGERS *and* HJALMAR *are in the studio waiting for luncheon guests to arrive.* GREGERS *is looking into the attic.*

HJALMAR *(in a low voice)*: I think you'd better not stand there looking in at father; he doesn't like it. (GREGERS *moves away from the attic door.*) Besides, I may as well shut up before the others come. *(Claps his hands to drive the fowls back.)* Shh-shh, in with you! *(Draws up the curtain and pulls the doors together.)* All the contrivances are my own invention. It's really quite amusing to make things of this sort and to put to rights when they get out of order. And it's absolutely necessary, too; for Gina objects to having rabbits and chickens in the studio.

GREGERS: To be sure; and I suppose the studio is your wife's department?

HJALMAR: As a rule, I leave the everyday details of business to her; for then I can give my mind to more important things.

GREGERS: What things may they be, Hjalmar?

HJALMAR: I wonder you have not asked that question sooner. But perhaps you haven't heard of the invention?

GREGERS: The invention? No.

HJALMAR: Really? Haven't you? Oh, no, out there in the woods—

GREGERS: So you have invented something, have you?

Hjalmar has rigged up a curtain that pulls up from the floor to keep the fowls in the attic when the door is open.

Gina: *pronounce it Cheena.*

Hjalmar: *pronounce it Yalmar.*

For several years Gregers has been managing his father's business in the northern part of the country.

The Wild Duck is reprinted by permission of Charles Scribner's Sons from *The Collected Works of Henrik Ibsen,* Volume VIII, translated by William Archer. Copyright 1907 Charles Scribner's Sons. Original publishers of this play are William Heinemann Ltd., London.

[1]Based on a nineteenth-century translation, this material has been edited and arranged for scene study.

HJALMAR: It is not quite completed yet; but I am working at it. You can easily imagine that when I took up photography, it wasn't with the idea of making ordinary pictures.

GREGERS: No; your wife was saying the same thing just now.

HJALMAR: I swore that if I devoted myself to this trade, I would raise it to the level of art and science. And to that end I set out to make this great invention.

GREGERS: And what is the nature of the invention? What purpose does it serve?

HJALMAR: Now, Gregers, you mustn't ask for details yet. It takes time, you see. And you must not think that my motive is vanity. It is not for my own sake that I am working. Oh, no; it is my life's mission that is in my mind night and day.

GREGERS: What is your life's mission?

HJALMAR: Do you forget the old man with the silver hair?

GREGERS: Your poor father? Well, but what can you do for him?

HJALMAR: I can revive his self-respect by restoring the name of Ekdal to honor and dignity.

GREGERS: Then that is your life's mission?

HJALMAR: Yes. I will rescue the shipwrecked man. For shipwrecked he was, by the very first blast of the storm. Even while those terrible investigations were going on, he was no longer himself. That pistol there—the one we use to shoot rabbits with—has played its part in the tragedy of the house of Ekdal.

GREGERS: The pistol? Indeed?

HJALMAR: When the sentence of imprisonment was pronounced—he had the pistol in his hand—

GREGERS: Had he—?

HJALMAR: Yes; but he dared not use it. His courage failed him. So broken, so demoralized was he even then! Oh, can you understand it? He, a soldier; he, who had shot nine bears, and who was descended from two lieutenant-colonels—one after the other, of course. Can you understand it, Gregers?

Hjalmar's father had been convicted of illegally cutting government timber for use in the factory he and Gregers' father controlled. Having served his term in prison, he now lives with Hjalmar and Gina.

GREGERS: Yes, I understand it well enough.

HJALMAR: I cannot. And once more the pistol played a part in the history of our house. When he had put on the prison clothes and was under lock and key—oh, that was a terrible time for me, I can tell you. I kept the blinds drawn down over both my windows. When I peeped out, I saw the sun shining as if nothing had happened. I could not understand it. I saw people going along the street, laughing and talking. I could not understand it. It seemed to me that the whole of existence should be at a standstill—as if under an eclipse.

GREGERS: I felt that, too, when my mother died.

From his imagination Gregers needs to invent specific details of his relationship to his mother and the circumstances of her death.

HJALMAR: It was in such an hour that Hjalmar Ekdal pointed the pistol at his own breast.

GREGERS: You, too, thought of—?

HJALMAR: Yes.

GREGERS: But you did not fire?

HJALMAR: No. At the decisive moment I won the victory over myself. I decided to live. But I can assure you it takes some courage to choose life under circumstances like those.

GREGERS: Well, that depends on how you look at it.

HJALMAR: Yes, indeed, it takes courage. But I am glad I was firm: for now I shall soon perfect my invention; and Dr. Relling thinks, as I do, that father may be allowed to wear his uniform again. I will demand that as my sole reward.

Dr. Relling, a good friend, lives in the same building as Hjalmar. When he was convicted, old Ekdal was stripped of his commission and deprived of the right to wear his uniform.

GREGERS: So that is what he meant about his uniform—?

HJALMAR: Yes, that is what he most yearns for. You can't think how my heart bleeds for him. Every time we celebrate any little anniversary—our wedding-day, or whatever it may be—in comes the old man in the lieutenant's uniform of happier days. But if he only hears a knock at the door—for he daren't show himself to strangers, you know—he hurries back to his room again as fast as his old legs can carry him. Oh, it's heart-breaking for a son to see such things!

GREGERS: How long do you think it will take you to finish your invention?

HJALMAR: Come now, you mustn't expect me to have a time schedule. An invention is not a thing completely under one's own control. It depends largely on inspiration—on intuition—and it is impossible to predict when the inspiration may come.

GREGERS: But it's progressing?

HJALMAR: Yes, certainly, it is progressing. I turn it over in my mind every day; I am full of it. Every afternoon, when I have had my dinner, I shut myself up in the sitting-room, where I can ponder undisturbed. But I can't be goaded to it; that will do no good. Relling says so, too.

Gina, a realist who can maintain herself without either illusions or "ideals," says that Hjalmar takes a nap every day after dinner. Although Dr. Relling knows that the invention will never materialize, he encourages Hjalmar's fantasy because he knows that such an illusion is necessary to his self-respect.

GREGERS: And you don't think that all that business in the attic distracts you too much?

HJALMAR: No, no, no; quite the contrary. You mustn't say that. I cannot be always absorbed in the same exhausting train of thought. I must have something else to fill up the time of waiting. The inspiration, you see—when it comes, it comes, and there's an end to it.

GREGERS: Hjalmar, I think you have something of the wild duck in you.

HJALMAR: Something of the wild duck? How do you mean?

GREGERS: You have dived down and entangled yourself in the sea weed.

HJALMAR: Are you referring to the nearly fatal shot that has broken father's wing—and mine, too?

GREGERS: Not exactly that. I don't say that your wing has been broken; but you are in a poisonous marsh, Hjalmar; an insidious disease has infected you, and you have sunk down to die in the dark.

HJALMAR: I? To die in the dark? Look, here, Gregers, you mustn't say such things.

GREGERS: Don't be afraid; I shall help you up again. I, too, have a mission in life now; I found it yesterday.

It was yesterday that Gregers rejected his father when he discovered that Werle, although as guilty as Ekdal, had escaped trial and conviction; and that he had arranged Hjalmar's marriage to cover up his adulterous relation with Gina.

HJALMAR: That's all very well; but you will please leave me out of it. I can assure you that—apart from my easily explainable melancholy—I am as contented as anyone could hope to be.

GREGERS: Your contentment is an effect of the poison.

HJALMAR: No, Gregers, don't go on about disease and poison; I am not used to that sort of talk. In my house nobody ever speaks to me about unpleasant things.

GREGERS: That I can easily believe.

HJALMAR: It's not good for me, you see. And there are no marsh poisons here. The poor photographer's home is humble—and my circumstances are lowly. But I am an inventor, and I am the head of a family. That raises me above my mean surroundings.—Ah, here comes lunch!

Hedda Gabler

HENRIK IBSEN

Exploratory Analysis of a Scene from Act I: 2 women

Background   Because he was the first world dramatist completely to master the form of the social problem play, Henrik Ibsen is generally considered to be the "father of modern drama." *Hedda Gabler* (written in 1890) is accepted by many critics as his best work. In this play, as in earlier pieces, he is a searching social satirist, but he emphasizes more than previously the element of individual psychology. This emphasis is probably the reason that *Hedda Gabler* is the most frequently performed of Ibsen's plays and that leading actresses have welcomed the challenge of the leading role for almost a hundred years.

Hedda is the aristocratic daughter of an army general. She finds her marriage to George Tesman, a university professor, unbearable—not principally because he is an unstimulating companion, but because she is incapable of giving herself freely in any relationship. It was this trait that caused her, before her marriage, to dismiss a brilliant young suitor named Eilert Lövborg, thus furthering his propensity for drink and reckless living. Learning that Thea Elvsted, an old schoolmate, now in love with Lövborg, has restored some order to his dissolute life and helped him to write a successful book, Hedda exercises her destructive powers upon the pair, returning Lövborg to drunkenness and burning the only manuscript of his new work written with Thea's help and encouragement. Hedda's efforts lead to Lövborg's, and ultimately to her own, suicide.

The scene for exploration occurs early in Act I. Thea, searching for Lövborg and fearing that celebrating the success of his book may cause him to return to his former dissipation, has called upon the Tesmans to ask for help. She knows nothing of Hedda's earlier relationship with Lövborg; she comes because he and Tesman were colleagues.

Who   Eva LeGallienne, one of the modern actresses who has met the challenge of playing Hedda, writes that she "is a fascinating, tragic, hateful woman; a woman of the world—well-bred, of subtle intellect, cultivated, exquisite; but this calm, polished, cold (Ibsen called her 'ice-cold') exterior hides a demon—and it is vitally important to the performance of the play that the demon *be* hidden. There have been some actresses—some very great ones—who have played Hedda as an exotic *femme fatale;* but this is to make nonsense of the play. Ibsen has taken the trouble—which he does not always do—of describing Hedda quite specifically. He says: 'She is a woman of twenty-nine. Her face and figure show breeding and distinction. Her complexion is pale and opaque. Her eyes are steel-gray and express a cold, unruffled repose. Her hair is an agreeable medium-brown, but not especially abundant.'

"Perhaps Grant Allen went a little too far when he declared Hedda was 'nothing more or less than the girl we take down to dinner in London nineteen times out of twenty,' but the point is that she must not be in any way spectacular.

"Ibsen's description provides a very definite clue to his intention. Unless Hedda is able to convince people, to charm them, to inspire confidence in them—before proceeding to destroy them—there is no play. And is it conceivable that a good solid bourgeois professor like George Tesman—blissfully under the thumb of his two beloved aunts—would ever have become involved to the point of marriage with a neurotic scheming monster? It is precisely in the very gradual revelation of Hedda's true nature that the excitement of the play lies. . . .

"In different circumstances, surrounded by beauty and wealth, the center of a circle of brilliant, stimulating people, Hedda might have been quite a different person. It is her own spiritual poverty, her malign egoism, that generates the boredom which causes her to destroy herself and others. She is a creature without aim or purpose in life—a parasite on Society; and all her potential virtues have become warped and atrophied."

Hedda's breeding has given her tastes that she cannot afford and a desire for power over the lives of others that she cannot gratify. It has taught her to shrink from everything that is dull and ugly, but it has not provided her with the means to create the life of beauty she desires. It might seem that with the freedom women have achieved in the 1970s Hedda's problem would have become obsolete. There remains, however, a kind of timelessness about the play. Careers or remarriages do not fill the vacuum of spiritual poverty. Today the story of the play would be different, but the problem remains the same.

THEA is two years younger than Hedda. She is described by Ibsen as "a woman of fragile figure, with pretty soft features. Her large blue eyes have a frightened inquiring look. Her hair is strikingly fair, rich and naturally curly. She wears a dark visiting dress, tasteful but not in the latest fashion."

Thea is drawn as a contrast to Hedda in almost every particular, a contrast Ibsen establishes at the outset with his description of their hair. Thea's luxuriant blond hair is a symbol of her womanliness, her vitality, her humanity. Hedda's thinning brown hair—perfectly groomed, of course—is a symbol of her sterility and inner poverty. Without having Hedda's upbringing or her subtle intellect, Thea has a warmth and a willingness to sacrifice herself for others that, although she does not seek it, gives her the power that Hedda yearns for but does not possess. Thea also, in contrast to Hedda, has the courage of her convictions. She is, ironically, a more liberated woman than Hedda, willing to ignore conventional morality to be with Lövborg.

Character Relationships   The relationship between Hedda and Thea is based upon a compelling dramatic irony that means there is a striking discrepancy between what the characters expect and plan and what happens. Although the impact is not fully revealed until the end of the play, it must be anticipated in earlier scenes. Hedda, General Gabler's daughter, who had so many admirers and who used to turn all heads as she galloped about town on her own riding horse in her specially tailored riding clothes! Little Thea Rysing, whose hair had always irritated Hedda, but whom no one noticed especially; an old flame, in fact, of Tesman's! Thea has always been timid and ill-at-ease with Hedda. Hedda has always been scornful of Thea and treated her with an air of superiority. Yet, true to their characters, Thea will subject herself to Hedda's disdain to find Lövborg; Hedda will woo Thea to accomplish her purpose.

When and Where   The play was written in 1890, and while it can and has been done in contemporary dress, the superficial aspects of the behavior of the characters are of the nineteenth century. This period dictates a manner of dress, speech, and posture less casual than we are likely to find today. The place is the drawing room of a house in the fashionable section of Oslo (then called Christiania), the capital city of Norway. Ibsen describes the room as "spacious, handsome, and tasteful," giving many details about the furniture and accessories. For the present purpose it is necessary to discover only what furniture and properties are needed in this scene, and what arrangement of them will facilitate performing the physical actions.

The Actors' Work   Analyze the scene for intentions, obstacles, beats, physical and verbal actions, relationships, subtext, sensory tasks. After making the analysis, formulate a ground plan. Write the results in your script to provide you with a score for playing your role.

Hedda Gabler[1]

HENRIK IBSEN

(HEDDA *stands holding a large bouquet of flowers. A maid opens the door for* MRS. ELVSTED *and exits.*)

HEDDA (*receives her graciously*):   How do you do, my dear Mrs. Elvsted? It's delightful to see you again.

MRS. ELVSTED (*nervously, trying to maintain her self-control*):   Yes, it's a very long time since we met.

HEDDA: Thank you for sending such lovely flowers.

Earlier in the play Hedda has complained of so many flowers in the room and has asked for fresh air. Here she conceals her distaste.

MRS. ELVSTED: Oh, not at all . . . I would have come straight here yesterday afternoon, but I heard that you were away.

HEDDA: Have you just come to town?

MRS. ELVSTED: I arrived yesterday, about noon. Oh, I was quite in despair when I heard you were not at home.

HEDDA: In despair? I hope you are not in any trouble?

MRS. ELVSTED: Yes, I am. And I don't know another living person I can turn to.

[1]Based on the standard Archer translation, this material has been edited and arranged for scene study.

HEDDA *(laying the bouquet on the table):* Come . . . let's sit here on the sofa . . .

Hedda's prevailing upon Thea to sit down, here and again later in the scene, is important in establishing situation and relationship. How this is accomplished will reveal an important decision in regard to the interpretation of Hedda's character.

MRS. ELVSTED: Oh, I'm too nervous to sit down.

HEDDA: Oh no, you're not. Come here . *(She draws* MRS. ELVSTED *onto the sofa and sits beside her.)* Has anything happened to you at home?

MRS. ELVSTED: Yes . . . and no. Oh . . . I don't want you to misunderstand me . . .

HEDDA: Then you'd best tell me the whole story, Mrs. Elvsted.

MRS. ELVSTED: Yes, yes . . . of course. Well then, I must tell you . . . if you don't already know . . . that Eilert Lövborg is in town too.

HEDDA: Lövborg . . . !

MRS. ELVSTED: He's been here a week . . . a whole week. I'm so frightened that he'll get into some kind of trouble.

Thea must create her anxiety, and then make every effort to conceal it.

HEDDA: But my dear Mrs. Elvsted . . . how does he concern you so much?

MRS. ELVSTED *(looks at her with a startled air and speaks hurriedly):* He is the children's tutor.

HEDDA: Your children's?

MRS. ELVSTED: My husband's. I have none.

HEDDA: Have you seen Lövborg here in town?

Be sure to understand clearly Hedda's intention in asking these questions.

MRS. ELVSTED: No, not yet. I've had great difficulty finding out his address. But this morning I got it at last.

HEDDA *(looks searchingly at her):* It seems to me a little odd of your husband to . . .

MRS. ELVSTED *(nervously):* Of my husband! To what?

HEDDA: To send you on such an errand. Why didn't he come himself to look after his friend?

MRS. ELVSTED: Oh no, no . . . my husband has no time. And besides I had some shopping to do.

HEDDA *(with a slight smile):* Yes, that is a different matter.

The direction with a slight smile *indicates this line has an important subtext.*

MRS. ELVSTED *(rising quickly and uneasily):* And now I implore you to receive Eilert Lövborg kindly if he comes here. And that he is sure to do. Your husband and he used to be such great friends. And they are interested in the same studies . . . the same branch of science as far as I can understand.

HEDDA: They used to be at any rate.

MRS. ELVSTED: That is why I beg so earnestly that you . . . keep a sharp eye on him. But please, please don't say a word to him that I suggested it.

HEDDA: How could you think I would? And now sit down again and we'll have a cozy confidential talk. There is a great deal more to tell, I can see that. *(She forces* MRS. ELVSTED *to sit in the armchair by the stove and seats herself on one of the footstools.)*

MRS. ELVSTED *(anxiously looking at her watch)*:   But, really, Mrs. Tesman, I must be going.

HEDDA: Oh, you can't be in such a hurry. Now . . . you must tell me everything about your life at home.

MRS. ELVSTED: But . . . that is just what I don't want to talk about.

HEDDA: But to me, dear! Remember we were schoolmates.

MRS. ELVSTED: But you were in the class above me, and I was dreadfully afraid of you then.

HEDDA: Afraid of me?

MRS. ELVSTED: Yes, dreadfully. When we met on the stairs you always used to pull my hair.

HEDDA: Did I really?

MRS. ELVSTED: And once you said you were going to burn it off.

HEDDA: Oh, that was all nonsense, of course.

MRS. ELVSTED: But I was so silly in those days. And since then we've drifted so far apart. Our lives have been so entirely different.

HEDDA: Then we must drift together again. Why, at school we always called each other by our first names.

MRS. ELVSTED: No, I'm sure you must be mistaken.

HEDDA: No, not at all. I remember quite distinctly. So . . . now we are going to renew our old friendship. (Draws the footstool closer to MRS. ELVSTED.) There! (Kisses her cheek.) You must call me Hedda.

MRS. ELVSTED: I am not used to such kindness. (Presses and pats HEDDA's hand)

HEDDA: There, there! And I shall call you my dear Thora.

Pronounced Tora.
Pronounced Taya.

MRS. ELVSTED: My name is Thea.

HEDDA: Why, of course. I meant Thea. (Looks at her compassionately.) So you are not accustomed to kindness, Thea. Not even in your own home.

MRS. ELVSTED: No . . . no!

HEDDA: I don't quite remember . . . wasn't it as housekeeper that you first went to Mr. Elvsted's?

MRS. ELVSTED: I really went as governess. But his wife . . . his first wife . . . was an invalid, and rarely left her room. So I had to look after the housekeeping as well.

Thea needs to use her imagination to create specific details of her relationship to her husband and of her life at home. She needs to recall these details at each rehearsal.

HEDDA: And then . . . at last . . . you became mistress of the house.

MRS. ELVSTED (sadly):   Yes, I did.

HEDDA: Let's see . . . about how long ago was that?

MRS. ELVSTED: Five years ago.

HEDDA: To be sure. It must be.

MRS. ELVSTED: Oh, those five years . . . Or at least the last two or three of them! If you could only imagine, Mrs. Tesman.

HEDDA: Shame, Thea! (Gives her a little slap on the hand.) Mrs. Tesman!

MRS. ELVSTED: I will try . . . Well, if . . . you could only understand . . . Hedda.

HEDDA (lightly): Eilert Lövborg has been up there about three years, hasn't he?

MRS. ELVSTED (looks at her doubtfully):   Eilert Lövborg? Yes, he has.

HEDDA: Had you known him before, in town here?

MRS. ELVSTED: Scarcely at all. I mean . . . I knew him by name, of course.

HEDDA: But you saw a great deal of him in the country?

MRS. ELVSTED: Yes, he came every day. You see, he gave the children lessons. I had so much to do I couldn't manage it all myself.

HEDDA: No, that's clear. And your husband . . . I suppose he is often away from home?

MRS. ELVSTED: Yes, being sheriff, he has to travel a good deal in his district.

HEDDA *(leans against the arm of* THEA's *chair)*:   Thea, my poor Thea. Now you must tell me everything . . . exactly as it is.

MRS. ELVSTED: Well, then, you must question me.

HEDDA: What sort of man is your husband, Thea? I mean . . . you know . . . in everyday life. Is he kind to you?

MRS. ELVSTED: I am sure he means to be.

HEDDA: He must be too old for you. There is at least twenty years difference, isn't there?

MRS. ELVSTED: Yes, that's true. We haven't a thought in common . . . he and I.

HEDDA: But is he fond of you? In his own way?

MRS. ELVSTED *(evasively)*:   I really don't know. I am useful to him. And it doesn't cost much to keep me. I am not expensive.

HEDDA: That is stupid of you.

MRS. ELVSTED *(shakes her head)*:   It couldn't be otherwise . . . with him. I don't think he really cares for anyone but himself . . . and perhaps a little for the children.

HEDDA: And for Eilert Lövborg, Thea.

MRS. ELVSTED *(looking at her)*:   Why do you say that?

HEDDA: Well my dear, when he sends you after him all the way to town . . . *(Smiles almost imperceptibly.)*

MRS. ELVSTED *(with a little nervous twitch)*:   I suppose it must all come out.

HEDDA: What must all come out, Thea . . . ?

MRS. ELVSTED: My husband didn't know that I was coming.

HEDDA: What! Your husband didn't know it!

Tesman and his aunts have gone into debt to satisfy Hedda's extravagances.

At what point does Hedda know why Thea has come to town? At what point does she suspect the reason?

MRS. ELVSTED: No, of course not. He was away himself . . . he was traveling. I couldn't bear it, Hedda. I would have been so alone. So I put together some things . . . what I needed most . . . and then I left.

HEDDA: Without a word?

MRS. ELVSTED (rises and moves about the room):   Yes, and took the train straight to town.

HEDDA: Why, Thea . . . to think of your daring to do it. What will your husband say when you go home again?

These lines reveal a major contrast in their characters. Hedda is afraid to risk public disapproval and loss of security.

MRS. ELVSTED: Back to him?

HEDDA: Of course.

MRS. ELVSTED: I shall never go back to him.

HEDDA (rising and going to her):   Then you have left your home . . . for good?

MRS. ELVSTED: There was nothing else to do.

HEDDA: What will people say about you, Thea?

MRS. ELVSTED: They may say what they like. I've done what I had to do. (Seats herself wearily and sadly on the sofa.)

HEDDA (after a silence):   And what are your plans now?

MRS. ELVSTED: I don't know yet. I only know that I must live here where Eilert Lövborg is . . . if I am to live at all.

HEDDA (takes a chair from the table, sits beside MRS. ELVSTED and strokes her hand):   My dear Thea, how did this . . . friendship . . . between you and Eilert Lövborg come about?

MRS. ELVSTED: Oh, it grew gradually. I came to have a sort of influence over him.

Influence over others is exactly what Hedda wants for herself. How does Thea's line affect their relationship?

HEDDA: Did you?

MRS. ELVSTED: He gave up his drinking. Not because I asked him to. I never dared do that. But when he saw how unhappy it made me . . .

HEDDA (concealing a scornful smile):   Then you have reformed him . . . as the saying goes.

MRS. ELVSTED: So he says, at any rate. And he has made a human being of me . . . taught me to think and understand so many things.

HEDDA: Did he give you lessons too, then?

MRS. ELVSTED: Not exactly lessons. But he

talked to me about many things. And then I began to share in his work. He allowed me to help him.

HEDDA: Oh, did he?

MRS. ELVSTED: Yes, he never wrote anything without my help.

HEDDA: You were comrades, in fact!

MRS. ELVSTED: Comrades, Hedda, is the very word he used. I ought to feel perfectly happy, but I'm so afraid it won't last.

HEDDA: You're no surer of him than that?

MRS. ELVSTED (gloomily):   Another woman's shadow stands between Eilert Lövborg and me.

HEDDA (looking directly at her):   Who can that be?

MRS. ELVSTED: I don't know. Someone he knew. Someone he's never forgotten.

HEDDA: What has he told you about her?

MRS. ELVSTED: Nothing really.

HEDDA: Come now. What did he say?

MRS. ELVSTED: He said when they parted, she threatened to shoot him with a pistol.

HEDDA (with cold composure):   Nonsense! No one does that sort of thing here.

MRS. ELVSTED: No. That's why I think it must be that red-haired singer he once . . .

HEDDA: Very likely.

MRS. ELVSTED: I remember they used to say she carried a loaded pistol.

HEDDA: Then, of course, it must be she.

MRS. ELVSTED: And now, she is in town again, too. Hedda, I don't know what to do . . .

HEDDA (glancing toward the inner room): Hush! Here comes Tesman. (Rises and whispers.) Thea, all this must be between you and me.

MRS. ELVSTED (rising quickly):   Yes, for heaven's sake . . .

Hedda hopes *she is the woman.*

Hedda knows *she is the woman. Her pistols are important later in the play.*

A Note on Playing *Hedda Gabler*

It may be said that, almost without exception, the greater the character in dramatic literature, the wider range of choice he provides the actor in regard to interpretation. As stated earlier, some actresses have chosen to play Hedda as an exotic *femme fatale,* while others have chosen to play her as "the girl next door." Still others have seen her somewhere between these two extremes. It is important to recognize that actors must make conscious choices about the interpretation of their characters. The choices are based, not just on intuition, but upon a careful study of the play and due consideration of existing critical commentary. It would be rather interesting and valuable to play this scene in different ways, finding out how different interpretations affect the scene as a whole and the relationship between the characters. It would be a challenge for Thea to adapt to Hedda's different approaches.

A Month in the Country

IVAN TURGENEV
Adapted by Emlyn Williams

Exploratory Analysis of a Scene from Act I, Scene 3: 2 women

Background In 1850 Ivan Turgenev wrote a dramatic masterpiece, a play that departed from accepted patterns by shifting the dramatic action from external to internal conflict. *A Month in the Country* is the forerunner of the plays of Chekhov and embodies qualities now considered to be the essence of modern drama. Keenly observed psychological truth underlies the delicate surface that deals with a tangle of amorous complications.

The major complication concerns Natalia Petrovna, wife of a healthy landowner; her adopted daughter Vera; and her son's tutor, Beliaev. Not truly in love with her husband and bored with the loyal devotion of an old family friend, she develops a passion for the young teacher. Rightly suspecting that Vera may love him too, she attempts to arrange a marriage between her daughter and a middle-aged neighbor. At first Vera is uncomprehending. When she comes to realize the situation, she tells the innocent Beliaev of his predicament. Attracted to both mother and daughter in different ways, but not in love with either, the tutor departs leaving Natalia with her unromantic husband and Vera with her neighborly suitor.

The scene for exploration is an early encounter between Vera and Natalia.

Who NATALIA PETROVNA is described as a "beautiful, exquisite creature of twenty-nine." She is cultured, well-bred, accustomed to the best of everything. She is in no sense a *femme fatale*. Her behavior is not coldly calculated although it is capricious and unpredictable. It troubles and puzzles her that her feelings have got out of control. After the encounter with Vera she says to herself: ". . . I don't know myself any more—what am I doing? Shall I tell you, Natalia Petrovna? You're trying to marry a poor orphan girl to a foolish fond old man . . . What is happening? *(After a pause, slowly.)* Unhappy woman, for the first time in your life—you are in love."

VERA is a "beautiful immature girl of seventeen, timid and highly strung." Her first responses to Beliaev are similar to those of ten-year old Kolia's. She enters into their sports and games, and she is captivated by the new tutor's ability to climb trees, jump ditches, and fly a kite. During the play as she recognizes the true nature of her feelings, she grows from childhood to womanhood.

Character Relationships Natalia has always been kind and generous to Vera—a fact that Vera recognizes and appreciates, but there has been no real affection or understanding between them. Natalia enjoys playing the role of a "lady bountiful," taking satisfaction in supervising Vera's education and caring for her in a rather extravagant manner. Vera has been treated like a child—sometimes indulged, sometimes scolded; and having been treated like a child, she has behaved like one. Before Beliaev's arrival, she had never dreamed she could play a role in Natalia's life other than that of the adopted orphan; and it had never occurred to Natalia that the orphan child could become her rival in a love triangle. In a climactic scene, however, Vera says: "Don't you think it's time we dropped all this . . . this talking to me as if I were still a child? From today on, I'm a woman—a woman like yourself . . . And will you please not throw any more dust in my eyes because it just won't be any good—for the simple reason that I'm no longer your ward, watched over by a tolerant and elder sister—I'm your rival."

And Natalia pleads for Vera's friendship: ". . . believe me I am just as unfortunate as you . . . It's time we came back to reality . . . instead of mortifying each other, shouldn't we be trying to rescue ourselves from an impossible situation?"

Where and When A large country estate near Moscow in the 1840s. The *where* and *when* affect the behavior of the characters both physically and psychologically. They are a wealthy, leisured class who fill their time with cultural pursuits (as long as they are not too serious), games and sports (as long as they are not too strenuous), and amorous adventures. They are beautifully mannered and handsomely dressed. It is the period of the hoopskirt with its corseted waist, a garment that was not designed for practical work. Since it is summer, there is the frequent raising of parasols and the flutter of fans. It was a time in Russia when French influence was everywhere apparent among the upper classes. Several times in the play a Chopin mazurka is heard from off stage. Listening to the music of Chopin should be helpful in an effort to realize the quality of *A Month in the Country*.

The Actors' Work Analyze the scene for intentions, obstacles, beats, physical and verbal actions, relationships, subtext, sensory tasks. Write the results of your analysis in your script to provide you with a score in rehearsing the role.

The Ground Plan The play is divided into several scenes which take place in various locations inside the house and in the garden. For this scene choose the particular location that seems best and provide the necessary elements for carrying out the physical actions.

A Month in the Country

IVAN TURGENEV
Adapted by Emlyn Williams

(NATALIA PETROVNA *is comfortably seated.* VERA *enters carrying a piece of music.*)

VERA *(timidly)*:   Did you want me, Natalia Petrovna?

NATALIA *(starting)*:   Ah, Vérochka!

Pronounce: nä täl'ya   pĕ trōv'na

Vérochka is a diminutive form of Vera, a familiar or "pet" name. Earlier Vera asked Beliaev to call her Vérochka. (ver' utch ka)
Natalia's appearance or behavior must motivate Vera's line.

VERA: Do you feel quite well?

NATALIA: Perfectly, it's a little close, that's all. Vera, I want to have a little talk with you.

VERA *(anxiously, putting down her music)*: Oh?—

What is Vera's thinking when she says "Oh?" As yet she has no notion why Natalia has sent for her.

NATALIA: A serious talk. Sit down, my dear, will you? *(As* VERA *obeys.)* Now—Vera, one thinks of you as still a child; but it's high time to give a thought to your future. You're an orphan, and not a rich one at that: sooner or later you are bound to tire of living on somebody else's property. Now how would you like suddenly to have control of your very own house?

VERA: I'm afraid I—I don't follow you, Natalia Petrovna—

NATALIA: You are being sought in marriage. *(VERA stares at her. A pause.)* You didn't expect this? I must confess I didn't either; you are still so young. I refuse to press you in the slightest—but I thought it my duty to let you know. *(As* VERA *suddenly covers her face with her hands.)* Vera! My dear—What is it? *(Taking her hands.)* But you're shaking like a leaf!

What Vera is thinking is fully as important to the scene as Natalia's lines.

Copyright 1943 by Emlyn Williams. Copyright © 1957, Acting Edition, by Emlyn Williams, revised and rewritten. Reprinted by permission of Samuel French, Inc. Copies of this play, in individual paper-covered acting editions, are available from Samuel French, Inc., 25 W. 45th St., New York, N.Y. 10036, or 7623 Sunset Blvd., Hollywood, Calif., or in Canada, Samuel French (Canada) Ltd., 27 Grenville St., Toronto, Canada.

VERA: Natalia Petrovna, I'm in your power—

NATALIA: In my power? Vera, what do you take me for? *(Cajoling, as* VERA *kisses her hands.)* In my power, indeed—will you please take that back, this minute? I command you! *(As* VERA *smiles through her tears.)* That's better— *(Putting an arm around her, and drawing her nearer.)* Vera, my child, I tell you what—you'll make believe I'm your elder sister—and we'll straighten out these strange things together—what do you say?

VERA: If you would like me to—yes—

NATALIA: Good— Move closer—that's better—First of all—as you're my sister, this is your home; so there's no possible question of anybody pining to be rid of you—now is that understood?

VERA *(whispering):*   Yes—

Why is Vera whispering?

NATALIA: Now one fine day your sister comes to you and says, "What do you think, little one? Somebody is asking for your hand." Well, what would be your first thought? That you're too young?

VERA: Just as you wish—

NATALIA: Now now—does a girl say "just as you wish" to her sister?

VERA *(smiling):*   Well, then, I'd just say, "I'm too young."

NATALIA: Good; your sister would agree, the suitor would be given "no" for an answer, *fini*— But suppose he was a very nice gentleman with means, prepared to bide his time, in the hope that one day—what then?

Natalia frequently uses French words and phrases, but not as an affectation. French was quite commonly spoken by upper class Russians. It is part of an actor's job to learn to pronounce foreign words correctly.

VERA: Who is this suitor?

NATALIA: Ah, you're curious. Can't you guess?

VERA: No.

NATALIA: Bolshintsov.

Pronounce: bàl shĭn'tsawf

VERA: Afanasy Ivanych?

Pronounce: ä fä näs'ee ee vän'ĭtch

NATALIA: Afanasy Ivanych. It's true he's not very young, and not wildly prepossessing—

VERA *(begins to laugh, then stops and looks at* NATALIA*):*   You're joking—

NATALIA *(after a pause, smiling):*   No, but I see the matter is closed. If you had burst into tears when he was mentioned, there might have been some hope for him; but you laughed—*(Rising, smiling wryly)* The matter is closed.

VERA: I'm sorry, but you took me completely by surprise— Do people still get married at his age?

NATALIA: But how old do you take him for? He's on the right side of fifty!

VERA: I suppose he is, but he has *such* a peculiar face—

NATALIA: Bolshintsov—my dear, you are dead and buried, may you rest in peace— It was foolish of me to forget that little girls dream of marrying for love.

VERA: But, Natalia Petrovna—didn't *you* marry for love?

NATALIA *(after a pause)*:   Yes, of course I did— *Eh, bien, fini!* Bolshintsov, you are dismissed—I must confess I never much fancied that puffy old moon-face next to your fresh young cheek. There!— *(Sitting again, next to VERA.)* And you're not frightened of me any more?

VERA: No, not anymore—

NATALIA: Well, then, Vérochka darling, just whisper quietly in my ear—you don't want to marry Bolshintsov because he's too old and far from an Adonis—but is that the only reason?

VERA *(after a pause)*:   Natalia Petrovna, isn't it reason enough?

NATALIA: Undoubtedly, my dear—but you haven't answered my question.

(A pause.)

VERA: There's no other reason.

NATALIA: Oh— *(After a pause.)* Of course, that puts the matter on rather a different footing.

VERA: How do you mean, Natalia Petrovna?

NATALIA: I realize you can never fall in love with Bolshintsov; but he's an excellent man. And if there is nobody else— Isn't there *anybody* you're fond of?

VERA: Well, there's you, and little Kolia—

"The matter is closed." Be sure to understand the subtext and to think it as you are speaking the line. Subtexts are especially important in this scene since much more is implied than is spoken.

"Yes, of course I did—" Natalia wants to conceal her feelings rather than reveal them.

"Oh—" is a terminal point. The pause is a transition. "Of course" is the attack on a new beat.

Pronounce: kōl'ya

NATALIA *(with a hint of impatience):* Vera, you must know what I mean— Out of the young men you've met—have you formed any attachment at all?

VERA: I quite like one or two, but—

NATALIA: For instance, don't I remember at the Krinitsins' your dancing three times with a tall officer—what was his name—

Pronounce: krĭ nŭt′sĭn

VERA: With a long mustache? *(Smiling.)* He giggled all the time.

NATALIA: Oh— *(After a pause.)* What about our philosopher Rakitin?

Work with an image of the tall officer. Compare him with an image of Beliaev.
Rakitin is the "old family friend" whom Natalia trusts and confides in, but to whose love she does not respond. Pronounce: rä kee′tĭn

VERA: Mihail Alexandrovich? I'm very fond of him, of course, who wouldn't be—

Pronounce: mee hä eel′ à lĕcks ản′drō vitch

NATALIA: An elder brother, I see— *(Suddenly.)* And the new tutor?

(A pause.)

Natalia has been carefully leading up to this question.
Pauses must be "filled." What each is thinking is vital to the scene.

VERA: Alexei Nikolaich?

NATALIA: Alexei Nikolaich.

VERA: I like him very much.

Pronounce: à lecks′ee nĭ kō lĭ′ĭtch

(She has blushed; NATALIA *is watching her narrowly.)*

NATALIA: He is nice, isn't he? Such a pity he's so bashful with everybody—

VERA *(innocently):* Oh, he isn't bashful with me!

NATALIA *(after a slight pause):* Isn't he?

VERA: I suppose it's because we're both orphans. I think he must appear shy to you because he's afraid of you. You see, he's had no chance to know you—

NATALIA: Afraid of me? How do you know?

It concerns Natalia that she tends to make people afraid of her. What is it about her that causes this response?

VERA: He told me so.

NATALIA: He told you—

VERA: Don't you like him, Natalia Petrovna?

NATALIA: He seems very kind-hearted.

What is Natalia's subtext?

VERA: Oh, he is! If you only knew— *(Turning to her, enthusiastically.)* The whole of this household loves him—he's so warm, once he's got over his shyness—the other day an old beggar-woman had to be taken to hospital —do you know he carried her the whole way? And one day he picked a flower for me off a cliff—he's as nimble as a reindeer. D'you remember yesterday, when he cleared that tremendous ditch? And he's always so good-tempered and gay—

NATALIA: That doesn't sound a bit like him —when he's with me, he—

VERA: But that's what I mean, Natalia Petrovna, it's because he doesn't know you! I'll tell him how truly kind you are—

NATALIA (rising, ironically):   Thank you, my dear—

VERA: You'll soon see the difference—because he listens to what I say, though I am younger than he is—

NATALIA: I never knew you two were such friends. You must be careful, Vera.

VERA: Careful?

NATALIA: I know he's a very pleasant young man, but at your age, it's not quite— People might think— (As VERA blushes, and looks down.) Don't be impatient, my dear, will you, if I seem to be laying down the law? We older people regard it as our business to plague the young with our "don'ts" and "mustn'ts." But as you like him, and nothing more, there's no real need for me to say another word. (Sitting next to her again.) Is there?

VERA (raising her eyes timidly):   He—

NATALIA: Vera, is that the way to look at a sister? (Caressing her.) If your real sister asked you very quietly, "Vérochka, what exactly are your feelings toward So-and-So?"—what would you answer? (As VERA looks at her, hesitating.) Those eyes are dying to tell me something—(VERA suddenly presses her head to NATALIA's breast. NATALIA bites her lips. A pause.) My poor Vera.

VERA (without raising her head):   Oh dear— I don't know what's the matter with me—

NATALIA: My poor sweet— (As VERA presses herself closer to her.) And he—what of him?

Vera is unwittingly revealing what Natalia fears is true. What is Natalia thinking?

Take care to understand Natalia's real intention.

"He—" What is Vera starting to say? Think clearly what is in her mind.

Why does Natalia bite her lips? Is this physical action to reveal or to conceal?

Natalia is strongly pursuing her overall intention for the scene and bringing the situation to a climax.

VERA: I don't know—

NATALIA: Vera, what of him?

VERA: I don't know, I tell you—Sometimes I imagine—

NATALIA: You imagine what?

VERA (*her face hidden*): That I see a look in his eyes—as if he thought of me—as a special person—perhaps— (*Disengaging herself, trying to be calm.*) —Oh, I don't know— (*She raises her head, and sees the expression on* NATALIA'S *face.*) What's the matter, Natalia Petrovna?

NATALIA (*is staring at her, as if she were a stranger*): The matter?—(*Recovering.*) What did you say? Nothing—

VERA: But there *is* something the matter! (*Rising.*) I'll ring—

NATALIA: No, no—don't ring— (*Louder.*) —Please! It's passed off already. You go back to your music—and we—we'll talk another time.

VERA: You're not angry with me, Natalia Petrovna?

NATALIA: Not in the least—I just want to be by myself.

(VERA *tries to take her hand;* NATALIA *turns away as if she had not noticed her gesture.*)

VERA (*tears in her eyes*): Natalia Petrovna—

NATALIA: Please—(VERA *goes slowly back into the music room.* NATALIA *does not move.*)

What physical action for Vera is inherent in: "(*Louder.*)—*Please!*"?

The Sea Gull

ANTON CHEKHOV

Exploratory Analysis of a Scene from Act III: 1 man, 1 woman

Background *The Sea Gull,* in 1898 an early production of the Moscow Art Theatre, is for two reasons unique in modern drama. Its production assured the continuance of the most influential theatre organization of all time, and it was the initial success of one of the greatest of modern dramatists. For Constantin Stanislavski, co-founder with Nemirovitch-Dantchenko of the Moscow Art Theatre, it provided impetus for exploration of an approach to acting following the "law of inner justification" in which the actor eliminated the older heroic and rhetorical styles and sought to find the essence of a role in his own experience and personality. The production encouraged Chekhov to continue writing plays that have become the most convincing pieces of dramatic verisimilitude in the entire theatre. Both the writing and the acting depend for their effectiveness upon the accumulation of sensitively observed realistic details and imbuing lines and actions with an undermeaning that reveals essential truths. John Gassner calls Chekhov's art "the sublimation of realism."

Like Chekhov's other major plays, *The Sea Gull* deals with the tragedy of attrition, the frustration of unrealized potential. But the characters do not recognize defeat, they are not passive. They struggle with whatever resources they have to gain what they want, and Chekhov treats their disappointments and failures with humor and compassion.

Who *The Sea Gull* dramatizes a group rather than an individual, making all the characters a part of the same close environment, but at the same time giving individuality to each. Two of the characters in this group are MADAME IRINA ARCADINA and her son CONSTANTINE TREPLEFF.

ARCADINA is a famous actress of somewhat hackneyed plays. Although she boasts she can still play a girl of fifteen, she has reached an age when she is beginning to worry about retaining her position as a beautiful and glamorous leading lady. She is vain and selfish, not interested in whatever does not serve to focus attention on her, and jealous of anyone else's success.

TREPLEFF is twenty-five, an aspiring playwright seeking new forms to replace the stereotyped theatre his mother symbolizes. He is talented and has had a minor success in the publication of some short stories, but he lacks the drive to exert the influence and achieve the greatness of which he dreams.

Character Relationships As a child Trepleff idolized his beautiful young mother. And since a young son did not jeopardize her public image, Arcadina was caring and affectionate playing the role of mother with considerable satisfaction. But now a grown son is an embarrassment. In Act I Trepleff says: "I am a perpetual reminder that she is no longer young. When I am not nearby, she is only thirty-two; when I am, she's forty-three, and she hates me for that." He is jealous of his mother's admirers and resentful of her fame because it reduces him to a nonentity. Another cause for dissension between them is his contempt for the conventional popular theatre and her impatience with his efforts at reform.

Trepleff yearns desperately for his mother's love and approval. Her unconcern leads him to attempt suicide. He succeeds in afflicting himself with only a superficial head wound, and this is the situation in the scene for exploration. It is a comic touch that here (as well as in Chekhov's *Uncle Vanya*) a character frustrated by failure cannot succeed even at committing suicide. We must take note, though, that at the end of the play Constantine successfully takes his own life.

Where and When   A country estate near Moscow belonging to Arcadina's brother, Peter Sorin. The time is toward the end of the nineteenth century. Trepleff lives here with his uncle. Arcadina frequently vacations here. The scene is the dining-room. Stage directions designate a medicine cupboard with ointments and bandages, a trunk and hatboxes indicating preparations for a departure. Arcadina is about to return to Moscow.

Trepleff wears shabby clothes and has a bandage around his head. Arcadina is handsomely dressed for travelling. Late nineteenth century fashions require an elegance of carriage that should be helpful in realizing this character.

The Actors' Work   Analyze the scene for intentions, obstacles, beats, relationships, physical and verbal actions, subtext, sensory tasks. Make a ground plan which will enable you to carry out the physical actions effectively. Write the results of your analysis in your script to provide you with a score for playing the role.

The Sea Gull

ANTON CHEKHOV

ARCADINA: Your uncle had another dizzy spell. He quite frightened me.

TREPLEFF: It's bad for his health living in the country. He's miserable. Now if, in a sudden

Peter Sorin, Trepleff's uncle, is a middle-aged bachelor, practically exiled to the country because he does not have the means to live in town. He has just told Arcadina that Trepleff's life would be happier if she would get him some decent clothes, perhaps send him abroad for travel and study. She has firmly declared she cannot afford it.

From *Chekhov: The Major Plays,* A New Translation by Ann Dunnigan. Copyright © 1964 by Ann Dunnigan. Reprinted by arrangement with The New American Library, Inc., New York, N.Y.

burst of generosity, you could lend him a couple of hundred pounds, he would be able to spend the whole year in town.

ARCADINA: I haven't any money. I'm an actress, not a banker. *(A pause)*

TREPLEFF: Please change my bandage, mother. You do it so well.

ARCADINA *(Getting ointment and bandages from the medicine cupboard)*:   The doctor's late.

TREPLEFF: It's twelve and he promised to be here by ten.

ARCADINA: Sit down. *(Taking off bandage)* You look as if you had a turban on. A man asked the servants yesterday what nationality you were. It's almost healed up. There's hardly anything left there. *(Kissing his head)* You promise not to play at chik-chik again while I'm away?

TREPLEFF: I promise, mother. That was in a moment of despair when I had lost all self-control. It won't happen again. *(Kissing her hand)* You have the hands of an angel. I remember a long time ago, when you were still on the Imperial stage—I was quite little then—there was a fight in the courtyard of the house we lived in; a washerwoman who lodged there got awfully knocked about. You remember? She was picked up senseless. . . . You were always going in to see her, taking her medicine and bathing her children in the wash-tub. Don't you remember?

ARCADINA: No. *(Putting on a new bandage)*

TREPLEFF: There were two ballet-girls lodging in the same place. . . . They used to come in for coffee. . . .

ARCADINA: I remember that.

TREPLEFF: They were very pious. *(A pause)* These last few days I have loved you just as tenderly and trustfully as when I was a child. I have nobody left now but you. But why, why, do you submit to that man's influence?

ARCADINA: You don't understand him, Constantine. He has the noblest nature in the world. . . .

Pronounce: är kä' dĭ na

Arcadina is imitating the click of a pistol.

The lines suggest that when Trepleff was a child, Arcadina lived in quite modest circumstances.

Consider carefully the intention of Arcadina's "No."

"They were very pious." Think about the subtext.

"That man" is Trigorin, a popular novelist and Arcadina's lover. He trails along wherever she goes.

Pronounce: kän stan teen'

TREPLEFF: Yet when he was told that I meant to challenge him to fight, his noble nature did not prevent him from playing the coward. He is going away. It's an ignominious flight!

ARCADINA: What rubbish! It was I who asked him to go.

TREPLEFF: The noblest nature in the world! Here are you and I almost quarrelling about him, and where is he? In the garden or the drawing-room laughing at us, improving Nina's mind, and trying to persuade her that he's a genius.

Nina is a young girl living on a neighboring estate. Trepleff is much in love with her. She dreams of a glamorous life on the stage and does not return his affection. In the course of the play, Trigorin seduces her and deserts her.

ARCADINA: It seems to give you pleasure to try and hurt my feelings. I respect Trigorin and I must ask you not to abuse him to my face.

TREPLEFF: And I *don't* respect him. You want *me* to believe him a genius too; but you must excuse me, I can't tell lies; his writing makes me sick.

ARCADINA: That's mere envy. Conceited people with no talent have no resource but to jeer at really talented people. It relieves their feelings, no doubt!

TREPLEFF *(Ironically)*: Really talented people! *(Angry)* I am more talented than all of you put together if it comes to that! *(Tearing off the bandages)* You apostles of the commonplace have taken the front seat in all the arts for yourselves and call nothing but what you do yourselves legitimate and real; you persecute and stifle all the rest. I don't believe in any of you; I don't believe in *you* and I don't believe in *him!*

Trepleff is correct in his opinion that Trigorin is not a genius. Trigorin realizes, however, that his writing is second-rate.

ARCADINA: You're decadent!

TREPLEFF: Go back to your beloved theatre and act your pitiful stupid plays.

ARCADINA: I never acted in such plays. Leave me! You cannot even write a miserable vaudeville skit! Kiev hack! Sponger!

Kiev is a city in the Ukraine, much less sophisticated and cosmopolitan than Moscow.

TREPLEFF: Miser!

ARCADINA: Beggar! (TREPLEFF *sits down and cries quietly*) You insignificant nobody!

(Walking up and down agitatedly) Don't cry. Don't cry, I say. *(Crying)* Please don't cry. *(Kissing his forehead, cheeks and head)* My darling child, forgive me. . . . Forgive your wicked mother! Forgive your unhappy mother!

TREPLEFF *(Embracing her)*:   If only you knew! I have lost everything. She doesn't love me and I cannot write anymore . . . all my hopes are lost.

ARCADINA: Don't lose heart. It will be all right in the end. He is going away; she will love you again. *(Wiping away his tears)* Stop crying. We are friends once more.

TREPLEFF *(Kissing her hand)*:   Yes, mother.

ARCADINA *(Tenderly)*:   Be friends with him too. You mustn't have a duel. You won't have one?

TREPLEFF: Very well. But you mustn't let me meet him anymore, mother. It hurts me; it is too much for me. There! I will go away. *(Hastily puts the medicaments away in the cupboard)* The doctor will bandage me when he comes.

"She" is Nina. Both Trepleff and Arcadina are jealous of Trigorin's attentions to her.

The Rivals
RICHARD BRINSLEY SHERIDAN

Exploratory Analysis of a Scene from Act II, Scene 1: 2 men

Background   Although not enthusiastically received at its first performance in 1775, *The Rivals* was shortly to establish itself as one of the great comedies of English drama, a reputation that has endured to the present day. It has been frequently produced in England and America, especially with "all-star" casts because of the many excellent roles it affords. It is popular because it contains a number of basic comic appeals. It is, first of all, a comedy of intrigue with several interlocking plots. The main plot, and the one being developed in the scene for exploration, has to do with the courtship of Captain Jack Absolute, a young army officer, and Lydia Languish, a beautiful heiress. Jack's father Sir Anthony, ignorant of the courtship, has arranged a marriage between his son and the niece of his old friend Mrs. Malaprop. Confronted with the prospect of an arranged marriage, Jack insists he will follow the dictates of his heart; Sir Anthony insists he will yield to his father's wishes. What neither of them knows, but what the audience does know, is that both father and son are talking about the same girl.

Who   In addition to being a comedy of intrigue or situation, *The Rivals* is a comedy of humors, a type developed by Ben Jonson and frequently occurring throughout the seventeenth and eighteenth centuries. The word *humor* was applied to some excessive character trait (jealousy, greed, vanity) which made the person appear ridiculous and, consequently, comic. Nearly all of the characters in Sheridan's play are amusing because of a clearly marked "humor" that makes them more or less incongruous in their surroundings.

SIR ANTHONY ABSOLUTE is marked with extreme irascibility, a hot temper, an "absolutism," as his name implies. What he does is inconsistent with any standard of rational behavior, and he becomes especially ridiculous when he is outwitted by the young lovers. The danger in playing this kind of character is that he may become over-exaggerated and one-dimensional. We have all known overbearing fathers. Sir Anthony has dignity and authority. As he says of himself, he is always compliant until he is crossed.

JACK ABSOLUTE is witty and good-natured. He is essentially practical, and he deals with his father not by losing his temper but by using his head. Because Lydia has vowed she would not marry anyone interested in her money, Jack can successfully play the role of a dashing and romantic suitor, penniless and not concerned about acquiring a fortune. Through this artifice, however, he hopes to get both the girl and her property. Not that he doesn't love her, but it would be foolish to throw away a fortune. Besides there is both satisfaction and poetic justice in outwitting his father and Lydia's aunt.

Character Relationships   In their everyday conduct Jack and his father are somewhat formal with each other. Jack treats Sir Anthony with the polite respect that a well-bred young man is taught to pay his father. Sir Anthony, by no means insincerely, behaves like a stern but loving parent. This formal relationship is colored by Sir Anthony's *humor* which has determined his method of disciplining his son. When Mrs. Malaprop expresses the hope that Jack will not object to the proposed marriage with her niece, Sir Anthony describes this method: "Let him object if he dare ! . . . No, no, Mrs. Malaprop, Jack knows that the least demur puts me in a frenzy directly. My process was always very simple . . . in their younger days, 'twas 'Jack do this'; . . . if he demurred, I knocked him down . . . and if he grumbled at that, I always sent him out of the room."

Jack, however, has long since learned to take these outbursts in stride, even with a contained amusement, and he knows how to deal with his father. His tactic in this instance, when he learns Sir Anthony has arranged a marriage with the girl he loves, is to pretend to yield entirely to his father's wishes without revealing that he has learned who the girl is. In a later scene he says to Sir Anthony, who has been describing Lydia's beauty: "Sir, if I please you in this affair, 'tis all that I desire. Not that I think a woman the worse for being handsome; but, sir, if you please to recollect, you before hinted something about a hump or two, one eye, and a few more graces of that kind . . . now, without being very nice, I own I should rather choose a wife of mine to have the usual number of limbs, and a limited quantity of back: and though one eye may be very agreeable, yet as the prejudice has always run in favor of two, I would not wish to affect a singularity in that article . . . But I am entirely at your disposal, sir. . . ."

Where and When   The year is 1775. The place is Bath, England, a spa where the people came to "take the waters" from a mineral spring as a cure for gout, rheumatism, and other various ailments. It was also a social center for people in perfect health. The time and place affect both the behavior of the characters and the style of acting. The characters in this play, while not aristocrats, are rich and fashionable or are pretending to be. They have the means and the leisure to achieve a degree of elegance in dress and manner. It is the time of Colonial America; if you have visited Williamsburg or have seen other examples of Colonial architecture and furnishings, you know something of the taste and refinement that characterize the period.

Men wore powdered wigs, three-cornered hats, coats and waistcoats of silk and velvet (often embroidered), lace at the neck and at the wrists, knee breeches, silk stockings, shoes with silver buckles. Military uniforms, following essentially the same lines, were made of fine wool. The British uniform was especially striking with a scarlet coat, white or fawn breeches, and knee-length boots. These were handsome clothes, and men were proud of their appearance in them. It is not likely that full costumes will be available for scene study. However, knowledge of what the characters wore (see Suggestions for Reading at the end of the scene), how it affected their behavior, and possibly some semblance of a proper costume for rehearsal will help to realize the characters and the style of the play.

Since *The Rivals* was written toward the end of the eighteenth century, the period has some influence on the style of acting. The realistic approach, that is, the attempt to make stage life as much as possible like real life, had not yet come into vogue. This does not mean that the characters are not truthful, but that the actors are not required in all details of their behavior to be faithful to the generally observed facts of experience. They accept the play as a stage piece rather than as a "slice of life," and concern themselves with more directly communicating the play to the audience. Stage positions are more open, the rhetorical tone of the dialogue is exploited, movements and gestures are precisely executed.

The Ground Plan   The description of the scene is "Captain Absolute's Lodgings." Eighteenth-century dramatists did not provide details of the setting, nor give abundant stage directions. Since no requirements are stated, remain flexible about your ground plan as long as possible. Let it evolve from the needs you discover during rehearsals. Provide yourselves with what you need, but do not clutter the scene with "realistic" business.

The Actors' Work   Analyze the scene for intentions, obstacles, beats, relationships, physical and verbal actions, subtext, sensory tasks. Write the results of your analysis in your script to provide you with a score in playing the role.

The Rivals

RICHARD BRINSLEY SHERIDAN

ABSOLUTE: Now for a parental lecture—I hope he has heard nothing of the business that brought me here—I wish the gout had held him fast in Devonshire, with all my soul!

Jack Absolute has just been informed by his serving-man that his father has come to see him. The business that brought Jack to Bath is his courtship of Lydia Languish. Soliloquies and asides—in which the characters speak their thoughts—are common in plays of earlier periods. Depending on the overall style of the production, the actor may either appear to be speaking to himself or he may speak directly to the audience, sharing his thoughts with them.

Enter SIR ANTHONY ABSOLUTE:

Sir, I am delighted to see you here; looking so well! Your sudden arrival at Bath made me apprehensive for your health.

This line is a polite expression of concern for Sir Anthony's health. Jack is saying: "I was afraid you had come to Bath seeking a cure for an attack of gout."

SIR ANTHONY: Very apprehensive, I dare say, Jack—What, you are recruiting here, hey?

Jack's military duties included recruiting young men into the army.

ABSOLUTE: Yes, sir, I am on duty.

SIR ANTHONY: Well, Jack, I am glad to see you, though I did not expect it, for I was going to write you on a little matter of business—Jack, I have been considering that I grow old and infirm, and shall probably not trouble you long.

Since Sir Anthony is clearly healthy, his intention is to solicit an expression of sympathy from Jack.

ABSOLUTE: Pardon me, sir, I never saw you look more strong and hearty; and I pray frequently that you may continue so.

SIR ANTHONY: I hope your prayers may be heard, with all my heart. Well, then, Jack, I have been considering that I am so strong and hearty I may continue to plague you a long time. Now, Jack, I am sensible that the income of your commission, and what I have hitherto allowed you, is but a small pittance for a lad of your spirit.

ABSOLUTE: Sir, you are very good.

SIR ANTHONY: And it is my wish, while yet I live, to have my boy make some figure in the world. I have resolved, therefore, to fix you at once in a noble independence.

ABSOLUTE: Sir, your kindness overpowers me—such generosity makes the gratitude of reason more lively than the sensations even of filial affection.

SIR ANTHONY: I am glad you are so sensible of my attention—and you shall be master of a large estate in a few weeks.

ABSOLUTE: Let my future life, sir, speak my gratitude; I cannot express the sense I have of your munificence—Yet, sir, I presume you would not wish me to quit the army?

SIR ANTHONY: Oh, that shall be as your wife chooses.

ABSOLUTE: My wife, sir!

SIR ANTHONY: Ay, ay, settle that between you—settle that between you.

ABSOLUTE: A wife, sir, did you say?

SIR ANTHONY: Ay, a wife—why, did not I mention her before?

ABSOLUTE: Not a word of her, sir.

SIR ANTHONY: Odd so!—I mus'n't forget her though.—Yes, Jack, the independence I was talking of is by marriage—the fortune is saddled with a wife—but I suppose that makes no difference.

ABSOLUTE: Sir! sir!—you amaze me!

SIR ANTHONY: Why, what the devil's the matter with the fool? Just now you were all gratitude and duty.

Jack recognizes his father's intention and obliges him.

This extravagant compliment shows the polite respect Jack pays to his father and typifies the elaborate manner of social conversation in eighteenth-century plays.

Note this rapid transition to a new beat.

It is within Sir Anthony's humor that he would expect no opposition from Jack in this matter.

The first part of the speech should probably be taken as an aside.

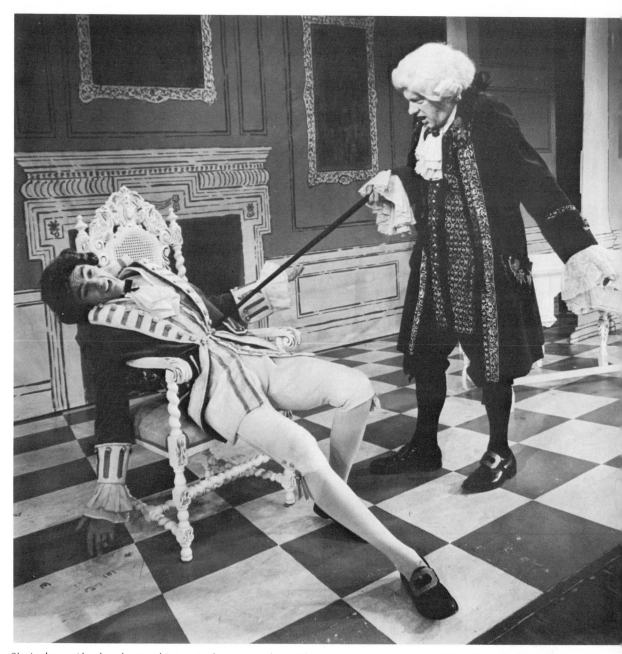

Sir Anthony Absolute berates his son Jack in a Goodman Theatre Center production of *The Rivals* by Richard Brinsley Sheridan. Production directed by Joseph Slowik. Note the eighteenth-century costumes, as well as the physical action. (Photograph: Voris Fisher)

ABSOLUTE: I was, sir—you talked to me of independence and a fortune, but not a word of a wife.

SIR ANTHONY: Why—what difference does that make? Odds life, sir! If you have the estate, you must take it with the live stock on it, as it stands.

ABSOLUTE: If my happiness is to be the price, I must beg leave to decline the purchase. —Pray, sir, who is the lady?

SIR ANTHONY: What's that to you, sir?—Come, give me your promise to love, and to marry her directly.

ABSOLUTE: Sure, sir, this is not very reasonable, to summon my affections for a lady I know nothing of!

SIR ANTHONY: I am sure, sir, 'tis more unreasonable in you to object to a lady you know nothing of.

The emphatic word is object.

ABSOLUTE: Then, sir, I must tell you plainly that my inclinations are fixed on another—my heart is engaged to an angel.

SIR ANTHONY: Then pray let it send an excuse. It is very sorry—but business prevents its waiting on her.

It *refers to* heart *in the previous speech.*

ABSOLUTE: But my vows are pledged to her.

SIR ANTHONY: Let her foreclose, Jack, let her foreclose; they are not worth redeeming; besides, you have the angel's vows in exchange, I suppose; so there can be no loss there.

Take care to understand the references to a business transaction.

ABSOLUTE: You must excuse me, sir, if I tell you, once for all, that in this point I cannot obey you.

SIR ANTHONY: Hark'ee, Jack—I have heard you for some time with patience—I have been cool—quite cool; but take care—you know I am compliance itself—when I am not thwarted;—no one more easily led—when I have my own way;—but don't put me in a frenzy.

Hark'ee *is* hark you, *a common form in plays of this period. Sir Anthony is saying:* "Now you listen to me, Jack."

ABSOLUTE: Sir, I must repeat—in this I cannot obey you.

SIR ANTHONY: Now damn me! If ever I call you Jack again while I live!

ABSOLUTE: Nay, sir, but hear me.

SIR ANTHONY: Sir, I won't hear a word—not a word! Not one word! So give me your promise by a nod—and I'll tell you what, Jack—I mean, you dog—if you don't, by—

ABSOLUTE: What, sir, promise to link myself to some mass of ugliness! to—

SIR ANTHONY: Zounds! sirrah! the lady shall be as ugly as I choose: she shall have a hump on each shoulder; she shall be as crooked as the crescent; her one eye shall roll like the bull's in Cox's Museum; she shall have a skin like a mummy, and the beard of a Jew—she shall be all this, sirrah!—yet I will make you ogle her all day, and sit up all night to write sonnets on her beauty.

ABSOLUTE: This is reason and moderation indeed!

SIR ANTHONY: None of your sneering, puppy! No grinning, jackanapes!

ABSOLUTE: Indeed, sir, I never was in a worse humor for mirth in my life.

SIR ANTHONY: 'Tis false, sir. I know you are laughing in your sleeve; I know you'll grin when I am gone, sirrah!

ABSOLUTE: Sir, I hope I know my duty better.

SIR ANTHONY: None of your passion, sir! None of your violence, if you please!—It won't do with me, I promise you.

ABSOLUTE: Indeed, sir, I never was cooler in my life.

SIR ANTHONY: 'Tis a confounded lie!—I know you are in a passion in your heart; I know you are, you hypocritical young dog! But it won't do.

ABSOLUTE: Nay, sir, upon my word—

SIR ANTHONY: So you will fly out! Can't you be cool like me? What the devil good can passion do?—Passion is of no service, you impudent, insolent, overbearing reprobate!—There, you sneer again! Don't provoke me!—But you rely upon the mildness of my disposition!—Yet take care—the patience of a saint may be overcome at last!—but mark! I give you six

The emphatic word is nod.

Zounds *is a mild oath, a euphemism for God's wounds. It has the same sound as* how. Sirrah *(accent on the first syllable) is a form of address implying inferiority, usually used in anger or contempt.*

James Cox *exhibited various mechanical curiosities in Bath in 1773–74. Among these was "The Curious Bull."*

Emphasize heart.

Exploit the contradiction between Sir Anthony's line and his behavior. Such incongruity is a basic element of comedy.

hours and a half to consider of this: if you then agree, without any condition, to do everything on earth that I choose, why—confound you! I may in time forgive you.—If not, zounds! Don't enter the same hemisphere with me! Don't dare to breathe the same air, or use the same light with me; but get an atmosphere and a sun of your own! I'll strip you of your commission; I'll lodge a five-and-threepence in the hands of trustees, and you shall live on the interest.—I'll disown you, I'll disinherit you, I'll unget you! And damn me! If ever I call you Jack again! (*Exit* SIR ANTHONY)

ABSOLUTE: Mild, gentle, considerate father—I kiss your hands!—What a tender method of giving his opinion in these matters Sir Anthony has! I dare not trust him with the truth.—I wonder what old wealthy hag it is that he wants to bestow on me!—Yet he married himself for love! And was in his youth a bold intriguer, and a gay companion!

Try taking a pause before and a half *and find a motivation for doing it.*

This speech is built in a series of stages to a climax. Maximum effectiveness requires careful planning.

SOURCES FOR EIGHTEENTH-CENTURY COSTUME AND MANNERS

Brooke, Iris. *English Costume in the Eighteenth Century*. New York: Barnes and Noble, 1964.

Davenport, Milia. *The Book of Costume*. New York: Crown Publishers, 1948.

Oxenford, Lyn. *Playing Period Plays*. London: Miller, Ltd. 1958.

Von Boehn, Max. *Modes and Manners*. New York: Blom, 1970.

Wilcox, R. Turner. *The Mode in Costume*. New York: Scribner, 1969.

She Stoops to Conquer

OLIVER GOLDSMITH

Exploratory Analysis of a Scene from Act II: 2 men, 1 woman

Background *She Stoops to Conquer,* first performed in 1773 before an approving audience that included King George III and Samuel Johnson, has continued to please theatre-goers for over two hundred years. "Making an audience merry" was Goldsmith's purpose, and he was not much concerned about some somber critics who condemned the play because it "tended to no moral." It is essentially a situation comedy, bordering on farce, as indicated in its subtitle, *The Mistakes of a Night.* The plot depends upon misunderstandings and mistaken identities. But the characters are attractively drawn, and the whole play bubbles with good humor.

Young Charles Marlow has come from London to get acquainted with Kate Hardcastle, to whom he has been betrothed by his father but has never met. With him is his friend George Hastings, who is in love with Kate's cousin, Constance Neville. Misdirected by a prankster, the young men mistake the Hardcastle house for an inn, Kate for a barmaid, and her father for an innkeeper. All mistakes are finally rectified, and the play ends with comedy's traditional invitation to supper and the prospect of a double wedding.

Who Young MARLOW, son of a wealthy titled father, is described to Kate by old Hardcastle as well-bred, a man of excellent understanding, generous, brave, very handsome, and "one of the most bashful and reserved young fellows in all the world." We learn from another source that while he is bashful and reserved among "women of reputation and virtue, . . . his acquaintance give him a very different character among creatures of another stamp."

This peculiarity of character—embarrassed and tongue-tied with a "woman of virtue" and amorously aggressive with a "female of the other class"—may seem somewhat improbable. It produces, however, some highly comic situations; and good farcical comedy makes us willing temporarily to suspend our disbelief so that the improbable seems altogether possible.

GEORGE HASTINGS is like his friend Marlow, except that he is comfortably at ease with women of all backgrounds. He is truly in love with Miss Neville and has come to the country to pursue this romance. To escape from Miss Neville's aunt, who opposes their marriage, he is planning an elopement to France.

KATE HARDCASTLE is a bright attractive girl, clearly a great favorite of her father and sharing his tolerant good nature. Given, like most girls, to thinking about romance and pretty clothes, she is level-headed enough to be neither sentimental nor extravagant. She cheerfully humors her father in his dislike for "gauze and French frippery" by wearing French fashions when she is calling or receiving visitors and by putting on simple country dress when she is at home with him. She and her father agree that any indignities they suffer at being mistaken for what they are not can be readily forgotten through an hour of good laughs together.

Character Relationships In the scene for exploration Kate meets Marlow for the first time. She has been prepared for the meeting by her father and is aware of Marlow's peculiarity. Although naturally apprehensive about meeting the man who may well become her husband, she has been favorably impressed by the report that he is young, rich, and handsome; and she is willing in good spirit to accept his shyness until she can get to know him and discover his real character. Anticipating the meeting, she tells Constance with youthful confidence that, although she may not be able to manage him, she is not going to worry and will "trust to occurrences for success." After the encounter she tells her father she will have none of him because of his "awkward address, his bashful manner, his hesitating timidity." Yet there is something about him she finds attractive, and this attractiveness determines her subsequent behavior and provides the title of the play. *She stoops to conquer* him by playing the part of the barmaid, thus encouraging their friendship until it turns into love.

Before the beginning of the scene, Hastings has discovered the prank that has been played upon them. He is anxious to keep Marlow from knowing because "the strange reserve of his temperament is such that, if abruptly informed of it, he would instantly quit the house" before Hastings' plan for eloping with Constance could be carried out.

Where and When The scene is an old-fashioned English country house in the 1770's. The period is the same as in *The Rivals* (see the

Introduction to the scene from that play), but Mr. Hardcastle makes no concessions to modern fashions. He says to Mrs. Hardcastle (not altogether with her concurrence): "I love everything that's old—old friends, old times, old manners, old books, old wine; and I believe, Dorothy, you'll own I've been pretty fond of an old wife." The atmosphere is warm, comfortable, and friendly. Although Marlow and Hastings come from the city—the great world—and Kate is a country girl, with her natural charm, beauty, and intelligence, she is in no way their inferior.

Although complete costumes are rarely available for scene study, a knowledge of the dress of the period (and perhaps some improvised garments) will help you to realize the characters. Typical men's dress was a knee-length coat, "cut away" in front to expose a shorter waistcoat (vest); knee-breeches; hose (usually white); shoes with silver buckles. The shirt had ruffles visible at the wrists and at the neck. Men wore either small powdered wigs or their own long hair tied back by a ribbon at the nape of the neck. Materials were often silk or satin, but since Marlow and Hastings have been traveling, they would more likely be wearing clothes of fine wool. Kate is dressed in what her father would call "French frippery," but, at least by eighteenth-century standards, it would not be elaborate. Essentials would be a long full skirt, a draped-back overskirt with matching bodice attached, the bodice boned to produce a slender waist. Flowered materials in pastel shades were popular. Attention to costume is important because it is difficult to get a feeling for period plays in jeans and sweat shirts.

Goldsmith wrote more realistically than earlier playwrights, but his dialogue is more formal than one would hear in everyday conversation. It is the actor's job to master the form and make verbal actions of the dialogue so he can use it to accomplish his intentions.

The Actors' Work Analyze the scene for intentions, obstacles, beats, physical and verbal actions, relationships, subtext, sensory tasks. As customary in earlier plays, Goldsmith gives few stage directions; physical actions must be invented by the actors. Make a ground plan that will enable you to carry out the physical actions effectively. The action takes place either in the reception hall or the parlor of the Hardcastle house. Write the results of your analysis in your script to provide you with a score in playing the role.

She Stoops to Conquer

OLIVER GOLDSMITH

(HASTINGS *onstage. Enter* MARLOW.)

MARLOW: The assiduities of these good people tease me beyond bearing. My host seems to think it ill manners to leave me alone, and so he claps not only himself, but his old-fashioned wife on my back. They talk of coming to sup with us, too; and then, I suppose, we are to run the gauntlet through all the rest of the family.

He is talking about the initial mistake. Mr. Hardcastle is treating him like the guest that he is; he is treating Mr. Hardcastle like an innkeeper.

HASTINGS: My dear Charles! Let me congratulate you!— The most fortunate accident!—Who do you think is just alighted?

MARLOW: Cannot guess.

HASTINGS: Our mistresses, boy, Miss Hardcastle and Miss Neville. Happening to dine in the neighborhood, they called, on their return, to take fresh horses here. They have just stepped into the next room, and will be back in an instant. Wasn't it lucky? eh!

Hastings is contributing to the mistake by making up an explanation of why Miss Hardcastle and Miss Neville are at an "inn."

MARLOW (aside):   I have just been mortified enough of all conscience, and here comes something to complete my embarrassment.

The aside is a convention in plays of earlier periods in which a character expresses thoughts for the benefit of the audience supposedly unheard by other characters onstage. It was frequently accompanied by the gesture of placing a hand near the side of the mouth and/or taking a step toward the audience away from the other characters.

HASTINGS: Well! But wasn't it the most fortunate thing in the world?

MARLOW: Oh! yes. Very fortunate—a most joyful encounter. —But our dresses, George, you know, are in disorder. —What if we should postpone the happiness till tomorrow? —Tomorrow at her own house. —It will be every bit as convenient—and rather more respectful. —Tomorrow let it be. *(Offering to go.)*

HASTINGS: By no means. Your ceremony will displease her. The disorder of your dress will show the ardor of your impatience. Besides, she knows you are in the house, and will permit you to see her.

MARLOW: Oh! The devil! How shall I support it? Hem! hem! Hastings, you must not go. You are to assist me, you know. I shall be confoundedly ridiculous. Yet, hang it! I'll take courage. Hem!

HASTINGS: Pshaw, man! It's but the first plunge, and all's over. She's but a woman, you know.

MARLOW: And of all women, she that I dread most to encounter!

(Enter MISS HARDCASTLE)

HASTINGS *(introducing them)*:   Miss Hardcastle, Mr. Marlow. I'm proud of bringing two persons of such merit together, that only want to know, to esteem each other.

MISS HARDCASTLE *(aside)*:   Now, for meeting my modest gentleman with a demure face, and quite in his own manner. *(After a pause, in which he appears very uneasy and disconcerted.)* I'm glad of your safe arrival, sir—I'm told you had some accidents by the way.

MARLOW: Only a few, madam. Yes, we had some. Yes, madam, a good many accidents, but should be sorry—madam—or rather glad of any accidents—that are so agreeably concluded. Hem!

HASTINGS *(to him)*:   You never spoke better in your whole life. Keep it up, and I'll insure you the victory.

MISS HARDCASTLE: I'm afraid you flatter, sir. You that have seen so much of the finest company can find little entertainment in an obscure corner of the country.

Actors should be alert to any costume suggestions in the lines. Here, however, Marlow may be offering an excuse rather than reason.

Support *here means* endure.
Hem! Hem! *calls for some vocal response, not necessarily a reproduction of the sounds indicated by the letters.*

During an aside the other actors hold their positions.

To him. *The stage direction might have been* aside to Marlow. *Miss Hardcastle appears not to hear the line.*
Her line is a response to Marlow, given without any recognition of Hastings' aside.

Goodman student Nancy Mellon as Kate Hardcastle in *She Stoops to Conquer* by Oliver Goldsmith. Appropriate costume properties—such as fans, walking sticks, eyeglasses—can aid an actor in creating character and in carrying out physical actions. (Photograph: Goodman School of Drama)

MARLOW (*gathering courage*):   I have lived, indeed, in the world, madam; but I have kept very little company. I have been but an observer upon life, madam, while others were enjoying it.

MISS HARDCASTLE: But that, I am told, is the way to enjoy it at last.

HASTINGS (*to him*):   Cicero never spoke better. Once more, and you are confirmed in assurance forever.

Cicero was a great Roman orator.

MARLOW (*to him*):   Hem! Stand by me, then, and when I'm down, throw in a word or two to set me up again.

MISS HARDCASTLE: An observer, like you, upon life, were, I fear, disagreeably employed, since you must have had much more to censure than to approve.

MARLOW: Pardon me, madam. I was always willing to be amused. The folly of most people is rather an object of mirth than uneasiness.

HASTINGS (*to him*):   Bravo, bravo. Never spoke so well in your whole life. Well, Miss Hardcastle, I see that you and Mr. Marlow are going to be very good company. I believe my being here will but embarrass the interview.

What is Hastings' intention? What physical action is appropriate to the line?

MARLOW: Not in the least, Mr. Hastings. We like your company of all things. (*To him.*) Zounds! George, sure you won't go? How can you leave us?

HASTINGS: My presence will but spoil conversation, so I'll retire to the next room. (*To him.*) You don't consider, man, that I am to manage a little tête-à-tête of my own.

Zounds rhymes with sounds. It is a mild oath, a euphemism for God's wounds.

(*Exit* HASTINGS.)

MISS HARDCASTLE (*after a pause*):   But you have not been wholly an observer, I presume, sir. The ladies, I should hope, have employed some part of your addresses.

MARLOW (*relapsing into timidity*):   Pardon me, madam, I—I—I—as yet have studied —only—to—deserve them.

MISS HARDCASTLE: And that some say is the very worst way to obtain them.

MARLOW: Perhaps so, madam. But I love to

converse only with the more grave and sensible part of the sex. —But I'm afraid I grow tiresome.

MISS HARDCASTLE: Not at all, sir; there is nothing I like so much as grave conversation myself; I could hear it forever. Indeed, I have often been surprised how a man of sentiment could ever admire those light airy pleasures, where nothing reaches the heart.

Here a man of sentiment *means a man of refined feeling with a strong sense of moral responsibility—an ideal much admired in eighteenth-century drama.*

MARLOW: It's—a disease—of the mind, madam. In the variety of tastes there must be some who, wanting a relish for—um-a-um.

MISS HARDCASTLE: I understand you, sir. There must be some, who, wanting a relish for refined pleasures, pretend to despise what they are incapable of tasting.

MARLOW: My meaning, madam, but infinitely better expressed. And I can't help observing—a—

MISS HARDCASTLE (*aside*): Who could ever suppose this fellow impudent upon some occasions. (*To him.*) You were going to observe, sir—

MARLOW: I was observing, madam—I protest, madam, I forget what I was going to observe.

MISS HARDCASTLE (*aside*): I vow and so do I. (*To him.*) You were observing, sir, that in this age of hypocrisy—something about hypocrisy, sir.

MARLOW: Yes, madam. In this age of hypocrisy, there are few who upon strict inquiry do not—a—a—a—

MISS HARDCASTLE: I understand you perfectly, sir.

MARLOW (*aside*): Egad! And that's more than I do myself!

Egad is another mild oath, a euphemism for Oh God. *Very common in seventeenth- and eighteenth-century plays.*

Men of sentiment were often satirized as hypocrites. Joseph Surface in The School for Scandal *is an outstanding example.*

MISS HARDCASTLE: You mean that in this hypocritical age there are few that do not condemn in public what they practice in private, and think they pay every debt to virtue when they praise it.

MARLOW: True, madam; those who have most virtue in their mouths, have least of it in their bosoms. But I'm sure I tire you, madam.

MISS HARDCASTLE: Not in the least, sir; there's something so agreeable and spirited in your manner, such life and force—pray, sir, go on.

MARLOW: Yes, madam. I was saying—that there are some occasions—when a total want of courage, madam, destroys all the—and puts us—upon a—a—a—

MISS HARDCASTLE: I agree with you entirely, a want of courage upon some occasions assumes the appearance of ignorance, and betrays us when we most want to excel. I beg you'll proceed.

Consider carefully Kate's intention in this line.

MARLOW: Yes, madam. Morally speaking, madam—but I see Miss Neville expecting us in the next room. I would not intrude for the world.

MISS HARDCASTLE: I protest, sir, I never was more agreeably entertained in all my life. Pray go on.

MARLOW: Yes, madam. I was—but she beckons us to join her. Madam, shall I do myself the honor to attend you?

MISS HARDCASTLE: Well then, I'll follow.

She means "I won't let you attend me, but I will follow after you." What is her intention?

MARLOW (*aside*):   This pretty smooth dialogue has done for me.

(*Exit.*)

MISS HARDCASTLE (*sola*):   Ha! ha! ha! Was there ever such a sober, sentimental interview? I'm certain he scarce looked in my face the whole time. Yet the fellow, but for his unaccountable bashfulness, is pretty well, too. He has good sense, but then so buried in his fears, that it fatigues one more than ignorance. If I could teach him a little confidence, it would be doing somebody that I know of a piece of service. But who is that somebody?—That, faith, is a question I can scarce answer.

Sola means alone; Kate is going to share her thoughts with the audience. What she says is a key to discovering her relationship to Marlow in this scene.

(*Exit.*)

See Sources for Eighteenth-Century Costume and Manners listed after the scene from *The Rivals*.

Index of
Authors and Titles